**Urban Futures
Observed**

Pergamon Titles of Related Interest

Related Journals*

Habitat International
International Journal of Intercultural Relations
Socio-Economic Planning Sciences
Urban Systems

   *Free specimen copies available upon request.

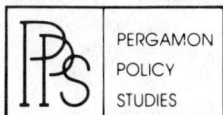

PERGAMON
POLICY
STUDIES ON INTERNATIONAL DEVELOPMENT

Urban Futures Observed
In the Asian Third World

Richard L. Meier

Pergamon Press
NEW YORK • OXFORD • TORONTO • SYDNEY • FRANKFURT • PARIS

Pergamon Press Offices:

U.S.A.	Pergamon Press Inc., Maxwell House, Fairview Park, Elmsford, New York 10523, U.S.A.
U.K.	Pergamon Press Ltd., Headington Hill Hall, Oxford OX3 0BW, England
CANADA	Pergamon of Canada, Ltd., Suite 104, 150 Consumers Road, Willowdale, Ontario M2J 1P9, Canada
AUSTRALIA	Pergamon Press (Aust.) Pty. Ltd., P.O. Box 544, Potts Point, NSW 2011, Australia
FRANCE	Pergamon Press SARL, 24 rue des Ecoles, 75240 Paris, Cedex 05, France
FEDERAL REPUBLIC OF GERMANY	Pergamon Press GmbH, Hammerweg 6, Postfach 1305, 6242 Kronberg/Taunus, Federal Republic of Germany

Library of Congress Cataloging in Publication Data

Meier, Richard L
  Urban futures observed, in the Asian Third World.

  (Pergamon policy studies)
  Bibliography: p.
  Includes index.
  1. Cities and towns—Asia. I. Title.
HT147.A2M44 1980   307.7'6'095   79-28624
ISBN 0-08-025954-5

Printed in the United States of America

Contents

Preface and Acknowledgments

As a youth I hitched rides over many thousands of miles of highways in the Great Plains and the West. When the next town on the road came into view I started noting the church steeples, grain elevators, water towers, and factory chimneys that rose above the understory of trees. I scrutinized roadside advertisements for family names: Was this to be a predominantly German community, emigrated New Englanders, Scandinavian, Mexican, the less frequent Slavic, or the more common melting pot? Institutions like colleges, county fairgrounds, prisons, and hospitals were also exceedingly important in determining the hospitality of the town.

In their regional setting all of these visual indicators generated a structured set of expectations. They provided me with a basis for choosing a pedestrian route through a settlement I had never seen before. The townscape for me resembled tree rings, with each prosperous era laying down a thick annulus of house types and the hard times only a few scattered tracts. The original center could be spotted by the old brick and masonry styles; the "strip," with its motels, filling stations, and coffee shops, was located so it could then be avoided. These features helped me decide how to pick up the next ride, obtain a cheap meal, or find a place to sleep.

Quite often I would have a chance to see what this town would put on the wrong side of the tracks, read the inscriptions on the monuments in the parks, appraise the social rank of the respective churches, or trace out a history from the dates on the headstones in the cemetery. Thus, the subtle differences among cities initiated in the 1820-70 period, which are highly repetitive in architecture and site development, came alive.

However the application of science and technology to economic and social development forced me to look at urban ecology seriously. In Great Britain and Latin America I had to learn a new set of cues in order to feel at ease. Greece and Turkey were still more complex and alien. Nevertheless it was surprising how quickly I could piece together stories about things the rest of the world would like to know, particularly about the development processes at work in a center.

These were interesting exercises, usually undertaken as a way of spending a holiday so that it might turn up some useful insight. The real test lay in the Orient; its urbanizing problems dwarf any experienced in the past. Could one comprehend an uncharted Calcutta or a Tokyo when their descriptions were largely untranslated? The Asian Third World must rapidly evolve unique forms of urbanism or sink into an oblivion of despair.

Half a sabbatical year in 1966 was spent in Asia, aided by a small grant from the Ford Foundation. A subsequent small travel grant was obtained to investigate the potentials for resource-conserving urbanism in the Orient. Other trips were partly aided by giving lectures under the sponsorship of the United States International Communications Agency and minor consulting efforts. It helps to have a former student in almost every port and the price structure in much of Asia is low enough to accommodate an academic salary. Gitta, my wife, studied family planning and approaches to dealing with mental illness, while each of the children made significant investigative contributions, so "finding out" was frequently a family enterprise.

The Institute of Urban and Regional Development of the University of California circulated numerous working papers; most of this volume is condensed from those sources. The AIP Journal published two papers on Tokyo (with Ikumi Hoshino) and one on Seoul. Some of the material on Singapore and Bangkok appeared in Leo Jakobson and Ved Prakash, Metropolitan Growth: Public Policy for South and Southeast Asia, Beverly Hills: Sage, 1974. Most of the section on Hong Kong was first presented in Issues in the Management of Urban Systems, H. Swain and R.D. McKinnon, eds., Vienna: International Institute of Applied Systems Analysis, 1975.

It is customary to acknowledge with gratitude the services of assistants and of typists, but in this case there would be well over a dozen. I am refraining from listing them because almost surely one or two would be overlooked. However, the elevation and plan of the idealized Korean house by Sungjung Chough, represents an independent contribution. It illustrates how one can obtain a visual record of urban ecology that is much less obtrusive than journeyman photographic techniques. I regret I do not possess the skill myself.

Of all the cities I investigated fewer than half are represented here. Some, like Casablanca and Ankara, were too far afield. Others, like Jerusalem, are already very familiar to Americans. Saigon, Beirut, and Tehran were dropped because outside forces combined drastically to change their trajectory into the future. Karachi, Dacca, Taipei, and Kanpur, although fascinating to me for various reasons, did not seem to interest colleagues and students. Manila was squeezed out for lack of space to do it justice. Similarly, the cities of Sri Lanka – Colombo and Kandy – will have to wait. Bandung, Jogjakarta, and Surabaya were drawn upon for studies on the future of Javanese urbanization to be published elsewhere.

The changes I see are rarely promising, yet it is impossible to despair in the face of so much vitality. Moreover there is a trend toward taking increasing control over the destinies of the cities, from the bottom as well as from the top. Some smaller scale interventions into urban process in the Third World are producing results worth transmitting to administrators, planners, and businessmen elsewhere.

Urban Futures
Observed

1 Finding Out: A Traveler's Quest

Tourism was once a kind of scholarship – a search for the roots of other societies while savoring life in their midst, partaking of their cuisine, using their conveyances, and living in their hostelries. A person on tour sought out those images and artifacts that were valuable enough to be preserved – cathedrals, castles, museums, restorations of antiquities, paintings, sculpture, tapestries, parks, lakes, vineyards, small harbors, and the like. Because so many of the leisure class took the challenge seriously the Baedeker and the Guide Bleu were created and the Cook's tour was organized.

By the mid-nineteenth century railroads and shipping lines began to produce tourism opportunities for the middle classes, while later the bus tour encapsulated some of this experience for the masses. The private automobile brought much more of the countryside – even the wilderness – into the itinerary. The jet age has been superimposed upon these other modes of movement, so that the whole world has been brought within the orbit of the tour. Honolulu, Kyoto, Den Pasar (Bali), Bangkok, Katmandu, Delhi, Tehran, Jerusalem, and Nairobi are doing their best to fit into the concept of tourism evolved between 1760 and 1929, while Tokyo, Hong Kong, Taipei, Singapore, Penang, Colombo, Bombay, and Beirut have added a fillip here and there. Each has been forced to emphasize the exotic, the unfathomable, and the splendorous. The attractions that represent a great tradition sweep the curious along paths already beaten by pilgrims.

Many new emerging nations originally set up barriers to travel, but the need for hard currency and the impatient demand for quick processing at the airport have somewhat smoothed the entry process in the Third World. A tourist is now commonly defined as a person who pays his bills with dollar equivalents and is allowed up to 15 days in the country before he must register at the police station. (There are, however, many variations and month-to-month adjustments in procedures.) Each country has begun to regularize its transportation system

1

from the international airport to the metropolis, set grades or quality standards for hotels, and supervise the services provided for tourists.

Once deposited in a hotel, the traveler is offered guided tours of the city, nightclubs, restaurants, and a listing of sights recommended for visitors. Most likely he has been enticed to the country by the images of the society as abstracted by color photography and presented with vibrant language in glossy brochures at the travel agencies or in the Sunday newspaper supplements. Video and film travelogues are less connected to the selling of air tickets, but are not unimportant. Those that have come on business cannot afford to ignore the scenic attractions; they could hardly face their social set back home and admit that they had not taken in the sights. It is a traveler's duty to go out and consume the local product.

Recognizing the artificiality of the sightseeing experience, professionals on tour bring along a list of names of persons to look up. Very often these people are their counterparts in the Third World metropolis and are sought out so the visitors can engage in gossip, talk shop, and perhaps get an insider's view.

However, the people on the list, most of whom have studied overseas, have found it necessary – because of a growing sense of nationalism – to standardize their intermediary role after meeting a few visitors. They have come to accept fully all the traditional European and American goals of tourism, so they will recommend the same trips and destinations as the commercial tours, or take a distinguished visitor there themselves. Moreover the explanations of what one sees are transmitted with the same cliches as provided in the literature stocked in the hotel. When challenged, the local host may express his personal distaste for the oversimplifications inpsired by the chamber of commerce and may offer a few cynical observations upon conditions in his immediate vicinity, but if he is honest with himself, he recognizes that he cannot generalize. The facts and the data, even in the mother tongue, are too sparse to permit persuasive contradiction of the myth or to put together reliable assessments of the total situation. As a result, the information obtained in the course of meeting friends or acquaintances while moving about the city and its environs is the product of mere happenstance; it offers few rationales for present and past events, and provides little more information about the current situation than can be found in the newspapers.

The few traveling professionals who have institutional connections with resident staffs can get glibly formulated appraisals of current trends, political background analyses, and forecasts of likely changes. In many ways they have a head start, frequently in the wrong direction. Old hands in government, international organizations, and the multinational corporations know that they are extremely vulnerable to carefully staged "snow jobs" in any society which they have not previously studied carefully. Many a politician, executive, and engineer has complained of being "brainwashed" by the resident staff after decisions made on the basis of the briefing have led to disaster. Experienced professionals recognize the need for some kind of independent and quite personal appraisal to place staff studies in perspective.

Students, dropouts, and recent graduates have found alternate paths leading away from the airport in developing countries. By wearing either blue jeans or loose-fitting oriental garments they are set apart from the standard tourists; in the trade they are known as backpackers. Although they avoid the touristic stereotypes and the intercontinental hotel milieu by regrouping at guest houses, pensions, camps, YMCA-YWCAs, hostels, and innumerable "crash pads," they still depend upon the "straight" tourist institutions for support. Therefore, many will be found in the American Express check-cashing line. Young people also arrive with names and addresses, but they depend very heavily on informally shared information rather than organizational affiliations. Any family that has been generous with a handful of strangers of this ilk may find itself swamped a season later, because the youth grapevine works with only a little less speed than the telex. Anyone over 40 can also move in these circles if he sheds all pretenses and can tolerate occasional discomfort, but he does not pick up as much information as his juniors, since the latter are more trusted by their counterparts within the society.

Following this alternate path through the metropolis, the visitor acquires an unromanticized view of the underside of a city. His sources of information – the younger bilingual "culture brokers" – are insecure, often rejected and bitter. Young adults are not infrequently affected by idealism, and so are strongly inclined to compare current conditions with the desired state of affairs. Then the present, and by extrapolation the future, are seen to be hopelessly deficient, regardless of the overall indications of economic and social development.(1) If visitors contact young people actively involved in the Establishment in Korea, Taiwan, Malaysia, Singapore, Nigeria, and similar rapidly developing countries, they are likely to find them working overtime, and unavailable for long discussions; perspectives based upon personal experience usually extend very little beyond the responsibilities of their post. Any youths that do have time to talk are likely to have marginal personalities, unimportant jobs, and no capacity to quantify – factors which influence their effectiveness as prophets. Thus the traveling "untourist" (a term that will be used routinely hereafter) is caught up in an interplay of circumstances and interests that prevents him from obtaining the kind of perspective that results in unbiased forecasts. Knowledge relevant for understanding the future course of the society is as elusive for him as for the conforming tourist.

The need for a better way of getting information while traveling first became apparent to me on an occasion when views were exchanged with the first behavioral scientists to tour the Soviet Union during the earliest thaws of the cold war. They speculated about how various propositions regarding the evolution of the Russian society could be tested even though their movements were controlled by Intourist. They were allowed a guarded look at several major cities and a few communities besides, such as a well-organized collective farm, a cluster of <u>dacha</u>, and a model city next to a dam. The first question raised was, "To what extent are the conditions representative?" Then, if bias were detected, "Is this bias an effort to represent the goals toward which the society is striving or is it an attempt to create a special sort of 'Potemkin' effect to satisfy the curiosity of the carefully programmed Westerners?" One discordant note in all the theorizing was the frequency with which English-speaking Russians had broken through to the visiting contingents with requests for clothes, printed matter, watches, and other items in limited supply. Were they really indicative of the sense of deprivation in the population? Or were they the special set of small entrepreneurs and marginal types that appear at the fringes of all societies and are the special bane of anthropologists seeking to get a representative cross section of a community? An experiment was therefore designed. One of the Russian-speaking members of the group undertook to enter a restaurant, choose a seat at random (he carried a table of random numbers with him), and engage the people at the table in conversation according to a pre-set schedule of topics. A similar procedure was used in the park. This rigorous technique for making contact yielded no startling findings, but it did serve to dispel the fears of those who held to the conspiracy theory of Russian behavior in dealing with guests.

Suddenly I understood that touring a strange city is, more than anything else, an immensely challenging game. It is as complex an engagement as chess, but involves many adversaries. A "good move" is one that reveals a hidden truth; "obtaining a checkmate" in the tourney is equivalent to a positive confirmation of a significant discovery that provides an advantage against an opposing point of view. One's opponents can be quite dissimilar. In some instances, the contrary version was presented as truth at home, and in other instances it was upheld by authorities in the host city.

Game-like qualities of the urban ecosystem itself also emerge at several levels. The metropolis is indeed a jungle, composed of stalking hunters wary prey, and those who maintain their camouflage and thus melt into the scenery. A touring professional is marked as prey by those who wish to strip him of his cash while he is trying to capture on color film the originals of the travel poster. On reflection, he sees himself as an urban naturalist seeking an economical way to outwit Nature, causing it to reveal itself. Because the stay is short he must employ techniques of wily reconnaissance rather than undertake studies in depth, and his strategy must be chosen accordingly.

How does a short-term observer develop expectations, even anticipations, regarding conditions that will not be reached for as much as a decade or more? He will need an extensive practical knowledge of social systems, something he has already acquired from his work as a professional person. He will also have acquired a greater grasp of urban systems than he realizes, since the advanced practice of any profession is carried out in a metropolitan milieu. At home he knows the urban system well enough to appreciate differential rates of change, often betting on some facet of its future when choosing a location or investing funds. It is quite natural, therefore, that the first attempt to "understand" – that is, to fit the new experience into some category of organized knowledge – is to compare the Third World city with those that were known previously. The initial task of the enquiring traveler is one of generating revealing experiences as fast as the memory can record them. Quite soon this flow of unexpected revelations slows; by that time, however, some intuitive generalizations have been formulated.

The basic strategy for obtaining an appropriate scale for the instruments needed for city watching is to use the city's own methods for observing itself. One does this by tuning into the urban communications systems because the persons engaged in big operations and those who promote large projects are forced to think in macroterms in much the same way as the city watcher. The international airport is one of these major operations, bringing together many strands of metropolitan life; as such it can be used as an early indicator of conditions in the metropolis. When the airport contains no newsstand, as in Karachi, it reveals this society's lack of awareness of external opportunity, associated perhaps with close central supervision of the media. Careful assessment of the bias in the communications system may be required. (It should be recognized also that the cause may well be trivial, attributable to a petty feud or a bankruptcy.) Some places, such as Indian airports, contain publications presenting content directed at national issues, but pay very little attention to international or metropolitan affairs. While in Katmandu, to choose another extreme, the whole world is reported upon as if it were a part of the city itself. Normally one has little time upon arrival to make such observations, but if the occasion arises, the airport can provide important first impressions.(2)

On an initial trip to a Third World metropolis any carefully considered and planned approach to a study of its future is exceedingly likely to fail. Communications are poor and misunderstandings frequent; the necessary arrangements and preconceptions break down at one point or another. Thereupon one should become opportunistic; usually starting from specialities that are best known to him. For example, an automobile executive might begin with used car sales and then expand to investigate the local competitors, including the substitutes for automobiles. These initial improvisations may be supported by daily reports on such events as a bus and truck drivers' strike occurring during the visit, illuminating quite convincingly some of the hidden relationships between transport and other activities within the metropolis. The result could lead to definite impressions of the directions in which the transport and communications systems will develop.

In the descriptions of procedure that follow this introduction three classes of personal interest predominate: 1) ways of making a living that are conditioned by a need to keep up with other cities, 2) advances in capability of public and private institutions, and 3) acceptance of new designs, images, forms, and living arrangements.

EARLY EXPLORATIONS

The first task is to discriminate among the indigenous ethnic species. Sometimes the differentiation can begin on the plane before arrival, but it starts in earnest when going through customs. Citizens returning may be observed as they unpack their personal belongings and display their "loot" to customs officials. Crowds waiting to welcome home the missing members of their intimate groups offer much diversity for observation. In the Third World and Japan the urge to visit the airport on leavetaking or welcoming occasions is so great many airports report ten visitors per passenger. The ethnic communities, as well as many of the religious ones, take care to distinguish themselves by at least one prominent visual cue, although at the airport many have compromised traditional dress with international fashions.

The tourist and the untourist almost always share the same transport in the transition from airport to metropolitan center. Both are faced with a complex strangeness. An extra bit of shock is induced in those countries where the signs cannot be read, and many of the commodities offered for sale are unknown by name or use. The first problem is to avoid becoming lost. Maps are useful, even if they are printed in an unfamiliar script and laid out according to strange conventions. They offer an orientation to bodies of water and mountains, if any, and from that alone much of the topography can be deduced. Also green patches are used to represent park or forest in all societies, so the relative locations of open public spaces can be judged. Even gentle slopes and small bridges can be depended upon for finding one's way.

Guides can be obtained in every city; often they are aggressive enough to seek out the stranger. They have at least a smattering of the common languages of tourists. If the visitor should look Japanese and does not wear a black suit, a guide is likely to appear who knows a bit of Japanese (his Chinese might be even better); those that wear black suits get the same treatment as Europeans. If one feels utterly strange, it might be worthwhile to invest up to a half day in a short organized city tour or with the least sleazy of these intermediaries.

In an organized tour one can mingle with fellow strangers who speak an approximation of one's own tongue and will share experiences, particularly in handling interpersonal contacts, decoding signs, and obtaining simple services. Guides will point out a few landmarks, pronounce their names, and sometimes translate their signs. These newly acquired percepts give a visitor confidence that he could not become completely lost. By taking advantage of the natural courtesy of the residents, he could find his way back to his temporary home.

Strangeness wears off quickly; within a single day in a totally alien city with an impossible language one can point out hundreds of sights and sounds which have become familiar, and hundreds more of borrowed Western items for which there are names in one's own repertoire of terms and images. Such a beginning can provide the mental security that is needed for further exploration.

All during the exploration of the physical surroundings, preparations should be made for the days that follow. Bookshops and newsstands are sought out. Offices for the airlines will usually be found clustered together in the high-rent district. Branches of international banks will hang out their plaques nearby. Restaurants with familiar cuisine will make themselves evident in all but the very poorest metropolises. Consulates will discreetly advertise themselves.

Most of the explorations of the structure of a city in the Third World must be undertaken during daylight. This is not because of the danger involved, since fears of personal harm are in almost all instances quite misplaced, although the presence of unaccompanied women in the streets after dark may be misinterpreted in some societies, just as it would be in the West. The principal reason is that the lighting is too poor to see much; since the energy crisis of 1973-74 the level of public illumination has been reduced, even in the lobbies and rooms of hotels. Thus the visitor may be prevented from perusing reading material in the evening unless he was forehanded enough to check the lighting and purchase a stronger bulb to replace the one provided by the hotel or guest house. Then it will be possible to use the time after dinner to analyze the reading materials that came to hand during the day.

Many indicators of the future reside in the English-language press. Virtually every metropolis relatively open to travelers, and even some (as in Burma) that are not, maintain an English-language newspaper, almost always on a daily basis. A few also produce French, German, and Chinese editions. The coverage of the dailies is heavily directed to world news, but they do allocate one-third to two-thirds of their attention to internal affairs. A stack of recent newspapers will allow a reader to quickly assemble a longer list of the principal actors on the local scene than he would get from the international press dispatches, to get a clearer idea of the respective arenas for action, and to identify the local issues of immediate public concern. Always remember that some issues are too sensitive to allow open public discussion – these may be identified by the visitor who was foresighted enough to review the foreign dispatches in advance and prepare a checklist of issues which can be compared with the list assembled on the scene. If restraints upon the press are serious, as they have been in Karachi, Jakarta, Manila, Delhi, and Seoul, a street market will exist in international English-language periodicals somewhere in the vicinity of the first-class hotels. Recent issues picked up by the hotel workers from among the discards of tourists provide the principal source of supply. Thus, without too much trouble, a fairly balanced (even though incomplete) appraisal of the newsworthy changes in the metropolis can be achieved.

The local press, publishing in the languages spoken in the metropolis, will pay attention to the full range of tolerated opinions, and occasionally introduce a few extra issues that are screened from the view of strangers in the manner that families keep some matters to themselves. Summaries of news stories and editorials from the vernacular press and items indicating other stories attracting attention often appear in the

English-language press. In general it is not advisable to query a long-term resident about topics that are certain to incur censorship unless he is a newspaper correspondent; old hands almost always exaggerate when responding, while a few ideologically committed nationalists will understate. However, once a formula for discriminating news acceptable to the current regime from that which is probably unacceptable has been worked out through application of ones own judgment, the expatriate residents and other bilinguals will be able to cite the cases that force corrections, thus enabling the line separating fact from fiction to be drawn more finely.

The importance of English as a medium of communication cannot be overemphasized. International traders, whether Japanese, German, or Arab, are forced to employ English when conducting business, when advertising new products, and when preparing technical manuals for operating new equipment. Virtually all modern medical treatment is carried on in English, or by means of direct translations. To an even greater extent, scientific teaching and research, modern technology, architecture and engineering design, and most of the youth culture are dominated by the language of their American and English origins. Anyone with technical or professional ambitions in a developing country – even on the other side of the Iron Curtain – must now master English. In fact, teaching English has become a major industry in all the large cities.

Written English is better comprehended than the spoken language. A note written in capital letters is much more likely to penetrate the normal layer of politeness and bashfulness in the presence of obviously illustrious – or unexpectedly unconventional, in the case of the un-tourist – strangers than any spoken inquiry or sentence taken from a phrase book. Language specialists, who, like the missionaries of old, were once engaged in translating English-language classics and tracts into increasingly minor languages and dialects, are now being taught to teach English according to the Michigan, Cambridge, or other standard approach. Proselyters for the communist ideology, both the Russian and the Chinese versions, must henceforth resort to English as often as the Christian missionaries if they are to gain converts. Virtually all foreign assistance, whether directly from other nations, or channeled through the United Nations agencies and the voluntary services, must work through the English-language medium. The law is one profession that sometimes provides an exception to this generalization, for societies, such as Iran or Thailand, which historically were never colonies or dependencies of either the United Kingdom or the United States.

Every new project – of the kind intended to improve production efficiency – has a requirement for imported capital and technology that necessitates copious translation into English, although very often the original conception and the detailed justification required presentation in the vernacular from an English version. The first drafts of five-year plans are almost universally prepared in English, because the technical components of plan formulation and advanced economic analysis are taught in that language. As a result, rumors about plan changing and target shifting filter through English-speaking bilingual circles. Popular values, social goals, and slogans are expressed in the mother tongue, but analytical structures, precision of statement, and sources of hard currency are contributed through English.

Quick comprehension of future potentials can be achieved by tracking down the full complement of literate English culture in the best library in the city. If the material is voluminous, the library will also have a modern cataloging and indexing system. A catalog allows a partially informed person to ask questions of the stock of recorded knowledge and reduce, step by step, the degree of his ignorance. Nevertheless it must be remembered that the creative thinking and the radical innovations for reorganizing the society seem to be carried out in whatever language is used for instruction in early elementary school; the translation of such novel thoughts into another language is often repressed for months or years and usually made available only after the concepts have gained a considerable following. Direct translations of these ideas into English make them seem primitive, naive, sloganeering, ungrammatical, meandering, inconclusive, and even incoherent, though in the original they are capable of kindling a flame. People heavily dependent upon the stream of English-language reports can, as a consequence, make huge mistakes in judging the prospects of the society; usually it is the resident correspondents, expatriate agents, technical assistance experts, and diplomats on the scene for a period much longer than 15 days who will be most vulnerable to this form of blindness. Local elites quite often have reason to employ a deceptive strategy in their dealings with the outside world, and any outsider who forgets that he can be a pawn in the struggle for power and status deserves to lose those exchanges.

Different professions have their own techniques for selecting from the output of printed materials those items which may be indicators of fundamental change. Each traveler draws from those techniques when constructing a personal set of expectations. Representatives of some organizations are required to put their impressions into writing as a report, while others are merely preparing themselves for the searching questions they expect from colleagues and friends after they return home. The most common varieties of professionals on tour in the Third World include those interested in technology and industrialization, public services (including public health, education, transport, power, telecommunications), and architecture. Each of these areas of expertise upon which future expectations may be based, will be taken up separately, assuming about three days of general orientation acquired by the means already described in the past few pages.

TECHNOLOGY: THE NEW WAYS TO MAKE A LIVING

A city comes into being because a few specialities were developed in that locale and its residents became so skilled in their production that other communities bought from them rather than produce for themselves. A metropolis distinguishes itself by developing a much larger number of specialities which are backed by a broad spectrum of standard services. The richest source of new specialities is from overseas, so the metropolis accumulates many international exchange relationships.

Most modern technology advertises its appearance in some way. (Up-to-date weaponry is the principal exception.) It must do so because modern goods and services are produced in bulk lots. Therefore, the visitor need only discover the respective media for advertisement to put together a relatively complete compilation of newly established technologies. However, an economical strategy for search is required.

One of the simplest procedures in the search for new projects involves hiring a car with a bilingual driver for a half day or so, setting out for the periphery of the metropolis and looking for recently finished structures and the new construction sites. Most metropolises in the earlier stages of development will have improved only a few roads at the growing edge, and these will support the new factories and warehouses. The medium-to-large construction sites are likely to display their source of expertise and funds in English as well as the official local language.

The territory in the vicinity of the international airport is particularly interesting. It will capture exporting firms with high value per unit weight, such as stylish knitted goods, electronic components, electronic subassembly, and perishables such as seafood, flowers, and newsworthy printed materials. The land behind the harbor will attract transport machinery assembly, food processing, and some plants dependent upon heavy imported goods. The blocks at the edge of the central business district will be taken up by warehouses and expansion of the "back-of-the-bazaar" industries, as well as new offices. A few scattered construction sites will also be detected, such as microwave relay towers, television transmission, telephone exchanges, new government office buildings, townships for government workers, and transport terminals of various kinds that will attract future industry.

Every visiting professional in the ranks of the technologists — whether engineer, manager, consultant, or investigator — possesses an irresistible urge to seek out his counterpart in a foreign metropolis even if he does not have an introduction. This itch should be repressed for at least several days if his objective is to construct a dependable set of expectations for the industrial future of the metropolis. As noted earlier, if the visitor succumbed to the urge immediately, he would be told the hoary cliches about the society as if they were everlasting verities. When he is properly prepared, the host can be diverted into more rewarding channels by being urged to explain some of the specific developments already observed that do not fit into any pattern as yet. Without such detailed preparation the meeting is likely to dissolve in bonhomie without any fundamental meeting of minds or transfer of basic information.

Any host who is asked to explain the presence of some specific facility, or the probable reasons for the choice of site, is thus enabled to display his full professional capabilities. He will draw upon little-known data and experience, the latest gossip, and the full extent of local knowledge of the technology or business to offer a plausible explanation. He does this because the visitor has changed his role from tourist (or untourist) to that of colleague-professional. One consequence of this change is that he is served with a curious "acronym soup" often delivered in a strangely accented English. The proper response on the part of the visiting professional is to feign some misunderstanding in order to get organizational relationships straightened out and sponsorships decoded.

After three to four days at this pace the flood of images, nouns, acronyms, public personalities, contexts, and special relationships would overwhelm the best of human memories. To prevent confusion the proper strategy is to employ odd moments for noting down stream-of-consciousness impressions and quick on-the-spot appraisals. Each of these notes is a knot of associations that enables one to make some sense of the multitude of impressions. Some time must also be set aside for writing a moderately organized subassembly of ideas, a few pages at a time. Out of these attempts at organization come interesting hypotheses for explaining the apparent path of development. For example: Can reasons be discovered for the apparent success of some capital-intensive activities in an urban economy where labor-intensive formulas would appear to be preferred?

Already at this stage the style of writing becomes important. Most visitors are strongly tempted to employ a colorful, idiomatic presentation of findings – a recapitulation of the impact all these surprises had upon himself as a potentially typical observer, followed by a more sober assessment of the findings. An easy formulation is to contrast the guidebook cliches with the reality that was perceived, lampooning them in many ways. However, intellectuals' egos are no more secure in the Third World than elsewhere so that kind of treatment – when read by residents for checking of details – causes deep resentment and invites angry backlash. It is better to identify a readership back home of one or a few people who are already quite knowledgeable and ask oneself what they might want to know about the near future of productive activity in a given metropolis. Then the expectations derived can be justified by marshaling the relevant facts; most of the interesting asides should be saved for informal verbal exchange with friends and colleagues elsewhere. Not only would the readers find the work more understandable, the tourist is saved the embarrassment of having his report cause his contacts and sources of information to lose face as a consequence of the flip, informal quality of the comment. His interpretation of the metropolis, which could be extremely valuable to all parties involved, might well be rendered impotent. The untourist is more likely to succumb to the temptation to engage in colorful comparisons because his organizational and professional ties are less strictly defined, yet the attempts of the untourists at gauging the future are at least as important as those of established professionals because their youth makes it likely that they will live through the future they see coming, and perhaps use their expectations as a basis for making policy while in responsible posts at some later date.

By the second week in a visit one should have accumulated enough concrete observations to overcome touristic impressions and be able to use interviews effectively. In making appointments a new factor enters that rarely had any influence on the visitor previously – the local holidays. These ritualized disruptions of routine are mileposts in the schedules of local professionals; they often influence the time – and somewhat less frequently the place – of an appointment. Is your local colleague fasting during Ramadan? If so he will have more time in the afternoon, but may be terribly fatigued or else edgy from lack of nourishment. The Chinese calendar is simpler to deal with, but national holidays are unexpectedly superimposed; holidays associated with political independence from colonial rule are often celebrated with enthusiasm, blocking many thoroughfares. The Hindu calendar is even more complex than it appears because each region places its own emphasis on designated holidays, almost ignoring more than half. If one's visit were to be chosen so that it terminated in a major holiday, the serious exchange of ideas, which is one of the principal reasons for making the trip, might well be missed.

Theoretically, a well-planned trip would avoid such a catastrophe, yet a call to the consulates of these countries rarely yields sufficient assurance of preventing it. Consulate personnel in New York, London, and elsewhere are most likely becoming used to celebrating the local holidays; they have a hard time reorienting to a lunar calendar, recalculating what this may mean within the international airline conventions for measuring the lapse of time, and making the simple informative reply that is expected of them. Most often an enquiry elicits confusion, at best a tentative response.

In a standard two-week visit that is calculated not to end on a national holiday or a religious fast, the last few days are most likely to be filled with appointments. Previous concerns with background and structural relationships give way to inquiry about the other person's role, experience, and the best means for getting deeper than pleasant formalities in a short time. A good strategy is to identify some development in technology elsewhere in the world that should be of interest to the person to be interviewed. The visitor is then in control of information relating to the technology while the local man serves as an expert on its equivalents in and around the metropolis. The visitor is likely to have seen the latest trade journals from America before leaving so he will have a number of possibilities to draw upon for matching wits in a discourse on a subject which may be very new in the Third World, where trade journals so often arrive by surface mail. He is able to point up the obstacles that such a technology would encounter in his own metropolitan environment, some of which may be important revelations of latent forces that affect the future. Once the conversation attains this level of interprofessional exchange, it can be directed anywhere that promises to yield insights.

In the last few hours of the visit, after packing, it is useful to recapture in the form of quick notes the flavor of these conversations. The best of them might be spelled out on the plane trip before fatigue sets in. They add human interest to what is otherwise a desiccated analysis of technology and trade.

THE NONMARKET SECTOR – PUBLIC SERVICES

What might be the strategy of search for future change in the public sector? The principal clue is found in sampling the talk regarding the setting up of new organizations. Old organizations have their course set for them, and the participants are fixed in their ways, but new agencies, cooperatives, voluntary groups, associations, clubs, political parties, and social movements make up for the deficiencies of existing organizations. Each of them serves a minor fraction of the population in a way it has not been served before. For example, tribalists coming to the city to work in the construction industry find that their animistic religion is not supportive in the new environment, so they look for a missionary who seems to have power and a message that injects some security into their situation. When one walks around a city, he should pay special attention to orators that can hold crowds and fill halls; they are worth making inquiries about when meeting bilingual contacts.

A revealing procedure, more available to the untourist than to others, is to interview students and start up a discussion about prestigious organizations to join after they have finished at the local university, hopefully with a first-class degree. Almost always the best students identify a public service which is handed the most challenging tasks in the society at that time. Forecasting is not for students; they merely distill what is being discussed in the homes of the elite. Any agency retaining this prestige has the opportunity to choose from among the best of candidates. As long as the bright minds keep coming, it is assured of remaining among the pacemakers and could continue in the forefront for an extra 10 to 15 years beyond discontinuation of the flow.

Probing further yields added surprises. For example, among the recent graduates high on the list for the elite Indian administrative service, some break away and opt for other jobs. Where do they go? For some years in the 1960s multinational firms were attractive, subsequently the banks, and later the public corporations such as airlines, shipping companies, and then petroleum production, had the greatest appeal. Why? A strong motivation was to get outside of India, if only on business trips, without being smothered in the protocol of diplomacy; this inclination was bolstered by the urge for power. The ambition to leave the mother country remains very strong among the English-speaking strata of South Asia, from Iran to the Philippines. But what are the more realistic options? Those who are independent of family decision making, that is, those who have the freedom to choose, are likely to have acquired quite knowledgeable views about the relative prospects of public agencies. Advanced students in capital cities where governments have been overturned, or nearly so, by demonstrations originating in the universities (Seoul, Bangkok, Kuala

Lumpur, Jakarta, and Katmandu) will be more knowledgeable about shifts in power and influence among the ministries and special agencies than other bilinguals, including the journalists. Students also talk more freely. One should believe few of the "facts" that they cite, but weigh carefully their estimates of relative potency and the possible coalitions for special ends. Americans will translate student views into pressure group theory, while Europeans and Latin Americans will draw upon their experience with elite-directed societies, in order to reach quite similar specific conclusions.

Related phenomena among intellectuals are easier for the visitor to understand. During the 1970s the environmentalist movement escaped from its colonial taint in the Third World, often taking on character-istics of a religious movement. Environmental pollution became a sin, and the malefactors were corporations, insensitive public agencies, special communities, and nameable individuals. Ecology of a very superficial sort became a doctrine. Calls for environmental action now fill the halls and gain excellent publicity. The consequences of this acceptance by the educated classes are quite predictable. Visible evidence of decay and the sources of stench will be attacked, usually with marked success. The maintenance of parks will be improved and landscaping extended to many other public facilities. The prevalence of litter in public places will appear to be unchanged, however, because the environmentalists comprise a tiny, scolding minority, whereas the public places are used by the masses who have not yet acquired the concept of "litter." At the same time they are encountering goods in paper and plastic packages that were formerly prepared at home or sold in bulk, so the uneatable or unusable portion is scattered to the wind, as are the handbills, cigarette boxes and stubs, and banana and pandanus leaves. Solid waste will remain a continuous challenge to the environ-mentalist, because as underemployment diminishes, the elaborately evolved traditional reclamation and reuse techniques based upon pari-ahs, untouchables, and unfortunates, begin to break down and leave mounds of refuse in prominent places.

For a stranger the composition of the litter of a city always provides a rewarding source of information about trends in consump-tion. How much is modern, represented by printed polyvinyl and polyethylene films, thin pastel-colored papers, grease-proof white pa-per, and unrecycled newspaper? What are their apparent origins in the city, according to product, user, occasion, and distributing establish-ment? Does the activity seem to be booming? The answer is strongly positive most of the time. Nevertheless these components of the litter are more like the dandruff released by preening, since much of the litter in public places is the detritus and excrement from urban metabolism. Addicts of tobacco, alcohol, betel, pan, and other common drugs will leave evidence of their habits in the most congested places, since high human densities attract their purveyors. In this instance the urban ecology will have provided a full set of salvage and reclamation specialists. Functions such as that of cigarette butt collector exist. In Jakarta, for instance, studies showed that an active person could find enough butts to support himself with greater security than if he worked as a field laborer in the overpopulated countryside, but the returns were too thin to allow the support of dependents. (The reclaimed tobacco is extracted for nicotine used in insecticide.) Old newspapers are cut and folded into envelopes and bags, low-grade cardboard packaging is processed into cinema tickets and bottles are redistributed as household containers to such an extent that the cooking oil is quoted in the market by the beer-bottle-full quantity, since that container is so frequently used. Larger tin cans are cut and flattened to be used as roof patches; the smaller ones are dissolved in acid in small industries behind the bazaar to manufacture hydrogen and carry out other chemical reductions. Vegetative wastes go to cows or goats kept in and around the tenements to provide milk for the babies. Fragments of unglazed pottery, brick, concrete, asphalt aggregate, and shattered glass are carted away for landfill. The litter that remains is too thin or worthless to keep alive the person who does the collecting unless he is subsidized by the public as a sweeper or sanitation worker. Techniques for analyzing dustbin contents and artisans' wastes waiting to be conveyed to the city dump were long ago developed by archeologists to establish the level of development of a civilization and modern versions of this analysis have changed little.

The reason I have placed so much emphasis on the analysis of the urban environment is that, though complex, the environment offers simple checks on the more precise but less dependable methods of detecting change which rely on translations of reports. People do not make up elaborate fictions to explain the composition of litter; in societies burdened with censorship and nationalistic propaganda the natural cityscape is far more unbiased than any stack of summaries and evaluations offered to the visitor.

It is important to understand the kind of future that can be forecast for the public sector. An outsider is aware of a multitude of possible next steps that fit the present states of development of a metropolis and are theoretically available. What the visitor will discover repeatedly is that some of the most promising pathways are blocked. Therefore the forecast is composed of many strongly negative assertions. Of a hundred possible advances, only a score or so will be permitted by current circumstances and only half of these will succeed. Also, political upheavals which the visitor finds too complex to probe will change the odds for or against a predicted trend. A set of expectations arrived at for the public sector is made up primarily of transitions that one expects will not happen, at least within a stipulated period, along with some that could occur because conditions are favorable.

SEEKING THE FUTURES OF DESIGN

A number of professions are interested in discovering the directions in which design is moving.(3) Architects are particularly concerned with the acceptability of new ideas such as abound in the studio and in the journals. Marketing specialists need to know what kinds of images are associated favorably with what kinds of products. Industrial designers and advertisers will want to know about the changing values of color, filigree, hand (of cloth), and plasticity, to mention only a few of the variables. Trends in the various metropolises move in utterly different directions in the Third World; apparently they depend heavily upon the kind of education obtained by the cohorts and social groupings now entering the marketplace. The new customers make judgments based more upon the image presented than upon past experience.

Arguing from the principle that the prestige attributed to an image causes it to be reproduced and imitated, thereby more common, diffused, and diluted, but also much more widely accepted, we have one theory that allows us to forecast a future. Prestige may be legitimized through acceptance by royalty, by some kind of specialized academy of critics handing out prizes or awards, by respected establishments, or it may merely be the fashion adopted by the elite. Almost always a prestigious image is given pride of place in the high-rent areas of the downtown center and the luxury hotels. This means that the attention of the investigator should first be directed to the clusters of high-rise buildings, wherever they may be, and the goods and trademarks they display.

Are the buildings modest variations of what may be seen in London, Paris, New York or Los Angeles? The glitter of the intended highlights has now been subdued in most Third World cities by the "browning out" brought on by the energy crisis, so the appraising eye can no longer depend upon illumination as a principal clue, or cue, to relative importance of their features. Whom do the new buildings represent? Banks are common virtually everywhere, multinational corporations are very important in free ports and other commerce-based cities, while prestige government corporations – oil, airlines, fertilizer, export promotion, and shipping are typical – recently have been crowding into the center. A few private entrepreneurial groups are usually also represented. What gesture does the building make to accommodate itself to the local culture? Is it by name alone, or are such elements as gateway or entrance, window outline, murals, internal decoration, furnishing, or, most complete of all, dedication to the local script, also employed? To what extent are these buildings defended against hawkers, beggars, and street sweepers? Are the brand names displayed in the windows mainly international, mixed, or determinedly national?

This inspection of the high-rise, high-rent blocks of the city yields some first impressions which are likely to remain uncontradicted throughout the whole visit. The openness of the society to external imagery, the sensitivities of the local versions of nationalism, the dependence upon strict policing of public areas, the capacity to maintain images and property at levels of definition approaching the original standard, and the uses for color combinations are all characteristic of those higher strata of the society which establish long-run attitudes toward design. Thus Manila reveals itself to be determinedly contemporary American (mostly Southwest) in its choices of architecture and manufactured products, although Latinized in clothing and heavily Tagalog in local inscriptions. Kuala Lumpur, on the other hand, despite a similar basic culture and an equivalent period of political independence, spends much more effort keeping up face; it has an architectural range that goes from spare, bland, and intercontinental to gaudy, golden excrescences – evidence that taste borrowed from the British is being displaced by cosmopolitan Chinese. Bombay sprouts several new urban centers which try hard to use their fronts to capture the essences of India, and are determined to maintain the presentability of the entrances themselves; at the same time these centers seem incapable of preventing hundreds of mud huts and shanties from rising next door, or keeping the beggars from dominating the promenades. Taipei puts up concrete boxes that maximize the cubic footage allowed by obsolete zoning provisions and along the main streets provides for shop houses on as much of the lower three floors as possible, or else it presents bulky recapitulations of old Peking.

An architect will closely examine the new construction in these central areas. The announcements on the hoardings that list the responsible firms are almost always in English. Are these turnkey jobs, with designs put out of offices in Rome, Athens, Singapore, or San Francisco, and prime contractors pulled in from the big international firms? Or are they joint enterprises with an overseas-trained local man delegated to handle the internal relationships, especially the payoffs to local politicians? Or has the capability become wholly indigenous, as in India or Korea? The architect can immediately understand the kinds of design proposals offered in the first two instances, but would have to study closely the options that are made available in the last, since much will depend, for example, upon such peculiar organizational features as whether the local design offices have been able to install their own air-conditioning specialists. The architect will also identify what equipment is imported, and what kinds of building materials are allowed to be brought into the country, because these items very much determine the quality of the detail.

Landscaping is equally significant. If some tradition such as Japanese, Chinese, Korean, Mogul, Arab, English, or Dutch, has been established, how is it used to best effect? What imported traditions are preferred? How is the landscaping respected by people? Do the poor regard it merely as a substitute for public toilets? What are the multiple purposes that the parks are designed to serve, and at what hours of the day and on what days of the week? What kinds of unintended users of urban open space can be spotted? Levels of park and open space policing are also worth noting.

Differences between cities can be astonishing. The formal park with zoo, serpentine pond, rock garden, and small amphitheatre with tea-house is intensely used by whole families in Caracas, but the equivalents in Bangalore, Tehran, or Bangkok attract less than 10 percent of those crowds, even though they are still viewed as successful. Maidans and parks in many Indian cities are grazed by milk cattle, buffalo, sheep, and goats, thus providing milk for the infants and elderly; in Delhi they are now trimmed by hand sickle and scissors, with the grass being fed to animals in stalls in the nearby juggees; in Manila and most Latin societies the trimming is done by prisoners and the grass is composted. Special children's parks that draw upon Mother Goose lore and mythic beasts of the Paleozoic era, as well as the heroes of the Ramayana, are found in most Indian and some Indonesian cities, while others in Southeast Asia build huge relief maps of the nation so as to acquaint school children with an image of the vastness of their national heritage. Heroes of the defeat of imperialism are also memorialized with statues and monuments, and parks are dedicated to the founders of the nation and the ideals for which they struggled. Historic cities will fit together ruins, restorations, palaces, museums, and grassy plots into a fenced and carefully preserved installation.

The next stage is to look at residential styles being installed at the growing fringes of the metropolis which sometimes includes the re-development of central slum or squatter areas, where the growth is upward. The city could be aggressively committed to high-rise apart-ments in the best international style, as in Singapore; or in a much less impressive, but more often livable, block, as in Hong Kong; or to a mixture of high-density walk-up apartments with tiny plots for free-standing tile-roofed houses, as in Seoul; or architectural compromises, as in most of Latin America. The vast majority of urban residents everywhere prefer one- to three-story buildings on separate plots of land but only the rich and lucky can afford it. (In much of the Third World major lottery prizes are set at a size which allows the winner to obtain the most popular middle-income housing combined with indepen-dent transport to work – either a motor scooter or a second-hand car.) What is the image presented to the public in the newest tracts being developed? Is it a blank wall, as in Muslim countries from Morocco to Iran; a low stone wall with iron fixtures, as in the Eastern Mediter-ranean; a privet hedge, as in some former British colonies; a barbed wire fence, as in some military dictatorships; a brief lawn, as in some former French colonies; or potted flowers, shrubs, and small trees, which could be arranged according to styles set by the Chinese, Japanese, Arabs, or Dutch? Usually only a restricted set of these images is popular with the occupiers of new homes in any particular metropolis.

The organization of peripheral shopping centers tells a great deal about the stage of development the city is reaching. To what extent are they made up of branches of chain stores, each unit with a presentation of stock virtually identical to the others and possessing predictable fronts? Why have economies which have evolved highly organized sectors, such as found in Japan, Brazil, and the Philippines, been the only ones to have organized a variety of chains? Wherever independent Chinese traders are dominant in the marketplace, the shop-house arrangement will be chosen; although, where the land rent is high, it may have to adapt to the lower floors of an apartment block.

Elsewhere one looks for controls – or lack of them – imposed by the land developer, public or private, who recognizes that a large share of the returns will be extracted from sale or rental of shops. For example, land developers must take into account the known measures for coping with the hawkers who creep in and use the public areas free of rent. Can these peddlers be restricted to the periphery, catering to servants and low-paid staff, as in Jakarta? Or do they use carts to encroach upon the parking lots and roadsides, as in Malaysia? Or are they able to keep makeshift stands permanently on the broader pedestrian ways with the backing of local politicians, as in South Calcutta? What attempts are made to keep the premises clean and attractive? Generally the Indians have the lowest standards (this is true even for the rich Indian colony in Hong Kong), but there are vast differences even among Indians.

What shops have an order or arrangement that would be understood and trusted by people arriving via the airlines? In virtually all metropolitan areas, for example, the pharmacies and shoe stores are designed to be comprehensible to strangers, while groceries and dry goods are seldom so accessible. The Japanese, Koreans, Iranians, and Filipinos put a lot of emphasis upon barber shops, while other societies take for granted the itinerant barber who plies his trade under a tree on the avenue, or on the pavements of a quieter side street. Supermarkets, superbazaars, and superettes are rare in Asia and Africa (common in South America), but they show up earliest in any society in the newer upper-middle-class shopping areas. What sales are they promoting: exotic package goods, perishables, or scarce luxuries? What is perhaps most significant is the way light is used after dark, since the most valuable portions of the shopping area are more carefully illuminated. Are the best lit areas cosmopolitan, national, or something else? Much of the time the images cannot be classified because the underlying economic base for social organization (smuggling is one example) is not known to the observer, but quite a large number of them can be registered and typical clusters become apparent.

Equal in significance are the schools. Are they turned out according to some standard design, as in Korean cities, to prescriptions set by holy orders of the Catholic Church and the Protestant sects, as in Latin America, or fitted to the status and subculture of the community, as in most former British colonies? How important are the playing fields in these new growth areas, as judged by their level of maintenance? In what way do the girls participate? What seem to be the rules about uniforms? The value of education itself is not at issue, but only its style and exclusiveness. Cosmopolitan education shows up in the display of children's art and in the bilingual readers sold in the shops that carry stationery and textbooks.

Thus far attention has been concentrated upon the designs already in place where the context or field can be perceived as well as the core image. These items only set the stage for what is to be proposed for the future. One of the places that explores future design is the school of architecture, where for the first time one is likely to talk to colleagues. There in the models and the renderings are found the conceptions of the upcoming professionals. Are they wishful dreams of Western luxury, as in Saigon where all male graduates were apparently destined to become military officers, or romanticized borrowings from books published by the great men of this century with a trifling accommodation to the local culture? The cosmopolitan schools reveal by their work that students and faculty have been studying the most recent journals. Their students will join aggressive local firms that are in competition with Western firms with international reputations. Occasionally one finds a fiercely nationalistic idiom, as in Bangkok, but even there each major public building on the drawing boards resembles in its forcefulness and bulk the Boston City Hall. (Students freely admit that since they obtained new professors with degrees from Harvard and Massachusetts Institute of Technology (MIT), they noted their mentors referring quite often to that standout structure, so very likely there will be several Thai equivalents over the next decade or so.) The work in the private offices of the professors makes up the best single indicator of the permissible range of design over the next five years, unless as in Bombay and Hong Kong the department has had declining prestige in the eyes of the leading practitioners. Usually it is the teaching staff, rather than the current producers of designs, who are trying to stretch the limits of acceptability for that culture.

Starting from the images that people use to present themselves to others in a crowd, how does one get a leg up on the future? The first clue comes from the differences between old and young. What styles are affected by the young, and from what part of the world have they diffused? What has been the lag? (It is most interesting to note the acceptance of denim, blue jeans, and Levis through the respective marketplaces, and the subsequent styles based upon copper rivets, bell bottoms, washed-out fading, patches, etc.) In some societies footwear is as sensitive an indicator as clothing; it would take some time to trace the significance of shoe-style choices in Manila, for example, but the result would be revealing because shoes are obviously important.

Another basis for prediction stems from the special capacity of the metropolis to produce education and accumulate educated immigrants. The future metropolis will have fewer illiterates and a much higher proportion with credentials that admit them to the administrative, technical and professional classes. What shifts can be noted as one moves from fish and vegetable markets, itinerant shoemakers, and poorly capitalized hawkers (activities which contain the highest proportion of illiterates) to areas with meat sellers, packaged groceries, plastic wear, mechanical goods (spare parts supply), cloth, and electrical appliances? (The foregoing list suggests a likely ordering according to increasing level of education of both agents and customers that can be found within easy walking distance of each other.) Book stores and prestige shops exhibiting the latest styles are not included because they fit into very different niches in the respective metropolises, so that Bombay is not like New Delhi, nor Osaka like Kyoto. There is a strong tendency for those who have been educated through secondary school and nonselective universities to become deeply involved in "catching up" with the world, but completion of the more elitist universities and professional schools sets up ideological compulsions (mostly nationalistic) in the youth that will for a while control their choices of style. As this leading class grows older, clothing styles become idiosyncratic, as in the West, where people choose their attire to fit their mood and the occasion.

One of the most fascinating exercises is to prowl around in the industries behind the bazaar which work with miscellaneous machinery in flimsy sheds or in odd rooms of poorly maintained buildings producing relatively traditional products for daily sale. What accommodations are made to the modern taste? Cleanliness, quality control, printed paper wrappings instead of old newspaper, waxed paper for dividers, labels in color, printed containers, trademark displays? The greatest disparities between traditional and modern styles in these craft-originated enterprises are found in Japan, but off the beaten track in Katmandu and Jogjakarta one will see surprising combinations that suggest many questions to ask about the dyeing of fabrics, metal working, printing, and painting techniques that are most likely to evolve novel forms (as in batik or rug patterns). The industrial estates almost always produce less interesting products, but they will have a high concentration of bilinguals engaged in the local production of Western or Japanese designs. Many of these people are bored enough to abandon secrecy and talk freely about the trends they perceive.

In general Third World design of artifacts is impoverished as compared to the West; their great minds have been at work on other subtleties. Therefore, the outsider is most rewarded by concentrating upon the few things with variable patterns that are locally valued, but also produced for export, such as the batik in Jakarta and Bangkok, rugs and carpets in Tehran and Karachi, and Bengali sweets in Calcutta.

AFTERMATH

What does one do with future-oriented assessments of cities? Presumably there will already be rough drafts containing the deductions reached. For what kind of audiences does one prune away the excesses and highlight the features that are appreciated? Who is interested in the futures of Third World cities?

The most serious audience will be footloose professionals like the writer. Therefore the material is initially shaped for the fellow professionals, but a shock is experienced when the reviewers' reports come back. Such articles are often reviewed by cultural specialists who will find the manuscript replete with errors. (Spelling of names and terms were not regularized according to the most acceptable system for transliteration; interpretations of an incident do not fit their knowledge about the context; key events which have a bearing upon the action recorded were not mentioned, etc.) Also, when studies are undertaken in this manner the investigator is pushed to take a more optimistic view than most of the intelligentsia because he observes problems already being solved at a local level. This means that the analysis frequently contradicts assertions made by the New York Times staff, the authoritative elite of American international journalism. On the other hand, a future-oriented overview may also encounter a new kind of threat and since the experts have not stumbled upon it themselves, they express strong doubt, and the new report is regarded as too misleading to print.

Eventually the tourist-futurist comes to recognize that he has been a bumbling amateur; others may label him as a bit of a crackpot, even if it is demonstrated that he had arrived at a superior set of expectations. Prophets are recognized belatedly — if they are heard at all. When such a person communicates through talking, however, rather than writing, people appreciate the account, because it depicts life that is far from the daily routine.

Occasionally he will encounter someone who has been to the same metropolis. It is then that the superiority of the future-oriented approach for seeing a city becomes apparent to all, because the standard tourist can only underline one or another feature that had already been described in the travel sections of the Sunday newspapers; an investigator of possible futures gets in the last word with observations having added significance. For example, he is likely to be able to suggest how a tourist attraction fits into the national development strategy, and he can identify alternative attractions that could well be catapulted into the international media.

If a decent published report is to be produced out of the effort, the returned professional must get to a good library near home and immerse himself in newspapers, current journals, and recent books concerning the area of interest. In that way the full roster of prominent institutions and principals is brought to his attention. He must then introduce himself to the nearby specialists, and identify which of the "futures" he has discovered arouse their interest. Then he must rewrite, usually several times, with specific publications, audiences, and urban elites kept in mind. In other words, the instant expert is transformed into a mature, though somewhat specialized, investigator after much added work. His article then has a good chance of getting past the referees. It should show up in print one to three years after his return, still relevant because only a portion of the future envisioned will have been unraveled.

Three courses of action then remain open. One of them is to retreat from this extraordinary level of complexity, that is, take a real vacation. The second is to continue to dig deeper into the culture by learning the language and deepening friendships with people from that area. Then it becomes feasible to move freely back and forth between two societies, serving as a link between their social networks. It may even qualify one for a position with an international agency or with foreign affairs in government, thus making some constructive contribution to the realization of potentials earlier envisaged. The third choice is to keep exploring, assessing futures of other cities and regions, discovering the ways in which these growing metropolitan areas interact with each other and produce an independent system.

The alternative of exploring several very different metropolises was not politically feasible before the dissolution of the world empires in the 1950s or physically possible before the introduction of dependable air transport in the 1960s. When multinational organizations (almost as many of them nonprofit, nongovernmental organizations as the more publicized corporations) responded to improved accessibility and set up offices in many cities a real need for "multimetropolis" people was created. The multinationals depend upon circulating managements.

Therefore in the 1980s and beyond we shall see many more people moving from city to city as their careers evolve. There will also be a quickened demand for the transfer of technical and social innovations from the Western and communist worlds, often accompanied by financial backing. The diffusion of appropriate technologies among the Third World metropolises is expected to accelerate.

The global system of cities is coming into being due to the extraordinary expansion of telecommunications and airlines. These metropolises are all also becoming voracious consumers of hydrocarbon fuels, drawing upon the world energy markets and bidding up the price, so their internal structure will be changing. Nevertheless, projections for world trade expansion (almost the whole of it intermetropolitan) range from 6 to 10 percent annually – doubling in seven to twelve years – when calculated so as to eliminate the effects of inflation. That would be a continuation of the rate of growth experienced over the last thirty years. The added opportunities for exchange will transform many cities.

Thus a worldwide network of interacting cities, the Ecumenopolis as envisioned by Constantinos Doxiadis, is already coming into being. It will require people who experience, and have come to know, a number of culturally diverse cities in depth. Today's urban adventures provide basic training for tomorrow's world.

2 Seoul*

Among all the cities in the Third World, planners and urbanists have the most to learn from Seoul. With the help and advice of international advisors, Seoul has pulled a Korean society five times its size up the steep path of economic development faster than any city ever before recorded. The international advisors have quite often expressed pride in the results obtained, not recognizing that by the time directions for specific action had been formulated in the Korean language, the policies carried out were quite different from the original recommendations. The extraordinary quality of the achievements in Seoul must be attributed to Korean public servants and entrepreneurs more than to the assistance which was offered.

With the aid of hindsight, therefore, it is no surprise that my first visit to Seoul in 1969 was eye opening.(4) The findings required that I return again and again to discover what developmental surprises this metropolis had in store.

The South Korean government in Seoul has been much maligned in the American press for intolerance shown to rebellious students and politico-religious minorities, but what prime minister, mayor, or editor from Asia or the island republics to the southeast is righteous enough to cast the first stone? Because journalists and other professional observers have been quick to criticize, they have failed to grasp what is being learned in this part of the world that is so important to the rest of civilization.

It would appear, from the numbers of publications about Korea, that the remarkable pace of development has been thoroughly analyzed. However, the major studies

*Estimated 1985 population – 13 million.

focus rather narrowly on the macro-economic and sec-
toral data, with very little attention being paid to urban
development, despite its acknowledged pace-making role.
The institutional analysis had been directed to origins in
tradition (predominantly rural ethnology) and national
agencies, leaving much significant material to be assayed.
The best recent sources are:

Adelman, Irma, and Robinson, Sherman. Income Distribution
    Policy in Developing Countries: A Case Study of Korea.
    Stanford, Calif.: Stanford University Press, 1977.
Chuk Kyo Kim, ed. Industrial and Social Development Issues:
    Essays on the Korean Economy, vol. 2. Honolulu: University
    Press of Hawaii, 1977.
    _____. Planning Model and Macroeconomic Policy Issues: Essays
    on the Korean Economy. Honolulu: University Press of Ha-
    waii, 1977.
Hong, Wontak, and Kruger, Anne O., eds. Trade and Development
    in Korea. Honolulu: University Press of Hawaii, 1975.
Kang, Hugh H., ed. Traditional Culture and Society of Korea:
    Thought and Institutions, Honolulu: University Press of Ha-
    waii, 1975.
Kim, Young C., and Halpern, Abraham M., eds. The Future of the
    Korean Peninsula, New York: Praeger, 1977.
Kuznets, Paul W. Economic Growth and Structure in the Repub-
    lic of Korea. New Haven: Yale University Press, 1977.
Suh, Dae-Sook, and Lee, Chae Jin, eds. Political Leadership in
    Korea. Seattle: University of Washington Press, 1976.

PROTOTYPE OF THE NEW MODERNIZATION

October 1969

Nowhere else in the world today are the processes of urbanization so
intense, so compressed in time, as in the capital of South Korea. The
flow of people to Seoul has been at flood stage for sixteen years. It has
had its competitors, mainly inland centers, that have also swelled mightily
in this interval, but none compare with Seoul. Its nearest equivalent in
recent history is Japan, where the surge began eight years earlier and
has by now transformed almost all rural people into urbanites. Japan
had, however, started with a much higher degree of industrialization.
This willingness to adopt new ways in a new environment creates a
pressure cooker for modernization in the metropolis.

The process by which Seoul added population was quite normal; it is
only the pace that was unusual. In the first three years after the war,
refugees returned and the population began to rebuild what had been
destroyed. Seoul was then supporting its prewar population. But the
refugees from North Korea, who could not tolerate life under communism, continued to move from camps and makeshift housing to the

metropolis. Retrospectively, we can see that Seoul profited from having been rather thoroughly destroyed because it was then able to obtain the highest priority when South Korea was reconstructed with massive foreign aid. During the completion of reconstruction, its population increased by 9 to 10 percent per year, with an extra million people added. In 1961, national development planning was instituted, which distributed capital investments all over the country. However, immigrants continued to prefer Seoul, so the city added another million population at a rate of growth of 7 to 8 percent per year, although a number of small cities exceeded Seoul's power of attraction during this period. Since 1966, the people in those smaller cities have been moving to Seoul, thus opening up niches for their successors from the countryside, but most migrated to Seoul directly from their villages. Seoul still grows by about 8 to 10 percent per year, which means absorbing 300,000 to 400,000 immigrants annually, and there is no sign as yet of a diminished demand for entry.

Why do they come? No longer are their urgencies compounded by homelessness or incompatibility with an alien administration, as in the 1950s. More than 80 percent of the immigrants indicate economic motives when they are surveyed; the remainder generally mention educational opportunity and medical facilities. The villages no longer seem to be able to accommodate the population explosion that has occurred in the countryside, even after extensive land reform. The second and third sons volunteer for the army or work on contract for construction gangs, some even in Japan. They begin to experience what the city has to offer and acquire confidence that they can put their newly acquired skills to work. Many, of course, have a brother or uncle already in the metropolis, and only need to bring them presents and hope that they can help a man "looking for work" to find something that offers better prospects than the village.

In the postwar years a remarkably rapid acceleration in construction employment was assured by foreign aid, yet support from overseas has been less important recently than in other countries, such as Israel, and now has a declining role as a stimulus to economic growth. Internal markets and foreign trade have risen to take their places as job creators.

At the time of this writing, the "Special City" of Seoul had an estimated population of 5,200,000 people. The planners now believe that it may level off at 15 million within two or three decades. This means that it is aiming at the dimensions of the New York City metropolitan area, as measured in population, although the income is expected to be a fifth of current American levels and the physical equipment needed to sustain the residents will be an even smaller fraction. The expectation of population equilibrium is reasonable, because the family planning program is beginning to be successful. Family size in Seoul itself seems to be under control in more than half the city's households, and the crude birth rate is now close to 18 per 1,000 – not much above that of California. Moreover, the eventual proportion of the capital region to the whole population of a small country – a fifth or a quarter at equilibrium – seems quite reasonable in the light of European, Latin

American, and Japanese experience with primate cities. The projections of the planners seem to be quite realistic when using all the tests we know how to apply.

Considering the average scale of development in South Korea, Seoul maintains an extraordinarily high level of income and standards for urban services. Reports to the countryside of the pay available to the full-time employee in Seoul are probably given greater credibility than are reports of living costs. The level of per capita income is about 1.9 times that of the rest of the country and about three times that of the villages and towns. This means that Seoul has managed to produce jobs for immigrants at least as rapidly as they have been arriving. Prices for services in Seoul are almost as high as in Japan and generally exceed those in places that have developed further, such as Kuala Lumpur, Hong Kong, and Taipei.

The Image of Seoul

The new immigrants see Seoul as the epitome of all economic, educational, and political opportunity. To those Koreans who took history, it is known as the capital of the Yi Dynasty, which ruled Korea continuously for over 500 years before it was finally subjugated by Japan in 1910. The royal palaces have been carefully maintained.

The national capital has a dome, as all capital buildings of its era should, but the dome symbolizes only a government and has no sublime or mystical connotations. The solid gray trapezoidal Seoul City Hall says much the same thing for itself. Other government buildings are also places to work and nothing more. Even Taipei has more lasting modern imagery than Seoul, although Seoul's ordinary standard for new housing appears higher.

What does the tourist see? Again we find that even a minor export industry, such as tourism, is well organized in Korea. The conscientious visitor can find a number of volumes of first-class photographs – the kind that treat a cultural object so well that it is hardly recognized later when viewed in situ. Because the truly popular images must be portrayed repeatedly, they should show up in the tourism monthly. Its publisher has had the initiative to bring in three Peace Corpsmen to find and catalog the events of the month, lecture to fellow countrymen about polite behavior in Korea, and straighten out tangled syntax. It records colorful Buddhist temples, Confucian shrines, and visits to the palace museums. The forts at the gates of the old city have been preserved and are noted in passing. On a standard short tour of the metropolis, the defenseless tourist is also shown a brassware factory, an exhibition hall, the Korea trade promotion office, a freedom center, and a women's university. The magazine suggests that during September, with its many brilliant autumn days and afternoon temperatures in the high 70s, the tourist should not even be in Seoul when the mountains to the east are so beautiful. Seoul is a delight only to the person who is thrilled by the prospect of progress and by rising structures that have been quite successfully planned and coordinated. The true image of Seoul today is change; since virtually the entire city is in the process of becoming, South Koreans themselves assume the city offers little to the tourist.

The successful Korean in Seoul aspires to a house that is simple, practical, and traditional. It is about twice the size he must now accept, and should be freestanding (see Fig. 2.1). The change has not yet produced many of these.

The Educational Prize in Korea

Educational achievement is greatly stressed in Korea for reasons that are more similar to those in China than in Japan. In China, the formal examinations for the civil service were highly classical and required a great deal of time and discipline on the part of a reasonably apt student, but a village often sponsored one of its bright boys during his studies so that the new entrants were not all drawn from the 1 to 2 percent that constituted leisured classes. In Japan, education was the most common function of the retired samurai, and ordinary villagers, even girls, were educated along with the children of the samurai and the landowners. Thus, education became widespread in Japan as a direct outgrowth of the rise of a nation-state from a fragmented feudal population. In the absence of revolution, the warrior class was free to teach. In Korea, the acquisition of education led traditionally to the yangban status, a kind of mandarinate achieved by passing an examination (kwako). However, access to the examination was restricted rather early to persons who could demonstrate no illegitimacy in the family line for four generations. A Japanese invasion in 1592 somewhat modified this ruling by allowing access by achievement, such as bringing in the head of a Japanese general or providing arms for the troops. Those excluded from the examination protested repeatedly over the centuries, arguing that they should also be admitted. Finally, just before the successful Japanese invasion (1910), the reform was legally achieved.

Japanese influence then tended to lay down a prestige pathway through the schools, with critical examinations at every step. Some schools maintained a significantly higher performance providing their students an inside track to government posts. Competition for the preferred schools became extreme, and many sacrifices were made by family and student alike to gain entry. Virtually all of these schools were in Seoul itself. The future social status of the family depended on the school in which its sons matriculated; the situation was said to be far worse than the public school system of England. Thus the paragraph in the annual report of the minister of education stating that the examination for entering the middle school was to be abolished and students would move freely into middle school was as radical a change as repealing the "elevens" examinations in England and fraught with even more political peril. But the minister had the evidence to show

ELEVATION.

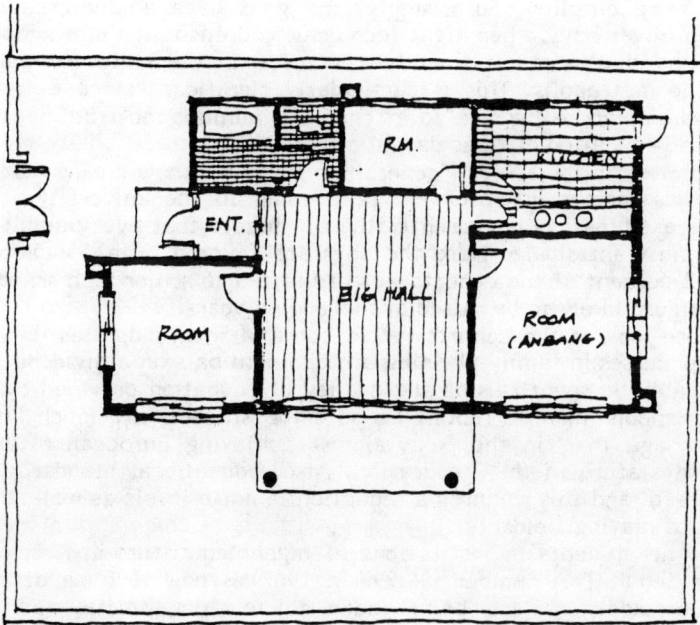

RM.

KITCHEN

ENT.

BIG HALL

ROOM

ROOM
(ANBANG)

N

FLOOR AREA: 738 SF.

0   6   12 FT.

PLAN

Fig. 2.1. Sketch of a typical house preferred by a successful immigrant to Seoul.

that the stress at the age of eleven in Korea caused a lag in physical development and led to a slighter and more nervous citizen.   This decision has changed the power structure in the school system, since it is now the middle school teachers who get extra "tuition" by coaching slower students in their homes. They are now making more money than university teachers.

Despite the rapid growth of Seoul, the capacity of the schools is keeping up, although perhaps at the expense of the quality of education in the rest of the nation, for teachers scheme to get appointments in Seoul even though the cost of living is higher. The school construction program seems well organized and average class size is slowly declining.   Statistics show that 96 percent of the population of elementary school age are in school, which leaves a standard number of blind, deaf, and feebleminded outside the system. There is also an interesting excess of about 5,000 boys in each age class who must have been sent from the countryside to live in boarding schools or with relatives to get a head start in Seoul schools.

Junior high schools are divided into two kinds – middle and technical. In 1967, about 71 percent of the students in the appropriate cohorts were enrolled. Surprisingly, the girls have a slight edge in enrollment over boys, when night technical school is taken into account. This means that a major shift has occurred in the status of women within the metropolis. This is particularly significant since even the public schools are expensive to attend, and families must be investing cash in the education of their daughters.

Enrollment in the senior ("general") high schools now means that the student has serious intentions of proceeding to the university.   The entrance examination is currently the big hurdle that every ambitious student must anticipate. Here the boys are favored by a 55:45 ratio. About 32 percent of the cohorts were admitted to senior high school in 1967, a figure likely to be raised in succeeding years.

A close look at the cohorts yet to come in Seoul indicates that the recent successes in family planning are about to pass on a dividend that will probably be spent raising the quality of education provided by the system. Schools must be rebuilt because the students are much larger for their age than in the past, almost achieving European rates of growth in stature in this generation. Also, educational standards are being raised, and this requires a reduction in noise levels as well as the addition of playing fields.

Half the students in institutions of higher education in Korea are living in Seoul. This number (86,999 in 1967) is now leveling off, but continuous additions are being made to teaching staffs, and new graduate enrollment is concentrated in the capital. This impressive level of educational attainment suggests that Seoul's schooling is not behind that of Tokyo, which has hitherto been preeminent in this respect in world history, although if we had the numbers for Moscow, they would be expected to be comparable.

Decisions about the pace of educational development in Korea were reached by Koreans, but the strategy is a result of extensive consultation with Americans. The Ministery of Education is one of the departments in the Korean government that puts out an annual report in English. It has also created a Central Education Research Institute (CERI), which has undertaken a program of international exchange on matters of educational administration; to the CERI has been assigned the task of planning the improvement of quality throughout the whole system.

Most unexpected, however, is the recent establishment of an Institute for Research in Behavioral Sciences. Its duties are to expedite talent identification, but its terms of reference include "research on child development, social development, organizational development, and test development." The major studies it has already launched include construction of tests for science aptitude, validation of tests for differential aptitude, creative ability measurements, and critical thinking. The institute is also concerned with the effects of cultural deprivation on cognitive development – a cross-cultural check on studies surrounding Operation Headstart in American ghettos. Behavioral science is expected to provide means for taking the stress out of the examinations, thus permitting measurements of something more than stamina.

I obtained a publication for instruction in the English language. Entitled the English Monthly (October 1969), this magazine had a Van Gogh cover showing a golden pastoral scene. Since nearly 80 percent of the print in the magazine is in Korean, it is not surprising that English generated by Koreans is troubled by multiple lapses mostly explained by the inadequacy of direct translation from the mother tongue.

Koreans nevertheless demand sophistication. For instance, their news deals with the Miss World contest, race relations in the United States, political hooliganism in Moscow, and cartoons about moon men discussing American litter. The poem published is a romantic frill by Shelley; the political item is concerned with the assassination of Rasputin; the Western classics are represented by commentaries on the role of grasshoppers in the lives of Greek gods and the invention of the term "bad egg" by Shakespeare. The contemporary scene shows a newspaper story with picture and headline of the eighth coed slaying in Michigan during the summer of 1969; the comic strips are the Flintstones and Emmy Lou; the gossip column mentions actor Lee Marvin's Las Vegas divorce and litigation, along with the landscaping of Beatle Ringo Starr's English mansion. There is a fable from Aesop as well as lectures on manners with quite satisfying explanations about the reasons for these customs.

The content of an English course in the general high school indicates that Koreans have gone much further than anyone in Asia to make their education relevant to the times and the popular culture. Perhaps the authorities have been conscious of the need to compete with the private enterprise, English Monthly. It teaches outside of class, the double entendre, the various forms of POW! expressed in words and simulated sounds, and revels in shocks implicit in American racial conflicts. Thus, English for the Korean offers an entry into a cosmopolitan world with

all its attractions and contradictions rather than the colonial Victorian-
ism of Hong Kong or Kuala Lumpur, the world of officialdom of India
and Pakistan, or the vistas of science in Taiwan.

It is clear why international firms such as Fairchild, Motorola, or
Toshiba can build up production so rapidly in the Seoul area. This kind
of education is raw material for effective organization. The reforms in
education were massively introduced following the Military Revolution
and the assembling of the administration under President Park in 1962.
The fruits should now be visible in the form of high productivity almost
equal to that of the Japanese. The fruits of reform will also appear,
however, in the organization of labor unions and in student politics. The
present strong dependence on authority to coordinate activities in a
large organization, such as a bureau, agency, or a corporation, must be
displaced very quickly by a policy of continuous consultation.

A new charter setting up goals for the reform of national education
has been promulgated and, as elsewhere in Asia, the order in the
wording is important. Appearance of the key terms occurs as follows:
sincere mind, strong body, development of innate faculty, national
progress, creative power, pioneer spirit, public good, order, efficiency,
quality, mutual assistance, love, respect, faithfulness, cooperation,
individual growth, responsibility, freedom, rights, participate, and
building the nation. Then, love of country, love of countrymen, democracy against communism, ideals of the free world, industry, confidence,
pride, make new history, and collective wisdom. It was framed after a
series of community meetings followed by a conference of leading
professionals and is intended to effect a transition from "slaves of
change" to "masters of progress."(5)

Builders and Planners of the New Korea

The Ministry of Construction moves at a feverish pace. Responsibility
for installation of infrastructure for Seoul has been assigned to this
highly organized body of engineers and planners. One can get a glimpse
of what is in store for the "Special City" by going to the city hall and
viewing the stirring photos and renderings stretched along two sides of
the building. Weary slums are displaced by white apartment blocks, and
roads break through rocky ridges leaving spectacularly blasted cliffs on
both sides of the future right of way. Most incredible of all is the
proposed intersection of a ring road with a radial road inside a mountain
so that the traffic exchange is carried out in tunnels. (Apparently, the
price of land has gone so high, and the technology of tunnelling has
improved so much, that this is now an economically viable solution,
particularly when the value as a bomb shelter contributes to the
benefits.)

But this is not "pie in the sky." The money is found somewhere
(government securities with a three-year term are paying up to 36
percent per year), bids are let, and the jobs proceed. Many strategies
have been found for overcoming difficulties encountered with similar

projects in other countries. For example, most cities are embarrassed by the fact that slums must be destroyed two years or more before the replacement housing can be ready. In Korea, most slums are on hillsides, where there is some access to water from wells. The solution is to build a road to the top, construct apartments there with greater accessibility than the slums highest on the hillside, and work downward. This means that the people being moved do not have to hunt for transitional homes. Because next year is election year, many more apartments are scheduled for completion than ever before.

The president, the mayor, and the economic planners decide what goes into the capital improvement budget for Seoul, and then the mayor and the minister decide on what jobs are to be done and when. The Koreans do not bother with a city council because it would slow down the action. The physical planners then price alternative means for getting the job done, and the project design with the best benefit-cost ratio is usually accepted.

It is hard to discover how the people react to this arbitrary approach but the planners resent it and allow their pique to show on many occasions in their working documents. The policy planning is not being implemented using the principles learned at Syracuse, Pitt, Penn, and other places in the United States. The people themselves, however, have rarely had it better. They have always been victims of those in power who wished to build monuments, but never before have the monuments resulted in such an improvement of creature comforts. Their sentiments are tapped by frequent small-scale polls conducted at the universities, and citizens do submit petitions when conditions are bad.

Physical planning is coming into being by stages because suitable land use data were not available before. Until recently, land was viewed by government as a tax resource, and not as something to be conserved and developed. The first of the regional plans was the Seoul-Inchon Special Regional Plan in 1965, with the toll road and the harbor development designated as major projects. Since then, four other regional plans have been launched covering 22 percent of the country, but the outline for the whole nation is also available. Now the plans for Seoul can be envisaged in the context of development of the entire country.

One interesting land use planning problem encountered in Korea is the allocation of land for graves. Since this restricts the growth of cities, a policy of land conservation encourages cremation in funerals and the design of "cemetery parks." In the past, the land in Seoul used for burial urns required very careful clearing procedures with payment to families for removal, while extinct families were transferred to temples constructed for the purpose. Even then, the original land was said to be haunted and was slow to be developed. Land scarcity is now so great, however, that no distinction is made between land formerly used as a cemetery and land used for other purposes. On closer inspection, one might possibly find that many more Christians are residing there and doing business because they are not disturbed by Buddhist and mixed ritual spirits.

Everywhere in the documents one sees comparisons with Western European countries and sometimes the United States – their standards, their consumption levels, their organizational frameworks. This is the way both Korean advisors and foreign-trained students have been taught. The method does not often lead the Koreans astray. Because the road to development has been heavily travelled, previously encountered traps can be bypassed. This tendency to follow faithfully leads to a special problem, which Korea, particularly Seoul, will have to face in the 1970s – the demand for "my-car." This term is a Japanese neologism transmitted to Korea several years ago (1964?) through advertising. It reflects the intense feeling of a materialistic society for the most prized possession of all – a private automobile. Most of the land readjustment is intended to raise circulation space in cities from 7.2 percent at present to 20 percent or more to accommodate the coming "my-car" days. Because Korea has no petroleum of its own, and because coal is quite expensive to convert to liquid fuels, foreign exchange problems are expected to frustrate this hope.

Another kind of designed scarcity may be found in the water and sanitation field, where planners want to install flush toilets in 30 to 50 percent of all buildings despite water supply difficulties in dry seasons. Seoul is supposed to get a sewer system in the third five-year plan. This is realistic because the night soil collection system will be breaking down then, due to the superiority of synthetic fertilizers for growing food. Japan's experience provides a very helpful guide in this direction for development. Due to the cold winters in Seoul, high-rate algae-culture ponds are not likely to work well here for sewage treatment and conversion, unless waste heat is available.

One factor that has gone out of control is the land price level. Wholesale prices have moved upward during the periods of maximum growth at a steady rate but land prices have skyrocketed. Speculators seem to be already assuming the values implicit in a metropolitan area of 15,000,000 persons. Seoul's commercial land was normally 400 to 600 times as expensive as rural land but now has risen to 900 times, according to the Ministry of Construction.

I carried out an analysis of the transport use in connection with land that had a mixed residential-commercial-manufacturing use. This is a part of the city that is very similar to parts of Taito-ku in Tokyo, which were studied by Hoshino and myself three years ago.(6) The land value then would be the equivalent for Seoul today ($10 to $20 per square foot). It is also comparable to parts of New Delhi, Taipei, Bangkok, and Kanpur, which were analyzed over the last year, at least with respect to function if not land value. Seoul is distinguished by the dual role of the bicycle, which operates both as a passenger vehicle and as a two-wheel cart that carries up to 300 kilograms in a trip. A higher proportion of passengers use the bus in Seoul since bus capacity does manage to keep up with demand most of the time. Climate is a factor that also favors bus transport, although one must remember that only a few years ago Koreans were almost without buses but kept an urban economy stumbling ahead. Thus, a strong cultural factor seems to be involved in the choice of vehicular mode (table 2.1).

Table 2.1. Vehicular Use in Seoul
(Adjacent to Wholesaling Area)

Passenger Type	Number	Propor-tion (%)	Share of Capacity (%)	Relative[a] Unit Cost	Index of Capital-ization
Bicycles	150	60	31	1	30
Motorbikes	24	10	8	10	80
Passenger cars	75	30	62	30	1,860
				Total	2,000[b]

Goods Movement	Number	Propor-tion (%)	Share of Capacity[c] (%)	Cost per Vehicle ($)	Capital per ton-mile-day Capacity ($)
Backpack coolie	17	10	2	5	5
Bicycle (allocated)	50	---	8	20	4
Cart	119	70	31	60	10
Truck, 3-wheel	6	4	9	3,000	13
Light van or jeep	15	9	10	2,000	16
Truck, heavy	12	7	38	5,000	7

[a] Multiples of a bicycle valued at $20.
[b] Compare with an equivalent index for the advanced parts of Seoul and Western Europe, where the index is 2,500-3,000. Old Delhi at 800, and subsistence level market towns at 250.
[c] This sets the coolie's capacity at 100 kg for 20 km, the cart at 300 kg for the same distance, the 3-wheeler at 1,500 kg for 150 km, the light van at 500 kg for 250 km, and the heavy truck at 5,000 kg for 150 km.

Source: Richard L. Meier, "Exploring Development in Great Asian Cities: Seoul," AIP Journal 36 (November 1970): 378-392.

There are some notable differences between Seoul and other metropolises. In the observed area, at least one-third of all bicycle use appeared to have light goods delivery as its prime purpose. Motorbikes appeared to be operated by young owners of shops or others in responsible positions. In Korea it did not appear to be proper for young women to ride the second seat. The backpack coolie is unique to Korea. These men have a sturdy wooden A-frame packrack, sometimes with a folding basket attached, which allows them to deliver goods even in a crowded marketplace. The coolie seems to be far more prevalent than is indicated by the statistics, perhaps because he is encountered as a pedestrian rather than a vehicle. The three-wheel truck is the same as the kind that was popular in the 1950s in Japan but has now virtually disappeared there. The most common version is equipped with a large bed about a foot deep that can be used even more than the light van because it is much more an all-weather vehicle.

The two-wheeled cart rear car is a far more efficient vehicle for drayage in restricted areas, perfectly designed for settlement patterns with 7 to 12 percent circulation space. It is basically a steel pipe frame for a box that could be as large as a cubic meter but is usually half that size. It has wire wheels the same diameter as those of a bicycle, but the rim width is twice the diameter. Although less graceful than the Tokyo version, it is better suited to hills because the tail can be dragged as a brake. It is normally pulled, but is readily pushed by a second person when a hill must be overcome. It offers an ideal form of goods transport for those parts of the city where one- to two-story buildings were constructed earlier.

The decision to plan a subway for the central section of Seoul has apparently been reached at the time of this writing. Most documents have treated the subject very gingerly, partly because it will be a feather in the cap of the Ministry of Construction. Again it appears that the new efficiency of tunneling in homogeneous rock is the deciding factor. It will be a short subway that will cross in midtown. One corridor will extend to the harbor and the back-of-the-port industries to the west, and the other to the satellite town of Suwon on the main route south. Very likely the problem of finding outside capital held the project in abeyance for so long. The presence of the subway, together with the very new housing estates, will create new subcenters in Seoul. The ministry has the power to use the profits from subcenter development to finance the sale of luxury houses with lots on a lakeside tract near Suwon. These in turn would help finance the toll road to the south. The subway will require much more integration of urban design than has taken place thus far in the ministry.

URBAN HOUSING POLICY FOR ECONOMIC DEVELOPMENT

A follow-up visit yielded further surprises. These edited field notes focus upon housing; they illustrate more clearly the kind of future-oriented urban information that can be assembled quickly.

June 1970

Seoul, of all metropolises in modern history, has come the closest to achieving housing and economic development simultaneously, neither at the expense of the other. Since 1966, metropolitan Seoul has exhibited the highest growth rate in gross regional product among all cities of over a million. At the same time, it embarked upon a colossal building program, hoping to get ahead of its present rate of population growth (attributable to immigration) and also hoping to make up some of the accumulated deficiencies.

Because this policy is still unfolding we must begin in the middle of the transition. Housing is high politics at the moment in the Republic of Korea. The mayorship of Seoul is one of the half-dozen top administrative posts in the country — one that swirls with highly publicized action. Last week the Mayor of Seoul, "Bulldozer" Kim himself, was forced to resign. He was toppled as a result of public indignation concerning the collapse of a publicly built apartment house. Scores died and many more were injured. Immediately subdued rumors about shaved standards, reduced safety factors, and corruption in government-contractor relationships came to the surface. The mayor had been taking credit for the extraordinary rate of construction in Seoul; now most people seemed to think it was time that he "take his lumps." Korean politics seems to require scapegoats in high places. According to the statistics on tenure in office, the Korean political system has a higher turnover rate than any other system in the world.

According to my informants, this is the first time that housing has been the issue that brought about changes in the front ranks of politicians. Usually the political controversies are more obscure and difficult to understand — even for other Orientals. This time the political process is more understandable to Westerners because urban housing was the nemesis of many a minister and mayor in Europe during the 1920s and 1930s, and in America in the 1950s.

Curiously, this specific catastrophe seems to be traceable to the compromises in the original housing policy that were made in deference to the demands of the intellectuals — mainly concentrated in the Opposition — who claimed that matters of amenity and conservation were being neglected. Therefore, the crowns of hills that were previously marked for five-story walk-up apartments which would be connected to the city by bus would now become common open space for the enjoyment of anyone in the city seeking air. Such housing was therefore extended down the hillside, displacing a patchwork of precariously perched squatter's houses. The collapse is said to have been caused by a slide of the clay that lies on weathered granite, the kind of fault that might have been identified by the engineers in the course of building a road to the top. All of this is surmise, however, because the investigations are still under way and all construction on similar sites has been halted.

Squatter Resettlement Housing

Apartments constructed in Korea are bulkier in frame than those elsewhere because of the high price of reinforcing rods for the concrete and a need to minimize the use of steel beams. Walls are infilled with very crude concrete block which is stuccoed or bricked over. Windows are kept relatively small because of the Siberian winter winds. The apartments themselves, in the lowest cost category, are built up about 20 inches from the floor in order to incorporate the cookstove-floor heater combination (ondol) that enables these people to survive. A coal briquette, a six-by-six inch cylinder with a half dozen one-centimeter diameter channels running through it to create its own draft, is used. The hot air proceeds under the floor which usually has some kind of tile or fiberboard surface overlaid by an oilskin-like material. Most apartments are allocated eleven pyongs, or 36 square meters, of floor space.

With the help of Kim Ban-gee and John Podgorsky I had an opportunity to see recently occupied housing aimed at alleviating the squatter problem. Kim is a graduate student in urban planning at prestigious Seoul National University. Podgorsky is a doctoral candidate at Syracuse University; he joined the Peace Corps and was assigned to the department. They had combined forces to make a modest survey that would cast light on the social effects of the housing policy.

They took me to an acropolis that had once defended the capital of the Yi Dynasty against Mongols from the north and Japanese pirates from the east. Little was left except a few steps cut into the granite and remnants of stone walls on the sheer cliff. Very likely every stone that could be pried loose had been put to work reconstructing the Seoul that had been destroyed by the communists in the 1950s.

Dropping down about a hundred feet on the other side of the cliff, a compact group of about 25 blocks of apartments, already rendered a uniform yellow, was visible. Occupation had begun only six to eighteen months ago. Spaces between the blocks were dug up because spring had come and it was possible to lay the sewers. Until now each block containing 120 units had a concrete box at its base which was used as a sump for sewage. In other places the terracing was under construction.

Sanitation seems to have generated a majority of the complaints registered by the occupants of these new flats. Waste lines were not insulated and so froze during the winter. Others would not work at all. The standards originally incorporated in the buildings allocated one cubicle with a pit toilet and a faucet to three families, but tenants could rarely come to an agreement on the responsibility for keeping it clean. This led generally to the practice of using the cleanest available toilet regardless of assignment. The managers and floor spokesmen resolved these difficulties in part by putting padlocks on the cubicles. Adults and older children were provided with keys; young children needed none, as the use of a toilet was not expected of them. It should be remembered that these sanitary facilities are far superior to those which squatters had before, particularly if they were manual laborers, as 90 percent of them were. Normally they brought their water to their homes in buckets from a standpipe or faucet, or by means of a plastic tube strung from an outlet, and then carried their sewage to the nearest cesspool.

The presence of a black-coated Korean with Occidentals was immediately interpreted as a metropolitan inspection team. Our questionnaire was designed to elicit verbal complaints, but this time one floor spokesman was at home and he insisted upon taking us to the roof and showing us some blisters that leaked water, some cracks in a beam, and the inadequacy of some of the chimneys when it rained.

The housing estates on this hill, already about 70 blocks of them, have an interesting history. A part of the hill was owned by a rich man, who lost control of it because of the squatters but nevertheless found a way to come out ahead. He gave half of his land to the government on the condition that they use the powers available only to the government to clear the whole of it. His land contains middle-class apartments, distinguished by their grey color, glassed-in balconies, and occasional potted plants. Also much less washing is in view. The size and arrangement of the apartments otherwise appear the same. The government is following suit and declaring all the blocks on premium locations to be middle class, peddling them at market prices.

The people who move in are predominantly in-migrants from smaller cities and the countryside of two provinces in the south of Korea. The heads of families have resided in Seoul an average of six to seven years, but the boarders are more often recent in-migrants. They are strongly upwardly mobile, so that many of the children somehow stay in school and move into the white-collar class, working in commerce and government. Perhaps half of the squatters have sold their rights to an apartment because they wished to go back to their villages or they had an opportunity to obtain another slum house close to the soil. Their replacements seem to fit the above characteristics even more closely than the resettled squatters themselves.

Home Finance

The basic apartment contract runs for 15 years. It costs about $6.50 per month, or about two days at organized manual labor, such as construction. Some subsidy is involved in this arrangement because it is said that the government is only charging 8 percent for money that costs 26, 32, and even as high as 36 percent per year for three-year bonds. However, the monthly payment is the least of the new occupant's worries.

First there is a charge for installation of services – water and sewer, electricity, window frames, etc., that costs $280-$300 in cash. Some of the cost can be delayed by making deals with the other residents; for instance, several flimsy wires carrying 110 volts may be strung along the dark halls.

In addition, there is the cost of "inside construction," including the precious ondol, doors, window glass, sink, shelves, partitions and the like. This generally runs $300-$350, but many people appear to handle most of it on a do-it-yourself basis. Again, hard cash is required. Finally the entering owner is expected to pay a monk, wizard, or priest to bring good luck to the house. One of my interviews was prevented by a hyperactive drummer who was trying to attract good fortune to a new household.

The money is not obtainable at a bank. The squatter household is forced to borrow on the average a little more than $150. The money is obtained in about equal amounts from loan sharks and relatives. The going rate from the moneylenders is 7 1/2 to 8 percent per month; from family 5 1/2 to 6 percent per month. There is a standard way to get out of debt, however. It involves finding boarders with capital. A home-owner can offer a place in his house for 100,000 won ($320), which is like selling a one-seventh share in its nominal value. The boarder gets his money back when he leaves. Boarders without cash negotiate for space, paying $10 per month and up. The average number of people living in these apartments is between eight and nine.

The fully developed apartment, with 14 ½ years yet to pay off the mortgage, can be sold on the open market. The offering price is usually $2,300. Nobody knows what the figure is when the bargaining is finished, but given the shortage of housing it is probably not much less.

Housing Policy from Here

The new mayor is Yang Taek-Shik, formerly governor of the third most important province in Korea. He is receiving advice from newspapers, chambers of commerce and professors regarding the way the city should now be run. The decision has already been made to push ahead on the subway and the first of the remarkable freeway exchanges inside the hills..Other than that it is evident that the new mayor must play his role in a way that is most different from that of "Bulldozer" Kim. For the moment at least there will be slowdown of new housing projects and a cleanup of any possible scandal left from the previous administration. The sensationalist rhetoric will be abandoned. City government and related ministries of national government will undergo basic changes.

The most fundamental decisions, in any case, are out of the hands of the mayor. Within the past nine months the word has gone out that Seoul must be deconcentrated. This is a theme that is raised every five years when the national plan outline is being formulated. I am willing to wager that it can be traced to United States and United Nations advisory groups, the members of which are high-grade intellectuals, and therefore horrified by the kind of housing described above and the way of life associated with it. They will concede that the housing program is popular with the Koreans themselves and that past housing policy delivered needed votes to the government; but, they argue, it is still not decent for people to be packed together so densely.

However, the alternatives have little to recommend themselves, either. An aided self-help housing project of some dimensions was started several years ago to the south of the metropolis; it is one of several in Korea, and none seem to be working well. The story of these decentralized tracts is the same as in India. The bus transport service had not been simultaneously improved (it is a free enterprise in Korea and subject to a special excise tax of 10 percent, so there are no incentives to development as yet); therefore, a large share of the parcels in the tracts are abandoned, particularly during the winter, and the settlers squeeze into the slums. The high turnover does not help community formation. This formation needs to be perfected before any sizable program of deconcentration can be launched.(7)

Other efforts will be made to keep the people in the countryside by providing much more infrastructure, particularly better roads. The argument is made that the income differential between the poorest province (with a population of 3,000,000) and that of Seoul is a factor of three, so it is a matter of social justice that something be done for them. Greater satisfaction in the rural areas should reduce the pressure for housing in Seoul, since 70 to 80 percent of the new immigrants say they have come for the economic opportunities.

Another contingent reports educational facilities as the key attraction in Seoul, particularly the secondary schools that have established channels into the leading universities. Perhaps a bonus must be paid to the better teachers to get them to teach in the market towns. All other programs, even electrification, are significantly less important than schools and roads.

Yet every scrap of evidence I could collect suggested that these decentralization policies could misfire and would actually worsen conditions in Seoul rather than improve them. For example, the construction workers drawn from the farms on the far end of the peninsula at Ulsan's new heavy engineering complex, drifted to Pusan and Seoul when the job was over, thus accelerating emigration. And again, virtually all the graduates of high school in the provinces flock to Seoul in search of college entry or clerical jobs, so that expanding their number and quality seems likely to stimulate more moves to the metropolis. The opening up of roads and new bus lines has the effect of allowing people to do more of their shopping in the city where the choice is much greater. Thus, local merchandisers suffer, sometimes closing up shop altogether, while new jobs are generated in the big cities. Electrification might bring television to outlying communities, and thereby increase satisfaction with life. However, television has not yet caught on with the working class (only 2 percent of the units in the block surveyed above had sets), a rather surprising phenomenon as compared to Latin America, Hong Kong or Bangkok. It may be noted that television viewers wanted to move to America. (Perhaps the greatest single force preventing wholesale migration to America from Korea is the strict application of the draft law – 33 months in service. The head of the family loses his status as a citizen if the son evades the draft. Rich men's sons are thus put into particularly difficult positions because draft-dodging on their part can bring down a whole industrial or commercial complex.)

Nevertheless, one method of decentralization has been found in recent years, although it has operated completely independently of government policy. About 100,000 people have joined two religious communes (shin yang chon) which provide houses and jobs for people who follow the charismatic prophet-organizer Park Chau-ro-kyo. He devised a Korean form of Presbyterianism, organized very much along the lines of the early Christian communities described in the New Testament. These people are diligent, thrifty, mechanically proficient, devout, and scornful of the fleshpots of the city. Their industries grow even faster than those of the metropolitan area. However, the government is constitutionally forbidden to propagate religion so it cannot take advantage of an established formula for success in deconcentration.

Thus, unless the new evidence takes on some completely different cast from that obtainable now, a policy of deconcentration would appear to be pure mischief. Vast sums could be spent in the countryside with zero, or at best, very small gains; and it could well stimulate migration to Seoul, where the government is less well equipped to service the migrants.

EVIDENCE OF TRANSFORMATIONS

June 1974

By this time centrifugal forces had already caused some decentralization. Monthly reports for Seoul itself, independent of its mushrooming satellite city, showed a drop from the original 10 percent annual growth rate to a rate of less than 3 percent, in part because of improved access to the city. Through an expanding network of roads, telecommunications, schools, and improved rail lines, whatever is Seoul's becomes the nation's; it is now accessible within a day for well over 95 percent of the people living within the peninsula and the islands.

Over the past year or so, Seoul has become conscious of its environment. The great reduction in the flow of immigrants enables people, along with the government, to catch up with housing needs, converting shacks that provided minimal shelter into substantial cottages for members of a stable working class. Meanwhile, the water lines have been extended, crude sewers installed, paving tiles laid down over them, and patches of land once filled with rubble have been landscaped. Seoul's ornamental horticulture is not comparable to other metropolises of its size, but the city is learning to take pride in its appearance. Tentative touches added here and there, some of them quite amateurish, amount to real progress in beautification. (Only one full-fledged landscape architect was found in the city or the country at large when the policy change became effective in 1972, and only two or three persons had some landscaping training.) The most outstanding improvement in the environment of Seoul has been a settling of the dust produced by construction, unpaved roads, and dirty streets in the central areas and the main corridors. Developed countries have forgotten about the effects of dust and mud upon the quality of life, but dirt is a much more immediate distraction than water pollution, litter, or destruction of wildlife. The latter are now the issues that dominate the attention of civil servants and independent professionals in Korea as well as in the rest of Asia.

Searching for Seoul's Squatter Houses

In earlier days it took a lot of scrounging to stay alive in Seoul. The houses of the poor demonstrated what kinds of opportunities existed and revealed the native enterprise for assembling some kind of protection from the elements. In 1968 and 1970 it was possible to see from the buses on many of the roads out of the city the heaps of scrap lumber, tar paper, tin sheet, tile, bricks, and unframed glass panes that made up a good fraction of the previously built self-help houses. Narrow lanes were choked with muck, unused gleanings from the city, and produce brought in to fill the daily pots. Even then, however, one could find a scattering of houses that were stucco finished, whitewashed, clean swept, drained, and topped by a carefully caulked tile roof with a short chimney that gave adequate draft but kept out the rain. Such a house was symbolic of the aim of rising above the low-class neighborhood standards and achieving full middle-class respectability.

The Korean equivalent of bourgeois lived inside the city walls of Seoul, while the round-topped thatched houses of the country people were found along the outside roads. There were always stories of exiled intellectuals and "radicals" who left the security of the inner precincts to live among the people. Their presence might have explained — directly or indirectly through imitation — the instances of urbanity among the squatter settlers of the previous decade. But now everyone is reaching for a level of respectability and almost all are within a few steps of achieving it. I sought out areas which had had the reputation of being the worst in the city during the 1960s and visited them to see if they would yield some clues to the transition.

Ogsudong is such a community. It is located on a granite outcrop adjacent to the road leading to the third Han River bridge. The proper urban side has a forest, official buildings, blocks of mansions, and a few of the lesser embassies. The minor road leading into it is dominated by a series of workshops handling dirty, heavy materials with simple machinery but interspersed with small retail shops catering to the working people. Rising behind, on the treeless landscape, are thousands of irregularly spaced cottages. At the edge, next to a small cleared space that retains traces of now-vanished tiny shacks, are newly raised stone-walled terraces supporting rich men's houses, landscaped with flowers, shrubs, and four young trees for each mini-estate. More are under construction. Are moneyed people displacing the original settlers of Ogsudong?

My wife and I started our walking tour by heading for a prized southwest facing slope upon which vegetables are grown. The night soil of the settlement was liberally administered upon the radishes, lettuce, peas, turnips, beans, and melons. Women and older girls were tending the plots, while small girls were cutting greens out of the tiny patches of wasteland. There were no prized black goats, no pigs, and very few dogs; only one clutch of chickens was noted. These last observations suggested that, though the gardens smelled and looked very much like a village, the cropping patterns had been urbanized.

All the houses adjacent to the garden plots were complete, but only a very few had become workshops. The latter were engaged in making cheap household furniture from the lumber and plywood manufactured in the tiny mills on the road below. The principal building material was a cast building block that uses cement to bind the sand derived from the weathering of the hill. A handful of well-built wooden houses left from the period preceding the squatter invasion were now adapted to store produce from the gardens – an indication that the pressure for living space on the part of the migrants had been greatly reduced.

The lanes of Ogsudong were freshly brushed and cleared of litter. Some solid waste had been used to inhibit the gullying around the garden (mostly clay cores remaining after the briquette had been burned in an ondol), but industrial waste was not really evident, nor were there any bottles or plastic containers lying about. Wrappings from candy and bakery goods were the prime source of litter; the detritus from fruit and vegetables was usually a minor contributor. Rusted tin cans were rare. What this means is that very likely a community cleanup effort was undertaken in the spring after the snows disappeared, and the original discipline had been maintained.

Under the lanes are sewer pipes laid in troughs dug out of the rock and covered again. These are used for waste water and storm drains, and not for sanitary purposes; indeed, in the small streams and channels down below, one finds remarkably clean and sweet-smelling water. Pollution at this time of the year came from the concrete block making plants which dispose of sand and lime dust by washing with stream water. No oil films or anaerobic sumps were found while poking around the improvised drainage system. On three instances sewer pipe breaks that had not yet been mended were noted, but they did not cause inconvenience. I was forced to conclude that an extremely rational and quite adequate sanitation and sewage system had been improvised at a site which only the rich could afford to occupy in an attempt to conform to international standards.

As with most Asian poor, the residents of Ogsudong are served by water carriers. At the top of the rock we saw a standpipe delivering a stream that filled a well-designed 20-liter container in less than two minutes. That rate of flow meant a high rate of productivity for the water carriers, since there was little waiting at the source. It also meant that there must have been some effective political pressure, because water flows freely at the top of a hill only after considerable public investment. There seemed to be different backpack specialists who carried fuel from the three-wheel lorries on the road up to the tiny shops that served as distributors. Again there were probably other coolie-type laborers for the collection and sale of the night soil. Whenever possible a coolie might use the standard rear car equipped with a 200-liter green tank for pushing and pulling around the lesser slopes, while still another specialist would use the same cart frame fitted with boxes to collect the rubbish in the early morning hours. Thus even a poor urban settlement has put together a complement of urban services that keeps it clean and liveable, although not one of those services employs techniques resembling those which have evolved in the West.

On a sheet of granite facing north stand a dozen examples of the Seoul city government's first alternative to squatter settlements. These are five-story flats (sometimes with a sixth and even a seventh story on the downslope side), with one family to a room and a tiny balcony plus a toilet down the hallway. Land and construction costs were packaged and paid for by the occupants over a fifteen-year period, while the task of financing the finishing of the apartments was left to the families. Their beginnings have already been described. Now, three to five years after moving in, some of the balconies are enclosed, while others are piled high with brown-glazed pottery jars of various sizes that exude the odor of kim-chi, despite their weighted lids. Tuesday's wash is out but seems to be made up of children's clothing only. Symmetrical red brick flashings on the piers ascend to the top floor, and there is faded green paint on the wood-framed windows. Perhaps a quarter of the windows have a grill to protect the residents from upper-story prowlers, most likely to guard television sets. The clutter is astonishingly small for working-class apartments; in fact, no junk at all is in sight. Although the halls are quite dark and narrow, housewives still stand in them to gossip. Bottom floors of the lower buildings are designated as shops, but no manufacturing artisans are present.

The nearest sources of employment are down a hundred to two hundred steps carved in the erodible rock and then along the streets served by buses and big lorries. Peckerwood sawmills with small drying yards produce thin-gauge lumber, dowels, and some plywood. Black-faced workmen overhaul Diesel engines, but they take pains to keep the oil and grease from entering the sewer in all but the rainiest periods. Tailor and other artisan shops hiring two to ten workers are distributed along the road at a density of 10 to 20 per hundred meters. All installations evince low capitalization, but all are electrified. The main sources of jobs for women and girls over 15 are the new knitting mills.

Thus, exports here have brought in the cash that allowed the self-help approaches to household improvement. This dependence upon world trade will become more important to Ogsudong in the future. Logs, the Diesel engines, and petrochemicals for the synthetic fibers and filaments made elsewhere in Korea are all imports. Ogsudong labor produces apparel from designs supplied by studios in downtown Seoul for countries moving into the postindustrial era which no longer wish to take the trouble.

So it seems that while looking for the worst in Seoul we came upon an outstanding success story. In the course of 10 to 15 years Ogsudong progressed from a haphazard shanty community of peasants and small-town people with little education or skill, although some possessed experience acquired in the military or in construction, all the way to an almost completed self-renewing set of neighborhoods with a stake in the metropolis, the nation, and even in world affairs. Most of the changes henceforth will be in the minds of the people – their loyalties, achievements, and associations – not in the physical environment.

Added income wil put tile on the last 5 percent of the roofs, add plaster to seal the last 10 percent of the walls, and install more dependable heating equipment in perhaps 50 percent of the houses. The lanes will be covered with tile or, more often, rough concrete. The steps cut into the rock or based upon loose boulders will be squared, and more fences and railings will be put up as accidents call attention to hazards. Water lines will be laid, and electricity will be installed in all the homes. The next community drives will probably encourage people to add trees (emulating the rich at the edge), if only in tubs. Colored paint, instead of whitewash, and ornamentation of fronts should follow. Trees have already been planted at some of the entrances to the community, and a dozen have survived the first winter.

Factory jobs for women reinforce the interest in family planning; later on a greater equality in sex roles is expected. The large cohorts of children we saw will move through junior secondary school and then into factories or shops, with only a few continuing in the direction of technical or higher education. In the future the community will collect more and more old people – citizens over 60 who have formally retired from active employment. But all the while the rich man's terraces and the apartment houses for the middle class will nibble at the edges of Ogsudong because of its fresh air and its views, both prized by those who wish to escape from the inner city.

Yet, if Ogsudong is like other self-improving communities in the world, this visible enhancement of the environment over relatively short periods of time is fraught with risk. Continued change for the better is taken for granted. At each stage further improvement requires integration with still larger networks and systems that extend far beyond a community that little understands them. If, because of circumstance in the larger sociopolitical system, the government or the employers cannot live up to expectations, the default is readily interpreted by local people as injustice. A major bus fare increase may be one such failure, and quotas upon exports imposed by America and the Common Market may be another. An accumulation of several such disappointments can lead to destructive collective anger. Ogsudung and two or three neighboring communities are enough set apart by natural boundaries and history from the remainder of the Seoul metropolitan area so that this anger can feed upon itself, escalate, and erupt. Political scientists and historians have noted repeatedly that urban unrest arises not among the destitute but among those who have progressed a good part of the way toward adequate levels of living. The youth and the very poor may join in later to take advantage of opportunities for looting.

It would be useful to know about the parts of Korea from which most of the Ogsudong people came, and more about their religious, recreational, and social institutions. That information requires an analysis that tunes into the speech of the people (Korean dialects are as differentiated as English or German speech). Those traditions would probably move Ogsudong away from the mainstream and point to a different kind of future. The needs of the people could then be better judged, and the likelihood for meeting them ascertained from a review of current plans in city hall and the departments in the national government. Investigations at that level, however, would require several years of study of the language before they could be undertaken – a rather imposing hurdle.

Note added two years later: We had been conducted to Ogsudong by a Korean student of an American university who discovered upon returning home that all students had been forbidden to speak to "poor people" (a ruling made after Seoul students had incited a street riot some months before). He dropped us at the boundary of the communities described above, not entering himself. Then he began to study Ogsudong surreptitiously. Later we heard by roundabout means that before the summer was over his principal contact and several others were injured in a confrontation with the police and the leader was subsequently evicted from his home. The last two paragraphs above were tragically prescient.

INSTITUTION BUILDING IN SCIENCE AND TECHNOLOGY

Korea Institute of Science and Technology and
the Korean Advanced Institute of Science

June 1974

In developing countries, scientists should be utilized to aid in the borrowing of appropriate modern technology – as in Korea. The Korea Institute of Science and Technology (KIST), since its inception in 1970, has been an example of employing scientists in this way. Curious to see if the institute was still adhering to its original course, I sought an opportunity for closer evaluation. At the United Nations Fund for

Population Activities, the mention of a proposal on the part of KIST to manufacture the ingredients for birth control pills – a subject which I had covered in a book assessing the social, economic, and cultural effects at about the time the pills were put on sale – introduced such an opportunity. I arrived at KIST carrying a copy of Carl Djerassi's report on pill manufacture in the People's Republic of China.

The Korean project seemed to have real merit. It reveals much about the organization. The proposer was Dr. Chae Yung-Bog, a Seoul National University graduate who had worked in Germany, getting a doctorate along the way, had spent some time at the Max Planck Institute for Cell Biology, and then was passed along to Severo Ochoa in New York City when Ochoa was running one of the fastest-paced laboratories in molecular biology and biochemistry in the world. His job in KIST is to develop the labor-intensive fine chemicals industry for Korea. In the last three years KIST has already carried more than a dozen projects to completion and has a much larger number well on the way. They were confident of their ability to push this project through because they had already brought an antituberculosis drug up to pilot plant production.

The method of organization employed at the institute is one of small teams, resembling the American rather than the older European system. They hoped to start from a cheaper raw material, cholesterol, and develop a slightly different method of synthesis using fermentation at a critical stage. They had an advantage over predecessors who had tried and failed because they had recruited a Korean who had studied in Japan with a university team which had converted cholesterol to estradione, from which the synthesis of the principal constituents of oral contraceptives is a relatively simple process. The university obtained a patent last year, but it is still unused by Japanese firms. They would not need a license to provide the contraceptives to the captive market supplied free by the government because the patent was not registered in Korea.

I introduced the idea of proceeding to the "paper pill" developed in Shanghai in 1972-3, in which the biologically active ingredient is absorbed in a square of water-soluble paper the size of a postage stamp. It is likely to be even simpler than standard pills for very poor and backward rural people. Producing the water-soluble paper is quite simple for the Koreans; the principal challenge would be to take advantage of the simplicity in the remainder of the formulation and packaging. Might it not be possible for Korea to be the first country in the noncommunist world to produce paper pills?

There was at least one hitch. KIST is not set up as a corporation. A proposal such as this would require a techno-economic survey, and the group responsible for such surveys in KIST needed a contract to make a study of the potential markets and risks. However most agencies request a thoroughly justified proposal before they will offer a contract or grant. Korean pharmaceutical firms are unable to make the commitment to a product that may be given away free. Thus the standard operating procedures of international, national, and corporate organizations do not fit together quite closely enough; and a potentially meritorious proposal may have to wait. KIST has some budget to gamble with, but balancing cost against the benefits of such a project involves many risks that remain uncontrolled. In all countries the interface between progressive ideas and the sources of funding has many cracks and crevices into which unlucky projects fall; undoubtedly more fail to traverse the gaps than succeed. Technical and economic merit are rarely enough to produce success. However, careful management and planning can rule out many of these extraneous factors – if the planning is not hobbled by lack of staff or budget – so that the odds for success are improving.

Vice-President Yang of KIST came into the office. He explained how his organization worked with the Korean Development Institute (KDI), which does long-range thinking for the Economic Planning Board, and the Korean Advanced Institute of Science (KAIS), whose function it is to retrain engineers and scientists who have studied and worked primarily in America.

For each of the government ministries a handful of private enterprises serve as designated agents, but for birth control pills no such firm could be identified by the chemists. There are pill fabricators using imported ingredients, but no pill designers. The know-how exists, however, in closely related fields, so KIST would probably have the task, through public relations or personal contracts, of setting up a designated corporate agent or two. A shift in the political winds may define this procedure as corruption, so at this point in time all parties are hesitant to move.

From my knowledge of science in Asia, the Koreans have the men, the equipment, and most of the organization needed to develop paper pills. Their deficiencies are much less than those of any other Asian country, except Japan, and they have some advantages over Japanese firms based upon their growing internal market. It will be interesting to see whether the bottlenecks are unclogged, and if so, how. If they are, a whole new class of fine chemicals would be added to the Korean repertoire.

The Challenge Facing KAIS

An opportunity to appraise the direction of the development of KAIS presented itself as a consequence of a lecture given to planners in the new School of Environmental Studies at Seoul National University. There, among other things, I presented the special challenge of developing a "cycle-based mode of transportation" along modern lines as the best single solution for a permanent energy shortage. Dr. Yoon, Duk, N., from KAIS was present; he disclosed that he had been thinking along parallel lines, but more according to the theme of appropriate technology, or "intermediate" as it was known until about two years ago, and therefore considering the design of devices rather than systems. He invited me to visit and give a talk to the Science and Technology

Society of KAIS. He admitted, upon being pressed, that his interest in human-powered transport was not shared as yet by his colleagues, so a topic thought to be of general interest (because advice to the government was being prepared) was chosen: "Long Range Planning of Science and Technology Education." Oh Byungho, an urban studies senior at MIT, came along to listen; his presence helped noticeably.

We were picked up by an Austrian, Henry Fuchs, a retiring professor of design in the Mechanical Engineering Department of Stanford University, who made the insightful comment on the way that the Koreans lacked much of the intuitive grasp of ingenious solutions that he found among Americans and Europeans. Koreans spent a great deal of time pumping new values for parameters into involved sets of equations, and often lost contact with the empirical world – a characteristic he attributed to their borrowed Confucian heritage. I could only agree that this was true from our Western point of view, but I detected a different kind of creativity, not ordinarily revealed to outsiders, which invented organizational shortcuts and alternative procedures that enabled the achievement of collective goals. Their organizational inventions often have general applicability, but they are still framed in particular referents within the Korean language. They can be diffused as analogs within a Korean bureaucracy, but remain trapped in an untranslated, or occasionally untranslatable, form in the subculture.

The KAIS building, situated on a low ridge to the northeast of the capital with a clear view of the peaks of Puk Han San, is the most carefully finished of any structure seen in Korea. Oh Byungho remarked that it could fit easily into contemporary MIT. This is an institution that was obviously launched with a space-age budget, i.e. United States Agency for International Development when technology was still high priority. Virtually all members of the staff were group leaders in American research and development organizations or had been teaching in universities before returning to Korea. Something like this building was needed to reassure this talent that Korea was rising out of the mud and poverty they remembered, and that their intellectual skills were likely to be of some value to the society as well as yielding some reward for themselves. Americans originally thought of KAIS as providing nuts and bolts know-how by retreading American-trained Koreans for semideveloped industry, and were becoming a little disturbed by the trend toward computerization and theoretical models that seemed to the Koreans to fit the context provided by the building. In this disagreement about institutional direction, my tendency to think in terms of long-range planning considerations put me on the side of the Koreans. But did they appreciate the systems that would consolidate their jump into the fully modern world?

My presentation itself revolved around the following arguments: Science and technology education contributed to net development starting about 20 years after the teachers were trained, and about 30 years after the policy was established. Yet policy was usually based upon the experience of the previous decades, with no careful assessment of how the society and the world would have changed before the returns were expected. An example of this phenomenon in the United States is space age education reform, which has already pushed students in a direction opposite to that intended. (Note that educational requirements projections for science professions have failed in all countries.) Places in advanced American engineering schools, once local youth showed lack of interest, were granted to the best applicants, about 70 to 80 percent of whom were Asians. These advanced degree holders are now working primarily for multinational corporations.

Meanwhile, the multinational firms have evolved a means of moving capital from one nation to the next, despite exchange controls of the nations. Therefore, in the future, the sovereignty of nations must decline further; they are losing control over both the capital and the people needed for extending technology and new social services. Moreover, the trend toward a postindustrial order will have been largely accomplished in societies that are open and interdependent, such as Korea. In view of this, a productive science education policy should anticipate an urban society heavily committed to providing high performance human services according to international standards set by multinational organizations much more than those set by nations. This is the most likely noncatastrophic future.

I used examples in the areas of food, transport, and communications to outline how this future would apply to Korean policy making.

The objection from the KAIS participants was that this kind of thinking was too broad for them. They thought that it was more appropriate to make simple assumptions about politics and then construct more short-range projections. They had not thought that their role might be to construct alternative projects and programs, particularly policies different from those generated in the Korean Development Institute.   However, if they did not accept the role, some institution similar to KAIS would have to take on the task.

They asked how one educates a person for the task of planning for science, technology, and social development. Oh Byungho described how it was done for urban development at MIT at present, and I added a few comments upon the strategy employed in graduate school education at Berkeley, which draws heavily upon peer group instruction rather than professional authority. This was obviously very different from conditions experienced when they had been in graduate school in America 6 to 15 years earlier.

Evaluation of the Advanced Scientists

KIST has found a niche for itself in Korea as an analog of the Battelle, Stanford Research Institute, and Arthur D. Little organizations. Enough Koreans had participated in these areas of research to see their roles in society quite clearly and establish themselves accordingly. Batelle's influence in the early stages of KIST was crucial.

KAIS does not seem to have found yet a place in the society which fits the intellectual capabilities and self-images of the members.   The policy roles played by leading scientists from MIT, Chicago, Berkeley, Stanford, and Cal Tech, as well as Lockheed, Boeing, IBM, and other space age firms, were incomprehensible to the Asian members of the laboratory. The Korean participants almost unanimously disapproved of policy-oriented activity engaged in by laboratory directors and independent spirits, such as Linus Pauling, unless the effort were directly aimed at getting money for the group. No other organization in Korea can become the voice of scientific and technological reasoning, yet so far the members of the KAIS are unable to identify an individual spokesman, nor is there a team developing. In that sense Korea is still behind Taiwan, India, and Pakistan.

3 Tokyo*

My first attempt to comprehend an Asian city was greatly aided by Ikumi Hoshino, a former metropolitan reporter for Mainichi, who had previously worked with a number of American social scientists and has since become a professor of urban sociology himself. In the immediate postwar period Tokyo's performance in reconstruction and economic development eclipsed all other metropolises in the world. Only since 1955 has the pace in Seoul begun to exceed that of Tokyo, but Seoul still has a long way to catch up and Tokyo's recent evolution may provide some clues regarding its future.

The program of investigation planned before arrival in the summer of 1966 was to analyze the same community that Ronald Dore, working as a social anthropologist, had studied in 1950-51.(8) I wanted to trace the kinds of changes that record-breaking economic growth induced in community structure. His "urban village" had been transformed into a metropolitan precinct in the interim. The creation of new and larger social entities forced Hoshino and myself to look at the ward, which is the most densely settled in Tokyo (260,000 persons in 10 square miles gross area) as a whole.

One of the methods we developed for discovering rates of change and sources of influence was to walk down a street in a specialized district and identify all the artifacts or images that could not possibly have been present 15 years earlier. Hoshino would challenge shopkeepers and townsmen to help us identify those landmarks for which we were unable to give a date. We also investigated the origins of the special districts themselves, discovering the

*Estimated 1985 population – 14 million.

53

special circumstances that caused each community of productive and social activities to settle where it did, and studying what adaptions enabled it to survive.

At that time our chief interest was to use the observed changes in these most urbanized portions of Tokyo as suggestions for what might happen elsewhere when high rates of economic growth were experienced.

CULTURAL GROWTH AND URBAN DEVELOPMENT IN THE INNER CITY

November 1966

How does the culture of a metropolis adjust during accelerated regional economic development? We know that many innovations must be adopted and widely disseminated in order to stimulate and sustain economic growth and that innovation and diffusion are cultural as well as economic and social processes. We know also that enhanced metropolitan economic opportunity attracts people from rural areas with highly diverse subcultures and that immigrants are subjected to strong acculturative forces. We recognize that large cities possess, almost without exception, a far greater range of cultural traits than smaller communities. Cities are built and rebuilt to improve the transmission of culture within urban institutions. Cities foster face-to-face interaction, public ritual, contact with the arts, and formal education. But which comes first – growth of economically productive capital or accumulation of culturally controlled behavior?

Cultural Additions Precede Economic Growth

Repeated observation suggests an answer, but it is one that is rarely found in economic plans. Additions to urban culture precede and are prerequisite to each project that increases urban economic growth. Cultural growth functions as a principal cause for expansion of income and wealth. In the process, novel ideas are recognized and accepted years, sometimes decades, before income derived from them can exceed expenditure. An increment to regional income can occur only if some persons have been previously instructed in the synthesis of a novel good or service and a much larger number has been persuaded of its advantages. New social roles, cultural traits, and especially imagery in the language, result from successful adoption of an innovation, while a new profit – a contribution to economic growth – is realized sometime later.

Cultural growth may be necessary to urban economic development, but some ideas, concepts, images, and behaviors are much more potent than others. Which of them has been associated with rapid development in recent years? What are their origins and pathways; by what channels do they enter the metropolis? What, if anything, do they displace or render extinct? How might a forecaster use this causal connection to infer future transformations of metropolitan society? How does it change planning strategy when development is the prime goal? These were the leading questions in our analysis of cultural change in inner Tokyo.

Admittedly, a general set of empirically tested propositions can be advanced only after cross-cultural studies have been undertaken, but analysis of a prototype could suggest a number of structural and procedural conditions that expedite conversion of cultural innovation into added income for residents. Because Tokyo is the largest and most dynamic metropolis in a country that has grown economically at a greater pace than all others in the postwar world, it is expected to provide the richest concentration of growth-related phenomena. Fortunately the extensive information available in its urban government, both at the ward and metropolitan levels, permits us to test many routine hypotheses and set them aside as being of insufficient magnitude to contribute to the known growth rate. The richness of its organized data in many instances greatly transcends that available in Western metropolises, thus permitting some important insights regarding the mechanisms of urban development.

Japanese culture presents special difficulties for observers because it has almost always valued the transitory and the ephemeral more highly than the permanent and the invariant. It has gloried in miniaturism rather than gigantism. Despite publicity about a few grandiose engineering and architectural works and oft-repeated statements of regret by a body of intellectuals, there is still no admissible evidence for a change in the general population's attitude. The core of Japanese urban culture is not epitomized by climactic institutional foci such as cathedrals, monumental terminals, or skyscraper corporate headquarters, but is elaborated on the microscale by the shifting mosaic of the street scene. These special cultural qualities induced us to experiment with a novel technique for illuminating mainstream trends in the city's life.

Changes in Street Scene Images

We depended most heavily upon a repeated walk-through, each time making a pedestrian's survey at different times of the day on different days of the week. Our notes were checked by brief interviews concerning meaning or source of more unusual items. We were especially interested in those images Dore drew upon as most revealing of typical city life in Tokyo during his residence in the cho. They were listed, and we attempted to discover what happened to them after a decade and a half. This involved a small amount of sleuthing, but most questions could be answered by educated persons who had resided continuously in the locale for the full period.

It is evident that, if hindsight were operative, we would have instructed Dore to be more systematic in his use of visual images since the full list leaves out many items now held to be potentially significant. Nevertheless, the features of life associated with the mobile street scene, as distinguished from structures and building styles, have frequently disappeared. Yet well-informed residents reported that the context and tempo of life in Hanazono-cho have not changed very much in the interim. Extended questioning about added services and new habits revealed, however, that respondents' lives had become steadily more cosmopolitan, so this idiosyncratic summary must be interpreted to mean that the community remained in step with life-style changes propagated by the total urban environment. It was neither a pacemaker nor a museum piece and therefore not subjected to unusual stresses. An important reason for the gradual quality of the change is that the community had been spared by the great fire raid of 1945 and even the great earthquake of 1923, and land use shifted one or two plots (comprising 400 to 2,000 square feet apiece) at a time. We found that 88 percent of Dore's images have been thoroughly modernized while those that remain are encountered much less frequently in the cityscape. Relics are most likely to be found in poorer parts of the metropolis and in provincial cities. Actually very little has been lost – the images merely become rarer and are finally found only in some private archive.

A major part of the effort went into identification of images added in the past 15 years. In this ecology of imagery, they occupy niches by invasion. Our method was learned as we proceeded, but if a parallel study were to be undertaken in a Third World city the following steps are recommended:

1. Choose at least two urban observers with experience. One should be intimately acquainted with inner-city changes and should have methods available for documenting dates of transition.
2. Conduct walk-throughs making notes of images that almost certainly have been introduced in the interim. These trips should occur (a) in the morning when many residents are going to work, (b) in the afternoon when school is out, and (c) on a weekend evening when marginal enterprises are operating.
3. Follow up by taking photos of typical examples of listed items.
4. In environments where little or no change in appearance has occurred the investigators should challenge responsible residents to identify the changes they know and ask if there is some visual indication.
5. Corroborate their statements, since the sense of passage of time is almost always biased, with most people underestimating the interval.
6. Classify images according to apparent purposes of display.

For example, in the category, homes, shops, and factories, we noticed such new images as garages, air conditioners, doors that open in, modern design lawnmowers, washing machines, plastic water hoses, plastic films and sheets, key-in-knob door locks, a Korean bakery shop, and fluorescent outdoor lamps. Signs make up a category that is particularly interesting and indicative of change. We noted signs and posters such as an advertisement for a diaper service, the Moon-Over-the-Waters Hotel, "purified vegetables" (a guarantee that night soil is not used), and Dash ("an antiphlogistic agent"), a poster put up by the Voluntary Association for Crime Prevention – Metropolitan Police ask, "Who knows this woman? 18,000 unidentified bodies have been found. We need your help! – and a poster displayed by the Human Rights Commission – "If you have trouble from blackmailers, loan sharks, or racketeers, see us in the ward office."

We were able to make a number of elementary inferences from the records of detailed inspections. First, most visible changes arose from growth of mass media, mass marketing, and innovations in luxury goods (a trend well under way when Dore resided there). Second, the ward government has undertaken a large variety of new services catering directly to individuals rather than councils for the respective cho as before. Third, the existence of metropolitan government (founded during the wartime emergency in 1943) now comes to the daily attention of active citizens as it attempts to achieve reforms.

If we trace back statistics for these channels for change, we see that mass media and marketing must have grown by a factor of almost 20 in the interim, while personnel expansion in government offices has increased by a factor of three, five, or more. Equipment intended to increase productivity of this labor was purchased and put to work, so quantity of service almost kept up with growth of the private sector.

The contrast between eras only a half generation apart signified rapid, relentless, but orderly change in the street scene. It meant also that the parochial character of urban precincts like Hanazono-cho was displaced by at least a veneer of cosmopolitanism. The greatly enlarged rush-hour traffic observed could only indicate that movements are wider and life is much less tied to the precinct. Thus we were induced to apply our technique to the hundredfold greater scale of Taito-ku, the ward of which Hanazono-cho was a sample representing uses for more than half its area. Since Taito-ku was foremost in wholesaling among Tokyo's 23 wards, most of the interesting locales were unique whole-saling districts. These districts were bordered by areas of mixed residence and small manufacturing, where enterprises not only supply wholesalers who distribute to the rest of the metropolitan area and other prefectures but also subcontract with larger manufacturing firms. The typical wholesaling firm appears to be an open shop with four to six meters frontage that spills out into the sidewalk, one among a cluster with a similar stock strung out along a wide street, often interspersed with grocery stores, coffeehouses, or wholesaling houses specializing in some other activity.

A search for new images in a wholesaling area becomes a quest for innovations. Extreme differences were encountered in the degree of acceptance of innovations. For example, among Buddhist paraphernalia suppliers (some with a direct line back to earliest Edo times), nothing is changed, although shop managers say that some demand is beginning to appear for plastic offering vessels. When these substitutes are seen from outside the display case, it is difficult to distinguish their appearance from traditional lacquered wood products. China and glass-ware designs are totally traditional (by which we mean that the images were introduced more than a generation ago), but plastic is beginning to displace metal on salt shaker tops. Initially, brushes appeared to us to be totally traditional, but on closer inspection many contained tapered nylon filaments – too regular to be produced in nature. An occasional rice cookie manufacturer has installed a postwar mixing machine, and some cookies are packaged in transparent vinyl envelopes with tiny bits of silica gel enclosed to keep them crisp. The crunchy "thunder" cookies and related types are still wholly traditional. On the other hand about 80 percent of the items carried by toy distributors did not exist 15 years ago. Indeed, two new trade associations have been formed to promote new products. Similarly, showrooms for Western furniture and timepieces present almost as high a proportion of novelty.

One of the most significant observations made is that sources of borrowed images found in public places of Taito-ku are 80 to 90 percent American. German influence could be readily detected in plastic toys exhibited; Swiss-French in timepieces; and British in formal clothing. Although a few basic stylistic contributions to toys, clockworks, elec-tronics, and clothing are Japanese in origin, this point is rarely stressed in advertising. The images obtained from Americans, in a number of instances, had themselves been borrowed by Americans either directly or through underlying concepts well before transmission to Japan.

The Content of Messages and Media

Japan is better equipped for conducting a comprehensive analysis of changes in symbolism than any other society. The Japanese language is sufficiently different from the Indo-European group to permit ready identification of loan words, and new words can be quickly sorted out of printed materials. Tokyo's major publishing houses produce a full range of periodicals as well as books, television programs, art prints, and research reports. Editors must make many daily decisions about what constitutes standard usage and what foreign images are well enough known to convey more meaning than mystery. They have made their task easier by commissioning dictionaries of new terms which, in their latest edition, have become remarkably comprehensive even on current usage. These dictionaries document additions made to the urban culture which call for adjustments in behavior by at least a significant component (about 1 percent) of the population.

Among the specialized jargons, recently evolved fields such as broadcasting and architecture are about 80 percent American in origin; the remainder are Japanese neologisms which often employ American abbreviations in Latin and Arabic symbols. It appeared that beauty treatment was highly Americanized, but a closer inspection revealed that new terms had been inserted into the vocabulary via television advertising. On the other hand, new fisheries' terms were totally Japanese; law was only 3 percent borrowed (despite the MacArthur constitution); few diplomatic terms were borrowed; and public finance, political theory, and labor terms did not exceed 10 percent non-Japanese. Educational methods and psychology are about 30 percent, almost all from America, and management practice and engineering are 60 to 80 percent foreign.

A chronological listing of introduced newspaper terms indicates that only 30 to 40 percent are complete importations; the remainder are permutations of local argots with each other or with some borrowed term. The straightforward loans are indicative of breadth of contact and illustrate the shift from an emphasis upon reconstruction and welfare. Additions in 1950 included red purge, teenage, case worker, Freemason, patrol car, trolley bus, auto race, and "oh, mistake." In 1955, no horn zone, mambo, after-ski, juice stand, jet coaster, aqualung, swimming glove, key puncher, one-dollar blouse, and jamboree showed up. In 1960, mass leisure, funky, winkie doll, leisure boom, revival boom, dump car, and credit card were recorded. In 1965, we see bunny girl, eroduction, wandervogel ("wangel"), zero meter (zone), racing car, convention, money dance, beauty cycle, sneak preview, and blue film. The additions seem to become less concrete and more sensual as urban culture becomes more complex. They may also be attributed to the fact that the babies born during the boom of the late 1940s joined the labor force just prior to 1965 and were making their influence felt.

Young men intent on becoming junior executives and administrators are urged to acquire vocabularies that enable them to discuss the latest worldwide developments in technology, management methods, public administration, marketing, and so forth. They ply each other with questions, jokes, and jeers aimed at familiarizing all parties in this conversational game with new images. A thorough understanding is believed to be required to pass examinations, impress company interviewers, and thus qualify for the most desirable jobs. Large companies and government prefer professional employees with a cosmopolitan outlook.

Forces Shaping Future Imagery

Virtually all the changes wrought in Hanazono-cho were set in motion by outside forces — foreign and megalopolitan, technological and cosmopolitan. A few traditions, still honored and preserved, were supported by outsiders. A teahouse maintained by the Edo Tea Ceremony School was designated "an important cultural property" by the Tokyo metropolitan government. A teacher of traditional Japanese singing has moved into the community. A school for Karate opened some time after the peace treaty was signed. A society for the preservation of ukiyoe prints set up its headquarters in a well-maintained house. Indeed, the whole area had been designated a "scenic district" with considerable power to prevent rapid commercialization, but this is due to the proximity of the very popular modernized zoo in neighboring Ueno Park.

Perhaps the most powerful influence in the future will be the impact of a huge increase in automobile ownership that is now under way. The attendant extension of overhead expressway construction, decentralization of offices, shops, and other places of employment, and new forms of recreation will all change the street scene. Much wholesaling is expected to move out of Taito-ku, for example, because better access to retailers and producers will be available on ring roads, and the metropolitan government is preparing a site. Present activities are likely to be displaced by industries and residences. The continuing rapid growth of per capita income is leading to a demand for residential floor space that can be met only by building upward, which is achieved in a tasteful way by reconstructing temple grounds as apartment houses where the top floors and penthouses are dedicated to cemeteries and temples, respectively. A high priority is also assigned to technology of "internal climate control" as a means of moderating discomforts of Tokyo's numbing winter and steamy summer. All of these changes fit into the government's goal of more fireproof construction, which it achieves through local merchants associations' self-renewal programs.

Megalopolitan forces will transform some locales in Tokyo. Airports, microwave relays, mass transit terminals, and blocks of executive offices will stand out on the skyline. Less imposing structures will house greatly expanded research laboratories, graduate and professional schools, and conference centers. Publishing, television production, and advertising are likely to regroup along the same lines as in America. These exogenous entities are forced to negotiate with local interests at the places they squeeze in, so "local autonomy" has a considerable influence upon the street scene. The unique Tokyo form of ward government assures that residents' opinions will have some weight.

Ecological Structure

The respective ecological communities often have formed trade or ethnic associations. If they are well organized, they collect data and may even formulate their own proposals for future urban development. Otherwise, a secretariat of some kind will have already formed which has detailed knowledge of extent of influence, resources, and potentials. Information of this sort is subject to many more sources of error than government-collected data so the kind of bias must be ascertained from independent informants.

More difficult to cope with are the disorganized "non communities" that one expects to find in such wards. A social structure exists, but it is a loose web with weak social controls and is easily stretched to the breaking point. Due to the unreliability of sampling techniques and incoherent, often conflicting, verbal responses, data for such noncommunities are rarely better than gross estimates. The implementation of plans in such areas involves either the use of coercion (police powers) or very extensive case work, both of which are inordinately expensive.

The best organized trade group in Taito-ku appears to be the Ueno Merchants Association, which prepared plans for the redevelopment of the Ueno Station area in 1963 and again in 1965 — plans substantial enough to gain the backing of the metropolitan government planners. The Asakusa merchants have greatly improved the presentability of their commercial area by adding new arcades. In 1962, they proposed a thorough redevelopment, with a high tower as a landmark, which was constructed in 1967. Even the Sanya hotel owners undertook an interview survey of the residents in their area, seeking to discover characteristics of the family unit, source of income, and employment security.

The major noncommunity of this sort is in Sanya, although a thousand or so floaters may be found in the vicinity of Ueno Park and Ueno Station. The numbers are difficult to estimate because the rice ration registration used as a means of keeping a monthly check on population shifts in Japan is evaded. These people do not cook their own rice, but live out of cheap restaurants for months at a time. Alcoholism and narcotics addiction are known but are not yet the major problems they are in America and Europe. Much more needs to be done in the future to reestablish sympathetic contact with these populations and resolve as many personal instances of injustice as can be found. Sanya also needs more public facilities, such as hiring halls, reading rooms, bathhouses, and small parks, all of which should introduce more organization into this semitransient population.

Growth Potential

A review of metropolitan institutions and activities with very high growth should also be undertaken to discover whether the ward will serve some new function in the near future. Instances of rapid growth in a city are very visible and much discussed, so there is little likelihood that a survey of current publications would overlook something important.

Most of the forthcoming changes in Taito-ku will be effected by exogenous forces — economic, technological, metropolitan, megalopolitan, and perhaps geophysical, in probable order of importance. National policy promotes rapid economic growth, along with more equal income distribution. New industries, just now emerging in the United States, will be installed in advantageous sites. High priority is given to the rationalization of Tokyo on the National Capital Development Plan. Megalopolitan development is a new challenge with novel implications. Natural disturbances, such as earthquakes or typhoons are becoming more predictable and therefore warrant more protective measures when risk is high. However, such changes have a momentum of their own, subtly shifting popular values and producing modifications in consumer behavior, swings in politics, and willingness to relocate.

The economic plans anticipate that the rate of growth will slow down somewhat but that nevertheless the per capita income in 1975 should reach the levels achieved by the United States in 1950. These plans have thus far moved ahead of schedule. Recalling the ways in which Taito-ku and other inner wards typify all Tokyo and even urban Japan, the plans imply:

1. A two- and threefold increase in autos, or equally expensive "automobile substitutes" yet to be perfected.

2. A twofold increase in floor space per resident.

3. Rationalization of commerce in areas of high accessibility.

4. A multifold increase in cultural and recreational activities.

5. Electrical power use increased two or three times, with internal year-round "climate-control" primarily responsible.(9)

A consequence of this growth is the redistribution of some of the labor force to auto repair and appliance maintenance, together with a proliferation of small organizations in cultural and technical activities, instead of the present crafts and trades.

Technological obsolescence is no threat to Taito-ku's sources of livelihood, because its entrepreneurs are far too varied and flexible in outlook. Nor does there appear to be a large new industry on the horizon that would want to settle in the ward. The influence of technological change will therefore be indirect. For example, improved methods of printing, especially of small runs, is likely to displace a large number of the tiny shops working for the wholesalers. Also, the introduction of synthetic leather made from plastic will shift more shoe production to large factories, pushing the artisans increasingly into specialty shoe manufacture, for which there should be some increase in demand.

The anticipated expansion of the University of Tokyo into a leading graduate school and center of research may cause some of its activities and services to spill over into the western fringes of Taito-ku. The skyscraper boom now beginning for Tokyo may induce many small to medium-size firms in the central area to move into the inner wards. Also, landowners in a few neighborhoods endowed with greater than average amenities will be urged to build high-rise apartments. All of these external forces, however, are together unlikely to produce the amount of redevelopment needed to renew and modernize the structures in the ward, so internally generated action is required.

Planning Strategies

The construction of proposals and programs that map out the future is also strongly dependent on the powers delegated to the respective tiers of government. Often a ward has no authority whatsoever to plan, but it will always have some political influence and therefore can get much of what it wants for the future accepted by agencies with authority to take action. This de facto ability to implement a modest plan is often followed by de jure responsibilities.

With 100,000 or so firms, households, and other independent decision units within its small territory, the majority of them quite knowledge-able about their property rights and self-interest, Taito-ku is hardly able to move in concert to fulfill a master plan. Nor is central authority able to direct development to meet its own objectives on schedule. Elsewhere, for example, the land for a jetport or the right-of-way for an expressway requires years of negotiation and substantial bonuses for quit-claims before construction can begin. Therefore, a grand design for comprehensive urban renewal would be unrealistic. The relatively modest proposals of the Okui team from Keio University accepted this conclusion, although their report included a tentative master plan which featured: 1) a "new town in town" around a new civic center and a reconstructed Ueno terminal area, 2) completion of the redevelopment of the Asakusa shopping and amusement area, 3) a tree-lined "boule-vard" connecting the two, 4) concentration of the wholesaling activities in two 4-hectare plots with small central landscaped open spaces or temple grounds, 5) removal of the heterogeneous activities drawn into Yoshiwara, leaving open space, 6) elimination of barging from the Sumida River, converting the whole shoreline to park and open space, and 7) creation of a residential area in the western panhandle of the ward. Even with a planning horizon of 30 years, 60 percent of the ward (including half of its most dilapidated area) would be left to drift with minor attention being paid to it.   Their proposals respond to the pressures for improvement visible in 1964 but do not fit the available means for implementation, nor do they take into account the tremen-dous growth in income planned for the next decade and beyond by the national government.

The ward government of Taito-ku was one of the first in Tokyo to prepare a draft plan. The product was a review of current problems as identified by the ward government, followed by a short list of high-priority goals for improving life in the ward. The list is instructive because it proceeds from: 1) education, 2) promotion of small and medium-size industry, 3) welfare of residents, and 4) beautification to 5) rationalization of ward administration. The problem in education is the shrinkage in enrollment, with a coincident steep rise in per capita costs, as well as a general demand for improvement in quality of instruction. Study centers for high school and university students are desperately needed. The promotion of industry is effected by holding down congestion, providing parking, and participating in the financing of high- and medium-rise concrete buildings. Welfare improvements are to be diverse, but strongly increased attention is to be given to the quasiofficial Association for the Respect of Old People, established about 15 years ago and possessing 2,224 members in 1963. Day nurseries, home helpers, and child welfare are given somewhat more weight than the public pawnshop, the "livelihood assistance loans," and free legal counseling. Beautification includes street cleaning, promoting concrete structures, replacement of dilapidated structures by modern public housing, expanding the room available for families and for cars, with elimination of such public nuisances as noise, smoke, and river pollution. The rationalization of administration puts strong emphasis upon "window counseling" so that the public can find its way through the administrative maze.

Because annual improvements in productivity are so great and new opportunities are appearing on the horizon so frequently, a master plan for redevelopment would become obsolete about the time it was adopted. Possibly a specifically designed area development corporation could be assigned the task of improving the quality of land use, a concept for which a variety of precedents exist. It could promote, participate in, and sometimes create solely on its own initiative, a large number of self-sustaining projects. The ward administration would then undertake only those projects which have little chance of paying their own way but are popular with voters and remain strongly in the public interest. For example, the ward would find it easy to get support for a number of sub-branch libraries or study centers. All efforts must work within a common policy plan, with each developing its own medium-term objectives and program of operations.

Conflict Resolution

One warning needs to be raised at this point. Many inner wards are battlegrounds between communities so suspicious of each other that they are willing to resort to violence to prevent the other from getting ahead. When such a polarized condition exists, plans must give highest priority to reduction of the deleterious effects of this conflict. The planning strategy in a conflict situation is quite different.

Both ward plans omit any mention of Sanya, perhaps because it presented issues too sensitive to treat in a planning document. Mass riots took place there in the summer of 1960, November 1962, and the summers of 1964 and 1966. The riots were triggered by seemingly trivial incidents – a price rise in the cheap restaurants in the area, police treatment of a drunk, and a traffic accident case in the most recent instances. The metropolitan government did act by opening up the Johoku Welfare Center, which reduced the travel distance of people in Sanya for welfare assistance, but it did not seem to reduce the grumbling about "red tape." The white-tile image presented by the center seems to be regarded by the residents as an affront to their self-respect and cleanliness. The headlines given to the riots have created a sense of place identification rare in Tokyo, but the social distance between the middle-class social worker and the resident seems to be widening as a result. They understand each other less and less.

The riots in Sanya suggested at first that, of all the wards in Tokyo, Taito-ku may be the future site of such an endemic conflict. However, all the evidence we have assembled points to a collective outburst directed at the first target available. The population of the poor and insecure is not well organized, and no specific antagonist exists.

Conclusions Regarding Taito-ku

In Tokyo, the growth functions of the inner wards like Taito-ku in the formation of a greater metropolis or megalopolis can now be proposed:

1. They distribute goods and services to consumers in the cities and their hinterlands but are chiefly responsible for exploiting the popular innovations (artifacts and images) borrowed or invented by the taste makers in the central wards.
2. They transform rural immigrants into established urbanites capable of making a living elsewhere in the metropolis.
3. They provide convenient locales for the residence of persons not committed to suburban living who maintain the alert, aggressive, opportunistic subculture necessary for rapid economic development.
4. They offer sites and local support for major educational, research, and cultural institutions which must grow more rapidly than the economy as a whole but do not have the resources to displace neighboring institutions in the central wards.
5. They export internal savings to a far greater extent than is normally mobilized from outside sources. Due to this unequal exchange, the physical equipment ages and debilitates relative to the core of the metropolis and the outer residential areas, so that an increasingly severe urban renewal problem results.

Tokyo's task is simpler than that facing most other cities because the minority ethnic and religious groups have already been integrated into the culture, but the riots in Sanya are evidence that serious civil disorders will occur even then, and thus stimulate a search for techniques of rehabilitation.

New development corporations at the ward scale appear to be an appropriate device for remedying the situation. They can be linked quite easily to megalopolis-scale planning by administering the projects vital to this new level of urban organization. They should be able to serve as agents for organizations in both the public and private sectors on a contract basis. The multipliers inherent in the demand for higher-quality services, such as postgraduate education, advanced medicine, convenient middle-income housing, urbane amusements, discernible in the developing urban regions can then be put to work renewing the inner wards.

CREATING JAPAN'S INFORMATION INDUSTRY

October 1969

Tokyo has been created by the most mature forces of the Industrial Revolution, upon which has been superimposed the new communications and information revolutions. The Industrial Revolution is no longer a net producer of new jobs in Tokyo. Its institutions have begun what is expected to be a long period of slow decline, while the communications trades make steadily increasing demands upon the labor force and the information-based activities virtually explode. Tokyo's advancement into the postindustrial era is certainly behind that of New York, Washington, Los Angeles and San Francisco, but it has probably moved ahead more rapidly than any Western European metropolis. The statistics available are of quite good quality – generally superior to those available in the United States because Tokyo's household registration, operated in Oriental fashion by police, is kept up-to-date, month by month.

A meeting of the International Advertising Association in Tokyo was the occasion for a series of current reviews of the impact of both the communications and the information revolutions in the English language newspapers. Fumiko Maki, formerly professor of urban engineering at Harvard, recognized that the dynamo of the megalopolis is the "knowledge industry." Since confidence in others involved in the transmission of this knowledge is obtained only in face-to-face interaction, the megalopolis requires some type of air shuttle or a Tokaido Super Express train to bring key people together. The handling of information technology ("the use of computing power") requires the availability of specialized private capsules in the central city area for the support of individuals or small task-oriented groups, while the face-to-face interaction of acquaintances requires "chambers" with greater range of numbers present and capable of serving an increasing variety of contexts for coming together. These are assembled by designers and administrators into "activities nuclei" or specialized urban districts, compared by Maki with Greenwich Village, White Plains and Harlem in New York.

The human problem presented by the current transformation is occasioned by the distortion of the channels and the threatened anesthetization or polarization of portions of the population. The rate of obsolescence of education requires that megalopolitans must plan to undertake several successive careers in a lifetime.(10) Other experts emphasize the immediacy of the threat because the telecommunications media are now moving into a period of accelerated diversification, particularly when they combine with information technology, as with earth satellite communications.

The information industry in Japan includes six manufacturers, but there are also about ten software firms which have grown up within the past ten years. Although the hardware is only a few years behind the United States in quality and scale (computers installed are now producing 0.9 percent of the gross national product versus 2 percent in the

United States), Japan plans to catch up before 1980 by implementing a growth rate of 34 percent per year in computer hardware. However, the real gap is in the software division, where growth is planned for a rate of 150 percent per year. The 17,740 system engineers and programmers in March 1968 (probably two-thirds live in Tokyo) are projected to increase to 99,200 by 1972. To do this, Japan must create a copyright system, a fee system, a credit system, and an on-line use of telephone channels. The telephone company is strong enough to prevent on-line connections of computers through its exchanges, so it is bitterly attacked by computer enthusiasts. Predictions are that the Japan Telephone Company will retreat from its exposed position in less than a year – or, mid-1970.

Almost all the leading Japanese urban planners have become communications theorists, but each uses a personalized, fragmentary approach. For example, Tosio Sanuki, economist at the Japanese Development Bank in Tokyo, has been elaborating the data on the production of symbols by all the media in Japan. He has also constructed a set of indexes drawn from current statistics which allows him to plot the degree of communications intensity in Japan. Thus, Tokyo scores 200 (all Japan is 100) while Osaka comes in at 160 and Nagoya and Kyoto are around 130 and 150, respectively. He argues that international information and communications technology will create what is called in Japan "the 24-hour city," but location of such an unusual community is problematic since it should be close to the Narita International Airport. However, there is a proposal to connect the new airport at Narita to central Tokyo by a fast nonstop express. Perhaps the solution is a one-stop express. The alternative is to construct a city in Tokyo Bay to get around the "lags" in land acquisition. Round-the-clock operations will simultaneously evolve and diffuse gradually into the three central wards by forcing subways and taxis onto a 24-hour basis. Later a number of office buildings and stores will be operated by multiple shifts of workers. By 1985 Tokyo might well have a satellite city and its inner three or four wards operating on a 24-hour basis. Each step in that direction would enable it to compete more effectively on the international scene, so this direction of development is quite likely.

Postscript 1979: Continuing Frustrations

The visit in 1969 caught very early a major trend in Japanese national planning which reached its zenith in the Tanaka plan. Tokyo and the other large metropolises were to be reorganized by means of communications and computing technology. Dirty industries were to be deemphasized. A prodigious amount of research, development, planning, and coordinating effort went into the program that would allow Japan to catch up with America by 1980 or 1985.

The students were the first to interfere with this dream. They allied themselves with the displaced farmers at Narita International Airport. At last report the big stake in the ground preventing the landing of airplanes was removed by police. Though the student resistance has virtually dissolved or moved underground, the farmers remain intransigent. The government initiated a gradualist campaign and succeeded in opening the airport finally in 1978. The express railway was frustrated by an inability to obtain land for right-of-way; even the pipeline from the harbor carrying jet fuel has been halted. However, the freeway connection to inner Tokyo works much better than anticipated.

Japanese electronics firms carefully sighted where their American competitors were going and then made concentrated dashes in that same direction. However, by 1972 it was already becoming apparent that American progress had sharply veered to new directions with the aid of new components, so that the Japanese also were forced to change course. They were at least as far behind as when they started. One coup arising from that shift in planning surfaced in 1975 when it was announced that IBM's designer of the third-generation computers had set up his own firm (Amdahl) in California with the backing of Japanese capital and intended to produce fourth-generation computers in competition with his former employers. Any inroads made through Japanese-financed firms in California upon the advanced technology created by IBM, Hewlett-Packard, Hughes, Fairchild, Intel, and others will be promptly transferred to Tokyo.

The Japanese Ministry of International Trade and Industry (MITI) assembled a high-level research and development group from a combination of government, industry, and university laboratories which would be given unlimited financial resources in an attempt to achieve a breakthrough on a wide front in computing and instrumentation.(11) Many of these scientists and research engineers had spent an important amount of their time at American technical meetings and visiting American laboratories over the preceding two years.

American response was immediate. Advanced Research Projects Agency, one of the advanced research agencies of the Department of Defense, was instructed to formulate the reply. An integrated five-year program, aimed at creating the computing system of the 1990s was formulated in a matter of weeks and distributed among the leading laboratories within a few months. The American hosts of Japanese visitors were sent immediately to Japan to reciprocate. Without doubt, a great scientific contest has begun, with California's "Silicon Valley" (the term used in the electronics trade for the Santa Clara Valley and the peninsula region south of San Francisco) and its university research institutes pitted against Japan, Inc. in Tokyo.

The early and very personal prognosis of Japanese chances of success made by American research leaders was not promising for the Japanese. If the path of development of scientific thought could be programmed, the investigators noted, the single-minded Japanese would surely reach their goal, but it took all kinds of imagination exploring in many unusual directions to solve problems as difficult as those found on this frontier. The greatest hindrance to the Japanese is the lack of cultural diversity. All their great minds rush down parallel tracks. They don't have the odd Hungarian, Turk, or Basque, symbolic of all those cultures that insist upon seeing the world differently, in the laboratory.

These Americans had forgotten, when making their appraisal, that a deputation of Chinese, drawn from all the subcultures of China, is expected to join the Japanese, and they should thrive intellectually in Tokyo at least as well as in American metropolises. Tokyo may have still other stratagems unrevealed.(12)

LIVING SPACE AND CULTURAL CHANGE

April 1970

"My-home-ism" (my-home-shugi) is a relatively recent syndrome in Japan. It is certainly not a full-fledged philosophy, as with Maoism or conservatism. Because even the researchers for Mainichi end up vague about its origins, implications, and its correlates when they editorialize on the subject, I suspect my-home-shugi represents a mood more than anything else. It could arise from developers' advertisements on trains and subways, and the household goods merchandised by the department stores, interacting with a need to decide how the next bonus should be allocated, and a feeling of disquiet about one's present environment.

People are said to be more discriminating about housing today in Tokyo than ever before, and my-home-shugi is believed in some quarters to be a principal factor. At least, the term was invoked in 1969 to explain the greatly diminished enthusiasm for the new middle-income housing provided at the Oshima-yonchome Housing Estate of the Japan Housing Corporation during that year. Instead of 20, 30, or more applicants per dwelling unit being on hand at the time of the lottery which decided who the lucky tenant should be, there were only 1.6 to 1.8 for each unit of the most common sizes. So many of the winners later reneged that a spate of vacancies remained and a special drawing had to be held to fill up the empty units. Was this due to the mood or to the qualities of the housing, or to some combination of both? Such a question is not readily settled, but a brief inquiry on the spot can clear away a number of intellectualized explanations and produce a restatement of the nub of the problem that should assist the planners.

The Japan Housing Corporation shows this land to be 35-40 minutes from Tokyo Station, the heart of the metropolis. The official brochure warns people that the site is separated from the commuter station by a 15-minute walk. It also warns prospective residents of smoke and polluted canals. A location in the East Ward of Tokyo, an area often discussed in the newspapers as a place of "sinking lands" and periodic floods, had a meaning for Tokyo residents that hardly needed to be mentioned. Almost all local readers of the newspapers will recall the arguments made regarding the effects of drawing water from the aquifers immediately below the factory site while pumping the waste waters into concrete-lined canals. Factories slightly downstream would find themselves sinking further as a consequence. (By now their ground floors are two to three meters below the high-tide mark.) This particular ward is also frankly reported in the brochure as being ten times more vulnerable to fires and conflagrations in the event of a very serious earthquake occurring around dinner time than the wards on the west and north sides of Tokyo.

Inside an Apartment Dwelling

Dining, bath and kitchen areas were completely Western in style. The floor was carpeted, instead of tatami, and the air conditioning was limited to a small fan above the door. Heating was provided by a caged pressurized paraffin oil heater that could be carried from room to room, and a portable electric fire was stationed in the kitchen area. The piano was covered with a cloth, which allowed it to provide a shelf for the classic dolls, a cabinet for bric-a-brac, toys, etc. The living room contained a desk for writing and a wall lined with books. The overall living space was about 70 square meters and the rent about ¥28,000 ($80) with a monthly service charge of ¥1,100 ($3.20).

Cityscapes from the balcony are extraordinary; the sweep of the harbor disappears in the murk, and the new skyscrapers of the precincts around the Emperor's Palace stand out on the horizon. Unfortunately, the factory chimneys spew noxious gases at this level, and a half dozen of them lie to the windward within 500 meters. The rail of the balcony felt gritty with fly ash and particles of coke. Yet this apartment was better off than most in Manhattan, and wondrously clean as compared to others visited the following day which were unfortunate neighbors of a productive, but unregulated, foundry.

Men are the working members of these families and so are acquainted with few of their neighbors. Taira, an editor of a design magazine and in his late thirties, could recognize the faces of neighbors and next neighbors in his floor, but no others. The wife, even if employed, does the neighboring. Children, especially young ones, bring the wives together. The estate has a coffee house (called Dessert, in English script) that sells Coca Cola, pastries and soft ice cream, and is frequented by mothers with children. The P.T.A. is a significant institution, whether in the school next door or in the private schools through which the middle classes push their children in hopes of entrance to a first-class university. Luncheon engagements can be made with friends and relatives from elsewhere in the city at the Friend Restarun, which misspells the English far more than any unselfconscious Greek restauranteur in Canada. Shopping is carried out in branches of metropolitan chains with rather formal, rather than neighborly, contact between employees, who came in from outside, and the residents. The resemblance to the Mediterranean life-styles in high-rise slabs seems to be purely physical; Tokyo's loyalties are to organization, classmates, and perhaps a religion, such as the Sokka Gokkai, whereas the Italian and Greek loyalties are to family, and perhaps sports or politics. Nor did the Japanese bother to keep the landscape from accumulating a clutter of paper, plastic bags and discarded packages. The high population density is not an adequate excuse, for this – the Europeans and the

Chinese succeed rather well in their efforts at litter control. The lack of concern for neighbors seems to be strongest among the young to middle-age Japanese of all social classes when living as nuclear families.

From the balcony on the twentieth floor, it was possible to see the progression of housing efforts in Tokyo. A few hundred yards away were the regular brown roofs of the emergency postwar houses, unpainted wood-frame, free-standing houses, with an occasional gap due to some past fire. The lanes were 2 and 5 meters in width. The 0.5- to 2.0-meter strips of land on the plots outside the walls of the houses had some small trees, bushes and gardens, but had accumulated much more salvaged lumber, pipe, appliances and mechanical equipment. Poor-quality fittings were rusting away in the corrosive atmosphere.

Adjacent were two-story contractor-built houses, slightly newer (say 1947-1955), with brown tile roofs. Most of the residential area fell into this category. Where small industries had recently evacuated, one saw neat, ordered patches of bright blue tile, corrugated plastic porches and sunshades and flashes of aluminum framing dropped onto the site. The houses of the new development were built up two to three stories with garages, so 10-meter streets became common. Land coverage was perhaps 70 percent.

Perhaps 500 units of metropolitan subsidized housing were just being completed. At last, belatedly, the sewers were going in and the landscaping was being done, although the apartments and workshops had been lived in for a year or two. The dwellings were four- to five-floor walk-up slabs with 50 to 70 square meters of living space apiece and a somewhat improved courtyard in the center. Scores of small boys running about in the courtyard managed to keep its red-brown soil compact and devoid of grass. Land coverage was about 25 to 30 percent so the complexes were reasonably spacious in appearance, especially for residences of working-class Japanese.

Diffusing into the Kanto Plain

On a sunny morning, Rory Fonseca (an Indian architect-scholar studying for a doctorate at Berkeley) and I joined the thin counterstream to the suburbs on the Tojo Line, an electric route out of the Tokyo subcenter of Ikebukero. A private firm owns the railroad and the department store in the station, as well as much of the land in the countryside. We chose to get out at Kamifukuoka because it offered completed projects of the Japan Housing Corporation about 40 minutes from the Circle Line of the Japan National Railways. Therefore, it was a location on the fringe as nearly comparable to the Oshima Housing Estates as any that could be found. There we could see how Tokyo was growing out as well as up.

The transport service was impressive − smooth rapid transit with trains every 10-15 minutes. The path to the station from four-story walk-up apartments (with some terrace-type units) required only five to ten minutes. About 20 percent of the residents of the apartments seemed to own automobiles, as opposed to 10 percent at Oshima.

As one leaves the station courtyard he encounters at least eight luxurious (i.e., air-conditioned) competing real estate offices, most with an associated contractor willing to build a 12- to 30-mat house with blue tile roof and colorful fixtures. Small tracts spread out away from the town center to displace the onions and soup greens, the latter carefully nurtured under half cylinders of polyethylene. Villages are left here and there, 20 to 50 houses on ground raised above the flood plain, recognizable from the distance by a scattering of unpruned medium-sized trees and a few thatched roofs.

The principal reason for the desire of the Japanese city dweller to move out instead of up was most probably to find a place for "my-car." There was a chance also of getting a head start on the city traffic when undertaking a holiday trip. Since 1960 the numbers of passenger cars in Tokyo region must have multiplied by a factor of four or five. Now only the mailmen and a few delivery boys in the community were seen using motorbikes; all the principal trips were made on four wheels or more. However, hundreds of men from outside the town parked their bikes near the station in special garages. On Sunday Kamifukuoka must be a kind of garden city, with walkers on the graveled lanes taking in the relatively unpolluted air, but on this weekday we found a typical commuting pattern, since virtually no men were to be seen other than the construction workers and the farmhands.

Out here in Kamifukuoka one could see the dreams of "my car" converge with those of "my-home" to produce a space-consuming life-style for Japan. Fully two-thirds of the population of today's Tokyo is only one or two generations away from the village or farm, so it is to be expected that the new settlers would very likely be attracted to the market gardens and open spaces, even if those features will disappear within a few years when the density reaches 20 households and 15 cars per acre.

TOKYO VERSUS THE ENERGY CRISIS

January 1974

Some day the machines will stop, say the humanists. What then will be the fate of urban man? Would his complete dependence upon mechanisms be his undoing? When wires no longer hum from the current they carry, smelters have cooled, and refineries have ceased to pump fuel, would the survivors be forced back to the land that once succored man? Doomsayers have long anticipated such a cataclysmic fate, novelists have drawn up alternative scenarios and filmmakers have dramatized them. Conscientious scientists are plagued by the fear that applications of the knowledge they produce may add to the vulnerability of civilized man. A vision of many millions of people trapped in cold, immobile cities, passing through moods of false optimism, black despair, and apathy before succumbing to the inevitable is what holds the fixed attention of artists, journalists, and evangelists among us. In it skyscrapers and apartment blocks, as well as new suburbs, become ghostly jungles occupied by bands of unfortunate survivors reduced to subsisting upon the hidden boards of food and fuel they manage to dig up.

Such speculations are uninformed and nonsensical, say those who have studied the systems by which cities are sustained. A metropolis is not only a mass of people, it is also an organized web of inter-dependencies. If supply links should be cut, resort is made temporarily to stockpiles while other links are expanded to make up the difference. As stocks fall, substitutes are brought to the fore as soon as bids in the marketplaces of the world are increased. Thus the modern metropolis comes close to achieving the goal of an ultrastable system that can take virtually any shock, short of a cluster of hydrogen bombs, and still survive. Never before in history has civilization seemed so secure – an energy shortage of the kind that can really occur may be costly, but it would not be deadly.

The time of testing may now have arrived. Tokyo, the world's largest metropolis with an effective population of over 20 million, operates almost completely on imported oil. Energy is the labor force of a modern city, and the employees are merely part of the directorate. They are hired to focus its application to the tasks at hand. This is becoming true even in the cities of the less developed countries, but Tokyo has converted almost wholly to mechanical slavery.

The facts about energy are these: the statistics reported a few months ago for 1972 showed that petroleum imports were responsible for 73.5 percent of Japan's energy (the remainder is attributed to coal, hydroelectric, nuclear, and trivial amounts of charcoal and gas). The Arab Bloc provided about 45 percent of the petroleum, Iran 36 percent and Indonesia 16 percent. Within Japan the Tokyo region is more dependent upon oil for its industry and commerce than any other because it produces less steel, which requires import of coking coal. Thus the maximum "energy shock" that can be delivered by the Arabs seems to be an across-the-board reduction of about 30 percent. However, 1974 was planned to be a much bigger year than its predecessor and new petrochemical facilities, rolling mills, and plastics plants were being completed; diesel engines had already been built, and aircraft jets had already been imported. Together they had added about 30 percent to the petroleum delivery contracts for 1972. Therefore, the outer limit for a shock was about 45 percent of the capacity to consume. The task for government was to decide which 45 percent of Tokyo's mechanical slaves should be idled.

Rumors are unsettling, and they set off epidemics of hoarding. In Tokyo the disappearance of fuel into private stocks resulted in a shortage of kerosene in the bathhouses, and a limit of 30 liters per day for taxis. Protesters appeared, with signs and chants prepared in advance, before the doors of the Ministry of International Trade and Industry. The government strategy, it appeared, was to publish a body of regulations to take effect after a last New Year's fling.

One law was passed which allowed allocation of fuel to various kinds of consumers and another which assured the "people's livelihood." Since

Japan has only a skeletonized social welfare system, strong measures need to be taken to prevent abnormal price rises affecting the pensioners, handicapped, semiemployed, and other marginal components in the population. This generally is done through subsidies for rice and other essentials. The government proudly announced that its financial reserves would easily compensate for the 50 to 70 percent rise in oil price, so the main problem lay in lessening the impoverishing effects of the shortage upon low-income people.

The Internal Response

A constructive response to crisis is to use it as a pretext for the solution of many sticky problems that remain unresolved due to conflicting interests behind the scenes. One of these problems is the structure of the Japanese oil industry itself. It had to grow very rapidly so as to provide gasoline to match the record automobile sales (now about 80 percent of the number of units per capita per year reported for the United States). These firms purchased crude oil and refined it for local use, but they were also strongly encouraged to drill their own wells. The Japanese, being late on the scene in the world search for petroleum, were left with less promising leases or were forced to outbid the major multinational firms. This is not a way to make money quickly in an industry where the stakes are extraordinarily high. An examination of the books of Japanese oil companies would probably reveal an alarming debt structure, with standing demands for ever larger sums for exploration and drilling, without the profits derived from long-held oil sources that the major firms are registering. In Japan a measure of security has been achieved by installing a high duty on refined imports. This allows high prices to be charged to the urban consumer but not to the export-oriented industries that buy crude or bottoms.

This policy comes into conflict, however, with a deal arranged with Iran, where a large air-polluting refinery would be built in Iran and the refined products brought to Japan. The Tanaka government postponed decision so often and for so long that the Iranians accused them of insincerity and threatened to cut off all oil. Overnight the Ministry of International Trade and Industry, the master strategist for Japanese export industries, acted to get the duties reduced on kerosene, naphtha, and other refined products. It could do so because the OPEC move to raise prices had given the oil companies, all of which had nearly full inventories, a big windfall profit in Japan. Moreover, it was perfectly obvious to everyone that Japan should be in a position to buy oil freely wherever it might be obtained, even if it had been refined elsewhere.

Other such moves should be made wherever administered prices have accumulated large built-in subsidies. In noncrisis times a body of citizens may interpret a price rise in a familiar service as an attack upon the structure of its life-style, and they often explode with violent protest. In troubled times their attention is deflected elsewhere. Thus, the bathhouse operators were assured their kerosene, but they also were allowed a 14 percent price rise in order to pay for increasingly expensive labor and fuel. Then the taxi cabs were given a boost of 25 percent — starting after the holidays, of course, since no administrator wants to face a howling mob. I venture to predict that increases in railroad fares and the cancellation of branch-line trains that cost more energy than the use of the automobiles that normally provide alternate means of transport will be next. The Japan National Railways has just settled a difficult strike with too many compromises being made to intransigent railroad workers.

No doubt the executives of the postal service and of the subways will try to make the next move toward simplification. Thus within a few months price adjustments could be virtually completed. The shifts are necessary because most enterprises offering these services have a customer population that is declining, and the patterns of behavior that evolved for many decades can no longer be maintained because marginal costs have risen sharply wherever automobiles have taken away the customers.

If one had to choose between automobiles and inflation as fundamental sources of trouble in the urban services, surely the automobile ranks first. And it is the automobile which has been dealt the most direct blow by the price shock. Perhaps now the structure of urban services will hold together better, especially after the automobile has been disciplined.

Beyond 1975

The energy planners in Tokyo should find that a 15 percent cut in energy use for fiscal 1975 wil not be too difficult. No one need be out of a job for more than a few months. The principal projects that would be extended or dropped do not employ many people. The entertainment sector, supported by expense accounts, will be hit the hardest, but this sector has recently been desperate for personnel, so a reduction will not affect many households. The major effect might be to reduce the rents and land values in the "gay districts," which had been rising unreasonably. A 20 percent cut might cause backlash from unexpected quarters; therefore, a rent reduction would be postponed as long as possible, so as to get better clues concerning the effects of cutbacks even if the risk of a temporary 25 percent cut must be taken.

Energy planning carried out along national and metropolitan lines can arrive at these comforting conclusions. Exploiting a crisis mentality can lead to many long-needed adjustments and therefore a leaner economy, more flexible in commerce, technology, and the provision of public services. For Tokyo, such energy planning appears likely to be sobering as well.

But there is a flaw here which is still not recognized. That is the extent of interdependence of Tokyo with the rest of the world. The details of energy planning on a global scale are carried out in Manhattan, Houston, and London. The OPEC counterforce in Vienna is still miniscule. Tokyo is on the fringe, because it instituted a policy of keeping the big multinationals out of the country. Thus certain problems such as the shortage of bunker oil can remain unanticipated and hit with a suddenness that adds new jolts to the metropolitan economies. The Japanese national economy may be forced to join the world even more rapidly than MITI has scheduled the transition, and in directions that remain undisclosed.

Meanwhile it is also apparent that an urban economy which is fast to react, as Tokyo is, can make a number of profitable deals. Economic growth can feasibly proceed with less energy. At the same time sulfur dioxide, carbon monoxide, and particulate matter in the atmosphere can be reduced to an even greater extent. Coastal pollution should not get any worse, and the gradual completion of projects should bring about the same kinds of noticeable improvements as were recently observed for the threatened Inland Sea. Perhaps parts of Tokyo Bay will even recover. Thus, though alarms and alerts continue, Tokyo should become more livable.

Outcomes

A number of specific forecasts were charted in the foregoing report, together with hints of future trends. It is useful to recount what happened in these respects during 1975-78:

1. The cutbacks in petroleum delivery were quickly rescinded, but fertilizers, some plastics and fibers, and steel still showed output losses for the year because the precious hydrocarbons were directed into newly completed production facilities. The airlines suffered a particularly bad year, but much of the loss was due to diplomatic fiascos.
2. Financial reserves slipped away for a while at a rate greater than a billion dollars a month, but near the end of the year OPEC countries deposited a billion dollars in Japanese banks to stem the potential panic.
3. Rationalization of public services was interrupted by the high-pressure wage negotiations conducted more or less simultaneously throughout Japan between labor and management. The firms and public corporations capitulated and granted unprecedented wage increases which could not possibly be balanced, as in earlier instances, with increased productivity. Thus a world record rate of inflation was triggered for Japan as a whole.
4. The new prime minister of Japan, selected to reform the party that won the election through scandalous spending of Tanaka's industrial contributions, was the "aging Miki" who had been sent to negotiate with the Arabs earlier.
5. Because of the energy crisis and inflation in America, sales of imported Japanese automobiles fell off disastrously for many models. The makers of Mazda were pushed to the wall, and their survival was once uncertain. However they all came back strongly in 1977-8.

6. Land prices in Tokyo were reported down by 10 to 30 percent despite a rate of price inflation of more than 30 percent. The cause was attributed to a liquidity crisis for many firms and families, as well as a slackening demand due to increasing disillusionment with city life (and reduced expense accounts). The appreciation of the yen with respect to the dollar in 1977-78 was responsible for price readjustments thereafter.

7. Toward the end of 1974 the coordinated drive to sell manufactured products overseas began to take hold. After experiencing the deepest recession since World War II the Japanese economy showed its resiliency by promptly rebounding, achieving about 5 percent real growth per annum in the 1976-78 period.

Japanese planners find that the urban public has not abandoned its environmental values. Indeed the turbulence of the period after the energy crisis and the inflation that followed have if anything enhanced the emotional commitment to the environment. The sentiment against pollution of all kinds is much more strongly held by the young people and those of intermediate education than by the intellectuals, and it sometimes reaches a religious frenzy that astonishes politicians and intellectuals. One move that has been initiated is an attempt at computer-based participative planning which will be expanded greatly in the near future because the prefectural politicians ascribe their success in the recent elections to this technique. In addition, the national planners were given a charge to construct as one alternative to GNP maximization the abolition of contemporary Tokyo. It is to be replaced by a clean, quiet, intensely gardened civilization, an image of the future which resembles contemporary Switzerland more than any other place in the world.

4 Hong Kong*

Hong Kong is a fascinating, frustrating, incredible metropolis. It frustrates because so much of its life below the surface events that are freely reported in current publications; analysis of this city incites disbelief in reviewers because it survives, even prospers, under conditions we are disposed to believe are impossible.

Increasingly colleagues argue that comprehensive, or holistic, assessments must be undertaken because our affairs are becoming ever more interrelated. Ecological models seem highly appropriate to this outlook, since an ecosystem is defined as a set of interdependent populations interacting with the physical surroundings. Problems arise in both analysis and communication, however, when attempting to transmit such a holistic outlook. The discussion revolves at great length around tables of data, lists of species and interactions, and sequences of deviation from norms before future states of being can be discussed. Thus ecological discourse tends to be dry and technical, particularly when arriving at reassurances that most kinds of crises are not forthcoming. In Hong Kong's case the crises are likely, but not as yet believable.

What follows are selections from a paper presented at an international conference on "urban systems" held in Schloss Laxenburg, Austria.(13)

---

*Estimated 1985 population — 5 1/2 million.

URBAN ECOSYSTEM DEVELOPMENT

July 1974

In Planning for an Urban World,(14) when endeavoring to envisage a
world population at steady state, with a predominant share of the
people finding it necessary to reside in cities in order to live at a level
above subsistence, I was forced to consider the city as a habitat for
machines as well as for living things. Machines are continuously
occupying new niches, serving purposes previously filled by humans,
animals, and even plants; as human population expands and natural
resources become depleted the cities need a wider variety of machines
to extract a good living from the physical environment. Thus the urban
ecosystem fits the following hierarchy:

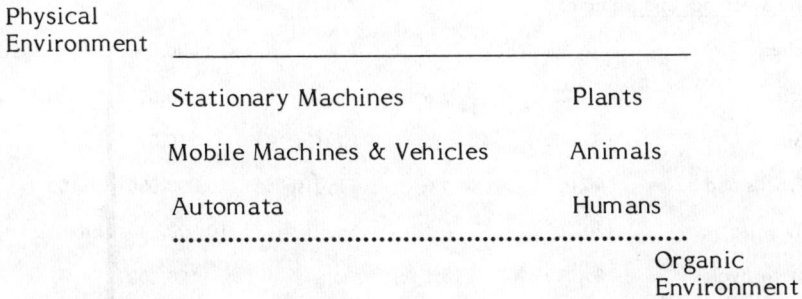

Physical
Environment   _____

Stationary Machines	Plants
Mobile Machines & Vehicles	Animals
Automata	Humans

··
Organic
Environment

What are the shifts in structure as the human component acquires added
competence, modernizes, and improves the security of its members?

Hong Kong, among all existing metropolises in the world, allows one
to obtain much more exact counts of the respective populations and fair
estimates of the current rates of change. The reason is that the
political boundary drawn around the Crown Colony encloses very little
rural hinterland and allows exceedingly little overflow into adjacent
territories. Hong Kong's population is 98 to 99 percent pure metropolitan.

Hong Kong operates very much like a self-sustaining city-state.
Much of the statistics-collecting apparatus was set up by British civil
servants, so the data are as reliable as any that are available for cities,
though far from comprehensive in coverage.

The notable populations involved in the developing urban ecosystem
have been estimated for Hong Kong and are presented in table 4.1.
Attempts were made also to estimate annual rates of change for the
mid-decade period, but these trends are often more uncertain or
variable. Inspection of table 4.1 shows that, although a great deal of
publicity is given to the rate of increase of human population, there
should be a great deal more concern for the growth in numbers of
vehicles — each of which requires as much concrete platform for its
"habitat" as 20 to 30 persons in a resettlement unit. Crowding caused by
the growth of vehicle numbers is much more imminent.(15)

Table 4.1. Population Estimates: Hong Kong Ecosystem (1974)

Stationary Machines		Trend	Plants		Trend
Electric motors (air conditioners, pumps, clocks, industrial)	700,000	+11%/yr[a]	Trees	2-3,000,000[e]	+5%/yr
			Brush and grass		?
Engines	30,000	+5%			
Electric generators	100	+10%	Vegetables and rice[f]		-2%
Mobile Machines and Vehicles			**Animals[g]**		
Watches	500,000	+20%[b]	Pigs	400,000	
Vehicles	285,000	+9%	Poultry	6,000,000	
Autos	135,000	+7%	Cattle	10,000	
Trucks and buses	40,000	+5%	Fin fish	10,000,000	+10% in biomass
Bicycles	150,000	?	Shellfish	10,000,000	
Motorcycles	25,000	+18%	Dogs	100,000	
Ships	10,000	+5%	Cats	50,000	
			Birds	50,000	
Automata			Wildlife (mostly fish and birds)		
Minicomputers[c]	100	+30%	**Humans**		
Computer centers[d]	1-200		Census	4,250,000	+1.4%
			Refugees[h]	100,000	+15%
			Tourists	15,000	+10%

[a] Electric power use was increasing 12 percent per year up to the energy crisis.
[b] Estimate from observations on the street and in the field.
[c] Estimate obtained from the Universities Joint Computer Center.
[d] Automata are sophisticated circuits controlling the machines; computer centers have much greater capacity, but their jobs are still mostly routine.
[e] Assumes forest averages 70 trees per acre, with more in banana and fruit orchards, a few in residential zones. A tree is at least 20 feet high or 1 foot in girth.
[f] Increase in output due to faster rotation; acreage has been reduced recently.
[g] Listed in approximate order of contribution to biomass.
[h] Many are illegal, so perhaps underestimated; a new wave has appeared since 1972.

Overall, the data from this community of humans and their artifacts depicting the population magnitudes and their trends suggest that Hong Kong is being stimulated to undertake extraordinary development. The growth of the respective populations could hardly be expected to stay in balance. Stated in still another way, the human population is very busy constructing and arranging a modern habitat convenient to itself, but in so doing it must draw increasingly heavily from the rest of the world for nourishment in the form of energy (food and fuel) and materials of construction.

Stresses of Growth and Change

Whenever a community undergoes rapid growth it should expect that some kind of price must be paid. Different components grow at their own rates. The identification of these differentials is a worthwhile enterprise. The respective growth rates have been estimated by making deductions from various annual reports of Hong Kong agencies. The official physical dimensions for Hong Kong have remained constant since 1861, yet the land surface is increasing about 0.2 percent per year due to reclamation from the sea. The human population is growing about 1.8 percent per year (counting refugees), and the number of vehicular trips by about 3 percent. The number of dwelling units is expanding by about 3 percent, as are the number of school places and the number of jobs. The amount of roadway is lengthening by about 4 percent, the amount of income available for consumption (in real terms) is increasing by 5 to 8 percent, solid waste produced, 10 to 12 percent, and electric power generated is about the same. The number of telephones installed advances by 13 to 15 percent, but the number of telephone calls placed is going up at a rate of 15 to 17 percent. The value of checks cleared is multiplying at a rate of 20 to 30 percent per year, while the additions to capital stock are more variable at 10 to 35 percent per annum. Each of these rates represents a different way of looking at internal growth: those mentioned earlier are more primitive and structural in nature; the intermediate ones involve transfers of consumer goods with a marked style, quality, or informational component; while those last mentioned measure transactions which have purely symbolic value with minimal demands upon space, so that they exhibit little friction with the environment.

A few indicators of the localized ill-effects imposed by the milieu upon its resident populations can be found within the current reports. Tuberculosis is still a big killer in Hong Kong, but the rates are dropping by 3 to 5 percent per year. Measles and chicken pox are episodic, but also show a major long-term decline. Traffic casualty rates are falling 1 to 2 percent per year based upon potential victims, about 9 percent based upon the population of vehicles. Overall crime reported showed a marked jump in 1973 (16 percent), but this indicated much more a willingness to record crimes that could not be traced to perpetrators as well as a redefinition of crimes against public order, such as littering public places. A noticeable increase in violent crime, particularly on the part of the growing population of juveniles, led to a special campaign with the slogan "Fight Violent Crime!" An increase in the number of crimes against property and the processes of exchange, such as theft, fraud, forgery, and corruption, reflects not only the vast increase in opportunity due to the extraordinary growth in securities transactions, but also increasing attention by the authorities concerning the corruption issue.

Data demonstrate rather uniformly that the individual and the family are becoming more secure against private disaster despite the increasing intensity of public interactions and an enhanced temptation for criminals. In part this improvement may be due to cooperation taking the form of public associations which allow people to defend themselves against sources of insecurity. Thus the Hong Kong of 1974 had significantly fewer bad things happening than the Hong Kong of 1973, and the trend promises to continue. Such a conclusion goes against the perceptions of the people themselves, even the educated stratum, because the mass media, particularly television, have taken up crusades against crime, accidents, and pollution, thereby exaggerating the number of incidents reaching the attention of the public. Very likely this increase in concern, which often changes to cynicism, is one of the necessary prices people must pay for enhanced communication.

Because Hong Kong's population densities set the world's record (still as high as 400,000 persons per square mile, or 600 per acre, with hundreds of thousands of households limited to 25 square feet per capita − 2.5 square meters − or less), they have caused architects and town planners to search for ill-effects due to crowding. The health and activity reports give no confirmation of these expectations. However, one argument commonly made is that the stresses may have been internalized, so that they may later release into the urban ecosystem some kind of collective frenzy that could gravely injure, perhaps destroy, the community.

Extraordinarily dense Hong Kong housing is not statistically associated with unusual levels of emotional strain, even down to a median floor space in resettlement housing of 23 to 26 square feet per person.(16) Analysis of the separate breakdowns provided by Mitchell's survey persuade one to believe that government policies for the construction and management of subsidized housing were consonant with user preferences. Although these major programs were aimed at preventing destructive fires and epidemics as well as opening up accessible land for more intensive use, they have not measurably increased levels of mental strain.

The conclusion to be derived from the sum of the evidence is that the Hong Kong habitat is presently favorable for man, animals, and some plants, more so than almost anywhere else in Asia. These conditions are encouraging a proliferation of growth together with the emergence of higher levels of organization. As noted earlier, local residents resist such conclusions; also professional opinions voiced elsewhere are not in agreement. Therefore, I have sought a number of corroboratory tests.

Migrants change their home environment for a better one. A local example is the moving of the water people from their boats and isolated houses on posts in tidewater villages. Jobs in factories and apartments in a tightly packed settlement have brought more than half of them into the metropolis over the past 15 years. Apparently they prefer that life to the uncertainties of fishing and the ties to a folk community with a long tradition. Almost all have the opportunity to move back again, but they are sticking it out in the heart of Hong Kong or its high-density appendages. The fisherman's life is much better now that diesel engines allow him to go out in all seasons, and the price of fish is up; nevertheless the number of water people continues to dwindle while the number of Koreans and Taiwanese in fishing expands.(17)

Similarly an increasing net flow is observed from China into Hong Kong, much of it moderately well informed because relatives outside provided contacts both before and after migration. Moreover, the flow to the United States, Canada, and the United Kingdom tends to select the locales in those countries that most resemble Hong Kong, such as San Francisco, New York, Vancouver, and London's Soho, even though jobs for bilingual Chinese are readily available in more thinly populated locations. Hundreds of thousands of voluntary choices of residence have been made over the past decade, and the great majority show a clear preference for Hong Kong-like communities, as compared to a variety of others.

These are personal and small group decisions made by people who are marginal to communities, and presumably more sensitive to the stresses than the mass, because it is the overstressed (or under-stimulated – a stress of another sort) who seek to escape. The totality of evidence, therefore, seems to argue that the quality of life in Hong Kong grades from average to good as compared to all the real alternatives open to human members of the community, even though it may be seriously flawed as compared to an ideal version of city life.

Alternative Pathways into the Future

The fundamental environmental issue facing Hong Kong as a community is not the relative goodness or badness at present, or even the threatened levels of pollution. It is the need to find a relatively painless path to a climax condition that exhibits zero population growth and zero energy utilization growth, together with flexible water usage and raw materials requirement. Three very different kinds of alternatives will be explored here, but a review of parallels in recent history will suggest a number of others.(18)

Goal-directed projection into the future

The simplest, most ecologically sound program for the community of Hong Kong presumes that the boundaries (which are virtually un-defended) will remain stable and that the lease for the New Territories can be renegotiated on much the same terms as at present. Immigration would be balanced by emigration.

The continuing investments in education make it likely that another 40 percent of the population will accept birth control as rapidly as the last 40 percent and that this acceptance will require perhaps 12 years. Thus if the one to two-child family becomes the norm and only unusual households bring the reproduction of the human population up to or somewhat beyond replacement levels, the population will grow older, with the average age shifting from less than 20 at the present time to about 35 a generation from now. The total population of Hong Kong would level off at a figure close to six million.

As a part of this projection it is judged that the dependent pig and poultry populations would by then have reached a somewhat higher level than at present, mainly because they can be fed on the wastes of the city and the by-products of the food processing industries, with supplements drawn from the cheapest rough grains on the world market.

The major population expansion is to be expected in fish, as an outgrowth of the borrowing of mariculture techniques from Japan and Hawaii. Floating ponds allow the recycling of human and animal wastes back to the pigs and the domesticated fish, instead of the present disposal into the tidal currents. These innovations are already proceeding in nearby Taiwan.

Under climax conditions rice growing should virtually disappear, but Hong Kong would be almost entirely self-sufficient in vegetables. The steep hill and mountainsides would be largely reforested, some of them becoming already quite dense and parklike a human generation hence. The mountain tops would support new and more digestible grasses, fertilized to increase the rate of milk production. Thus much more grazing would be carried out, but in a way that seldom detracts from the enjoyment of people on holiday, since the same peak areas are very precious for recreational use.

Some big stationary machines – oil, refineries, petrochemicals, plastics and fiber production, steel mills, and shipyards – are due to be installed in Hong Kong. Then its industry will become far more vertically integrated than now, but remain less so than in Japan, Korea, or Taiwan. Many intermediate products will still be shipped out and others quite similar will be imported. In this future Hong Kong must remain a very open system with worldwide relationships.

The automotive vehicle population must come under control well within a decade. As the annual increment dwindles to zero the diversity will increase, much as has already occurred in construction machines, vans, and in shipping. Private automobiles can be displaced by increasing the personalized transport services, such as "dial-a-ride." Fortunately, the era of the universality of the telephone is virtually upon Hong Kong. Its microelectronics industry will soon be capable of producing a portable telephone that would allow one to quickly obtain a ride from any origin to any destination at a price less than is paid for the same trip by automobile.

Bicycle populations will vastly increase in the new towns and environs, being assigned in many instances a separate network of lanes, based upon precedents now being established elsewhere in the world. The cycle population will also become quite diverse in order to fit the needs of older people.

The automata in this future will be largely invisible and embedded in the newest industries and services. If half of the new equipment in America will incorporate sophisticated automatic control systems by 1975 (a Business Week estimate) then the same level of use should come to Hong Kong 10 to 15 years later. Their introduction could save 20 to 40 percent of the energy and materials required per unit of output. A large share of the savings would be due to the expediting of round-the-clock organization which allows Hong Kong to be continuously on-line by means of communication satellite with America, Japan, and Europe.

The constructed physical environment must keep on growing much longer than the populations. In large part this is due to the unfulfilled demand for construction in this metropolis, but it is also needed to add flexibility to the economy, allowing it to adjust quickly to exigencies and opportunities in world trade. Thus a population of six million is likely to demand living space for itself and its organizations at least three times the present floor and road area and perhaps four times the enclosed volume. (One of the significant reasons is the growing body size of the resident Chinese that is attributed to improved diet.) A variety of water-borne structures is likely to be added a decade or two hence. The new structure must be designed for minimal air conditioning and maximal natural ventilation in order to save energy and gain flexibility of use under varying conditions of world supply.

Henceforth the emphasis everywhere must be on improved fit between the respective populations and the constructed physical environment. The engine and chassis of a vehicle may be quite standard, but the body and the auxiliary equipment will be increasingly adapted to the function it serves. Thus, in very little time, the body may change to fit a completely new function. Containerization starts with a standard exterior and introduces new liners and internal supports to handle many different cargoes. These approaches complement each other.

Similarly, the price structure for services, such as water and power supply, must be made still more variable so that real economies can be achieved during periods of regional or world scarcity that inevitably mean scarcity for Hong Kong. Thus if the world food situation becomes serious (less likely than presently publicized in the newspapers, but still a very real possibility) the pig and poultry populations of Hong Kong will suffer, the banquets will depend upon to-fu and textured protein substitute materials. Rice would give place to bread, noodles, and cornmeal pasties. In general it is much more economical for a harbor metropolis to invest in flexible consumption than in large buffer stocks.

Rupture of the boundary with China

This is an apocalyptic future that presumes temporary breakdowns of public order in China equal to or more severe than the Cultural

Revolution.(19) Then poor refugees will come crowding into Hong Kong at the same time that a large share of the cosmopolitan population and the financial resources they control (led by the tiny minority holding passports), would flee to safer cities. The population could very easily double, and the standard of living fall back to a subsistence level.

Population pressures are so great in Kwangtung, Fukien, and the provinces to the West that, once economic development is resumed, the conurbation of Canton should grow to a size larger than greater Tokyo. The number would at least be in the range of 30 to 50 million people, but probably even larger. The land forms require it to be polycentric, so that an enlarged Hong Kong might play a very significant role in initiating the enterprises and managing the technology as well as offering an opening to the world. Hong Kong might play the same role for the new Canton that Yokohama-Kawasaki did for Tokyo in the twentieth century, because Canton would almost certainly remain the center of political administration and be backed with the military police power. The small-scale manufacturing that still employs much of the labor force of Hong Kong would move onto new estates not yet populated.

Risks of further breakdowns along this pathway are very high. There may be repeated famines and revolutions in China until population distributions again come into rough balance with food production and with the capacity to distribute imports from the outside world. (The transport system of China does not allow it to depend upon food surpluses in America and Australia the way that India and Java can.) However, due to its high-quality harbor and docking facilities, and the great distance from the famine belt, the Canton conurbation should be better off than any other part of China.

During a period of hard times and disorganization in China the conurbation of Canton should remain a center of stability and become a base from which political power over a large hinterland could be exercised. Whatever is left of the identity of Hong Kong would play an important part in that renaissance.

A quasi-independent city-state

The accelerated decline of the United Kingdom's share of international trade makes it possible that it might divest the last traces of Empire in the foreseeable future. Then Hong Kong would be forced to pursue a course somewhere between that of Singapore and the future Taiwan.(20) Like Macao, it would have to take orders from Peking, but as long as the yield in foreign exchange is high there may be very little interference. Nevertheless, the demands upon its ecosystem would be much more dependent upon Marxist philosophies expounded in Peking than the Western ideas increasingly propagated in Hong Kong now. Short-run interests of an agressively developing economy, separated by a more permeable boundary, would predominate over the progressive evolution toward a steady state propounded by ecologically sophisticated planners.(21)

As a result the carrying capacity for biomass would be significantly reduced for a long time to come. The ability to adjust to shocks arising from political and environmental shifts would be judged from the point of view of the survival of the collective unit, the political economy of China itself, and much less from that of individual welfare. In recent history both emphases are common; neither can be claimed to be superior to the other.

5 Singapore, Bangkok and Penang*

Prior scholarship involving large cities has been extremely happenstance, often missing observations we now know to be highly significant, because it possessed an inadequate set of standards for reporting. Neither a humanistic nor an engineering approach alone is sufficient. We must ask how scholarship devoted to the study of exotic places can move away from the unraveling of detail and the analysis of myth — so typical of previous generations — and contribute to systematic extension of a growing body of knowledge.

Quality might be improved either by fitting the data and observations into a future-oriented systems network, as with the previous notes on Hong Kong, or by undertaking comparisons. In the comparative approach an investigator should identify salient phenomena in one locale, using them to raise questions about equivalent functions in the other. By shifting one's attention back and forth between several metropolises it is possible to discover shared destinies and fundamental differences. The naivete of parochialism is overcome. Methodologists believe, on the basis of experience with equally complex studies on personality and face-to-face communities, that eventually some defensible general theories will emerge from a body of comparisons.

Metropolises with similar trajectories offer an opportunity for such analyses of urban activity. I visited Singapore and Bangkok in 1969, 1970, 1971, and 1974, but Penang only in 1974. Some of the general arguments in the introduction were published earlier.(22)

---

*Estimated 1985 population — Singapore, 3 million; Bangkok, 7 million; Penang, 700,000.

A MEASURE OF METROPOLITAN PERFORMANCE:
SINGAPORE AND BANGKOK

October 1971-August 1974

Two metropolises lead the way in the modernization and economic development of upwards of 250,000,000 people on the southeast fringes of Asia. They provide niches for the powerful technological concepts of our time, allowing them to activate a series of quiet revolutions in ways of life, philosophic outlook, and human relationships. Increasingly the bearers of the crucial capabilities are the multinational corporations that can swiftly build up regional headquarters, now that the telecommunications facilities allow continuous exchange of information with the other leading metropolises of the world.

Singapore and Bangkok have accumulated skilled multilingual personnel who can be recruited to management, intercontinental hotels for entertaining important visitors, comfortable homes, a good standard of security from violence, and suitable recreation. In them world markets are translated into bids and offers for smaller transactions within the region; world interests in health, education, and welfare are reworked into metropolitan-scale programs implemented by public agencies, and advanced by newly organized scientific research and scholarship. Metropolitan enterprises simultaneously subdivide the larger managerial concerns into local projects and field operations.

The primary function of the pacemaking metropolis in Asia is that of broker. One cannot understand the dynamism of Singapore and Bangkok without recognizing the variety of milieux for middlemen that they maintain. Dealing in commodities moving in international and regional trade is a traditional activity that remains important. More recently quasi-markets in human skills have come into being. Consulting groups have established themselves as knowledge distributors. Organizers of information acquisition systems have advanced far beyond simple journalistic endeavors. Tourism has become professionalized with hundreds of specialities evolving which buffer the visitor, so that he is usually kept from experiencing severe cultural shock. The wholesalers of popular culture, whether American, Japanese, Chinese (from Hong Kong and Taiwan), or European, are also proliferating. When exchanges are effected with the hinterland, modern styles and cultural responses are very often adopted sooner in the boondocks than are the related technological improvements. Steps in the diffusion path can be traced back to locales in these metropolises where a small community of entrepreneurs, brokers, and agents has been learning how to distribute nonmaterial modern outputs.

Images of the Rugged Society in a Garden City

One exceedingly significant indicator of the place of a metropolis on the world scene is the image of itself that it presents to outsiders. This "face" appears in public statements by the prime minister, and is elaborated in detail by the output of the ministries wherever the leader strikes a chord of consensus and pride. Often the pictures speak louder than words; in the Singapore output they are very often glossy and in color, which indicates the priority level assigned to the maintenance of appearances. The imagery captured by the pictures raises questions of "Why?" and the explanations obtained from the residents are most often fragmentary accounts of recent history in the city-state. The items that follow are clearly important:

Singapore felt seriously threatened when the British announced they were pulling out altogether. Was a city-state viable in a part of the world where guerillas were attempting to take over two Asian countries to the north, and had just barely been beaten off in Malaya, when Singapore was the chief prize sought by the self-declared communists? The government decided that it needed to become much more like the Israelis – rugged and quick to react. The period of military service for young men was raised to three years, which is even more than for South Korea.

The rugged society has reached down into the schools. Physical fitness programs are emphasized, as well as parade-ground exercises. This shows up in the self-image of Singapore as transmitted through the Ministry of Culture's booklet for tourists. There is a remarkable degree of unanimity among the people as evidenced by the rather trivial scale of the May Day bombs and demonstrations. The Chinese, who once resented the built-in Malay control of the Malaysian government and took pride in the achievements of Mao Tse-Tung, now much prefer independence. Increasingly, Singapore is a nation worth fighting for. Business is very good, the schools are improving rapidly, and the government is sensitive to the needs of most specialized groups.

The rest of the booklet for tourists transmits the theme of modernity – an excellent environment for conducting business. Another message that comes through is only understood if one compares photographs of Singapore with other cities dominated or strongly influenced by the Chinese – Hong Kong, Taipei, Bangkok, and Saigon. Singapore has a clean and tidy image.

The younger professionals say the cleanup from the conditions of the Japanese occupation, which Westerners read about in novels of that period, began with indoctrination in the postwar Chinese elementary schools. Cleanliness came next to proper behavior in the presence of superiors. The other standard was set by the great houses and the clubs of the British colonial civil servants and the expatriate business class. They put great store in their gardens. Now perhaps three-quarters of those houses with sweeping lawns and manicured plots of flowers have Chinese names (printed in English) at the driveway entrance. Dust and smoke are also rare. Thus the tourist is very much reassured upon entering Singapore because he feels he is likely to leave with a functioning gastrointestinal tract. The local illness rate is, as expected, extraordinarily low, as is infant mortality.

The traffic circles are kept blooming the year round. Yellow, red, and green foliage predominate. Similarly, the fringes around the tall white slabs of housing are planted in relatively formal gardens. This is a place for the tourist to rest for a few days. There is nothing special for the tourist to do except eat alfresco on Bugis Street and watch the transvestites. The government has clamped down strongly on beggars and all the addictive vices from drugs to gambling. Hippies are shorn at the quarantine stations, and homosexuals are jailed if they are too visible.

On the other hand city life is relaxed and casual, so that coats are very rarely worn by men. Skirts can be mini, but not micro, as they often are in the centers and subcenters of Tokyo. A straitlaced Honolulu has been a source of inspiration for the planners of tourism in Singapore; not surprisingly, their advisors are drawn from among the most respectable professionals in Hawaii.

The street scene in Singapore is primarily automotive, with a heavy proportion of buses at peak periods. The pedicabs are the smallest seen anywhere and are relatively undecorated; they move around on the fringes of traffic primarily in the more traditional areas dominated by three-story tourist-oriented shop-flat combinations. Bicycles come into view more often in the early morning, before the nine o'clock rush, and in the evening at dusk. Light vans are common, trucks of two to five tons are concentrated around the harbor, while the heavier trucks are seen mostly around construction sites and industrial estates. The oddly shaped yellow American heavy-duty construction equipment is sometimes seen on the roads. Singaporeans, who have had a tradition of leveling hills ever since the nineteenth century, have been quick to import this equipment.

If the image of proper Singapore in the past has been a Southhampton and Torquay in the tropics, it is now surely a Tel Aviv-Honolulu restyling. No mention is made as yet of the future, when a strong influence will be the Osaka pragmatist. Singaporeans have gotten so used to looking east and west for visitors, that they are not yet used to the idea that Japanese from the North will comprise the principal flow of tourists in the future.

Already over a thousand Japanese are living in Singapore, as compared to perhaps 7,000 Americans. The Japanese families come in the second year of the residence of the employee. Since their salaries are double what they would make at home, they pick up the modern contractor-built houses in the suburbs. They concentrate their children in the same private nursery schools, and socialize in much the same way that the English did before the war. The women rarely learn English because they manage to get by with the Chinese characters used in the Japanese language, writing rather than speaking. Because most of the ultramodern technology installed in the Jurong Industrial Estate will come from Japan, this Japanese colony is likely to multiply by ten within a decade. Its institutions will be reinforced by the funds expended by tourists and sojourners.

It will be interesting to see what happens when a contingent of the Japanese "goes native" in Singapore and begins to interact with its culture. The urban Japanese are the most difficult people in Asia to hybridize. (It was accomplished in America and Hawaii because the immigrants were extremely poor, rural, and comparatively uneducated.) However, the Japanese tend to respect very highly a society that tries to be both rugged and "clean and green," so that a much greater degree of compatibility is to be anticipated than, say, with Bangkok or Kuala Lumpur.

Readying for the Future

To what extent can a city-state be a modern nation? There are insufficient precedents for Singapore to follow. Therefore, it will have to improvise as it progresses. The government has the desire to innovate, but what should it do? What policies and projects would a planner advise, beyond what is already being done, to make it possible for an isolated, independent metropolis to reconstruct itself and still maintain a viable form?

The most fundamental policy problems, now that economic development is gaining momentum, are political. Thus far the principal actions have led to an homogenization of the vastly different ethnic and religious groups, first in unions, then in the vote and in party unification, followed by urban renewal and schools, and now the military. Recently even the Malays, who make up an element not too far different in outlook from that of the Spanish-speaking population in California, have been responding well to the incentives for integration in schools, housing, and labor force, but after two years they had yet to take up the first small business loan from the allocation set aside for them. In the future, Singapore will need to capitalize upon its diversity. Each of its ethnic and religious traditions should be encouraged to evolve a modern component. These include British, along with the Hokkien, Hakka, Cantonese and Chiu-Chow, Malabar Muslim and Tamil, Sikh and Malay. Almost certainly Sumatran, Japanese, and Vietnamese will have to be added over the next decade. Fortunately the restrictions on immigration are relaxed for people who bring either a good education, a nest egg of capital, or a business opportunity. Therefore it seems likely that when the full force of the prospective labor shortage hits, the response will be more open than that exhibited by the Japanese, but more restrictive than that of Western Europeans when they imported millions of peasants from Italy, Spain, Yugoslavia, Greece, and Turkey to man the machines in their factories. Singapore is expected to accept immigrants as they are needed, but not before.

On the whole then, a city-state appears to be as viable as Wheaton argues in his "Singkong" thesis, but only if it bends its governmental efforts toward maximizing its freedom to jump, either to avoid the effects of disastrous tears in the fabric of world trade – such as the closing of the Suez Canal or the turn toward protectionism in America

- or to take advantage of unusual new opportunities.(23) Singapore should continue to have a strong developmental effect upon its suppliers because it could insist upon standards of accounting, quality, hygiene, and delivery that would raise the level of organization in its "hinterland" to a point approximating that of the rubber industry, and these improvements would feed back to support an organizing center in its own upgrading attempts. Telecommunications allow almost instantaneous adjustments to be initiated to keep the entrepot in equilibrium with the other financial centers. Given a balanced and agile policy, the gross domestic product could grow more rapidly over the next decade than Japan has over the last, despite the greater proportionate costs of defense. It has already come close to matching the Japanese rate, so that the foregoing claim is not an extreme one.

Modernizing Peasant Society

Bangkok is twice the size of Singapore, but in most features a decade or two behind. The effects of growth in population, income and organizational capability are everywhere evident. Most of the frustrations felt by the farang (the label applied to outsiders) with airport, telephone, transport, and governmental operations can be attributed to growth pains in the urban economy. Bangkok has reached a stage where the demand for such services is expected to grow much faster than the absolute dimensions of the residential population, which is about 4,000,000 (1974) and expanding by an estimated 5 to 7 percent per year. The gross regional product surely has been exceeding 10 percent per year prior to the leveling beginning in 1970. It is also one of the characteristics of Bangkok that the aggregate data are either not available or not trustworthy when reported.

Bangkok is different from Taipei, Singapore, and even Seoul, in that it has acted very much as a stopper that prevents further migration into the rest of the world. It has attracted many sojourners with the hope of finding a job. Formerly, most were carried in the boats that transported the rice, maize, jute, and minerals from the river ports upstream in the Chao Phraya basin. Now more common people arrive, like the students and educated people, on the buses and the trains. Most return home after a stay in the capital city, but quite a few do find reasonably steady employment and places to live in the soi (lanes) that invade the plantations surrounding the city. Almost all Thai students return to Bangkok. There are no important foreign colonies which exchange personnel with the mother country. The Thai elite, made up of top military officers, to a large extent, do get to Europe and the United States, but see little there to attract them for long periods of residence.

The physical installations and rolling stock needed to support a vastly increased circulation through the cities of Thailand have been largely completed. But this involves primarily the primate city, because Chiengmai, the second city, has only about 100,000 population, and the other cities are proportionately smaller. The focus on Bangkok, at the head of navigation on the Chao Phraya, is due largely to physical geography, but centralism is reinforced by the politico-military system. What can be projected regarding the resulting flow and counterflow? We are forced to depend heavily upon the performance of several key mobilizing institutions in the countryside.

At present, the influence of the capital upon the peasant villagers (almost all of whom own their land and are not permitted by law to lose it to Chinese moneylenders) is felt most strongly through the army. The Thai have a tradition of being military conquerers in Southeast Asia, so most families take pride in military service. The soldiers and police are most onerous in territories that had been conquered in the eighteenth and nineteenth centuries and have not yet been fully assimilated, such as the Muslim South and the Lao Northeast.

Bangkok rules through a chain that leads through 71 provincial governments (changwats), 539 districts (amphoes), 5,089 subdistricts (tambons), and 45,610 villages (mubans). The top two levels are filled by permanent government officials, but the latter two are selected from the community at the designation of the officials, but with the acquiescence of the local peasants. The tambon supports a wat, the Buddhist temple-monastery-school-hospital-meeting place complex (or a mosque in the South).

The equilibrium-maintaining feature of peasant society is the tie to the land. Social status among the peasants in the muban derives from the amount of landownership. The bigger landowners among them are more likely to innovate in agriculture, make more trips to town, and send their sons to school longer. Their opinions dominate the village councils for the simple reason that they are also more likely to be influential in obtaining Bangkok's help in restoring or improving the vicinity. Peasants normally wait upon government action and are reluctant to help themselves.

Buddhist monks in Thailand are not politicized, as in Vietnam, but are becoming increasingly influential in secular matters in the countryside. The most respected of these are the "permanent monks" who have served for more than ten years in the predominant Mahanikai Order.

Teachers are influential for many of the same reasons, particularly if they live in the village and if they are headmasters. They validate a great deal of the technical knowledge that villagers would not be able to distinguish from braggadocio or rumor, and they help write official reports.

Traders who are not Chinese are now appearing in villages. They appear to have acquired capital by working on construction projects, or in cities, and combine this capital with their expanded experience and contacts. Thus many village-based middlemen with ties to regional centers and to Bangkok have been created since World War II. It would not be surprising to discover that experience with organization and equipment during military service was exceedingly important.

Many Bangkok-based "politicians" (a term which includes higher military officers) maintain contacts with client villages to which they have an obligation, usually through possession of family estates. They may find means for installing new services in their villages earlier than the others and therefore serve as "outside" entrepreneurs.

These combined forces create a very irregular pattern of change for the peasants. They also insure that the standard approaches to planning by government continue to be ineffective. An AID administrator, after many frustrations, came to the conclusion that the proper model for implementation should not be based upon communications in an hierarchical pyramid but upon a pancake, a shape which forces the funds and information to diffuse laterally away from the center, but hinders them from moving very far.

I have yet to see an adequate explanation for the way that Thailand outgrew its feudalism and transferred title of the land to the peasantry. At any rate, the laws were carefully constructed so as to maintain a peasant society at equilibrium with its resources, even in the face of three decades of unprecedented population growth. It is evident that the system was refurbished after World War II when the grain collection channels were taken from the black market operators and centralized by the government. The government was aided by the food shortage in rice-eating countries during the 1950s and 1960s, because the sales were made on a government-to-government basis. But now, due to the "miracle rice" that has come out of Rockefeller Institute research in the Philippines, almost all Asian nations are becoming self-sufficient. The price of rice has dropped spectacularly and is likely to be driven even lower, so that it will sell again at only a slight premium over wheat or maize when measured as food value. The Chinese will continue to import wheat and sell rice until that equilibrium point is reached. This price drop forces the Thailand grain collection organization to put up huge subsidies, which probably cannot be sustained for more than a year or two. Already it is said that two-thirds of the farmers are in debt, almost all at usurious interest rates (say 3 to 7 percent per month) so the pressure on the peasant population will be extraordinarily severe, especially on the farmers living at a considerable distance from Bangkok.

This means that Bangkok and the regional centers are likely to receive an increasing flow of people who cannot make ends meet when living on their own land. A son or daughter will be sent to the city to get a job. They will join kinfolk or fellow villagers squatting on governmental land and will search for work as servants or in construction. The government's control over Bangkok development is far too imperfect to stop them from staying, once they enter as visitors.

Building a New Bangkok

Tracts of middle-class housing and squatter settlements are scattered along each corridor, separated by distribution centers, factories, private schools, and military specialization centers. All of these are remarkably automobile oriented, as is the Don Muang Airport to the

North. Round estimates (1972) suggest that as many as 50,000 house-holds are living in the squatter settlements. The number may well be an underestimate because it appears that neither the policy of registration nor the census can be assured of getting within 20 percent of the real figure.

How can the Thai government promote housing and infrastructure that expands at least proportionately to population? It has had housing experience in the recent past at Ding Doeng with pukka apartments for the middle classes, but they cost about $4,000 per unit. With a rent of $10 per month such apartments require a considerable government subsidy, which it can afford less and less.

More promising by far is the "site and services" approach to housing, where the minimum requirements are made available through loans as needed and the householders produce their own housing. It appears that up to 75 percent can afford the rent levels implicit in the "site and services" schemes, allowing 10-20 percent of income to be applicable to shelter. The remainder may be able to achieve the minimum level after acquiring more experience and skill in the city or they may return defeated to the village, as many do, to be replaced by an even larger number of young and adventurous individuals.

One other feature inherent in such data is often ignored. Windfall sources of income, and ill-gotten gains of all sorts, are rarely reported to interviewers. The fact that quite sizable sums are obtained shows up in the number of television aerials and motor scooters, but more is undoubtedly hoarded and would be invested in property with a clear title, should it become available.

Assessments of the cost of the "site and services" approach to housing reveal that one-half to two-thirds must be allocated to land. The considerable development costs for filling and drainage are far overshadowed by the price of the raw land.

Land price changes are an important indicator of confidence in the future of a metropolis if a land market is allowed to exist. Land price has not always been significant in Thailand because land was once almost totally in the hands of the Thai aristocracy, or the peasant farmer who was prevented from freely transferring his land. The government was the most common land developer, but it sold off plots to the private sector (after World War II reconstruction) at the same time that a demand for standing houses began to appear due to a new and rapidly proliferating middle class.

Over the past five years important amounts of official credit have flowed into real estate loans. At least two-thirds of this lending is concentrated in the Bangkok region. The uncertain nature of the land market is fostered by murky titles — the recording office is at least three years behind, and many holdings already built upon are merely shares in a scheme which does not make specific assignments of plots. It is amazing how much concrete and steel has gone up on such a flimsy legal base.

Perhaps the most troubling indicator that is relevant to the im-mediate physical development of Bangkok is the rapidity of growth of the population of motor vehicles. Roads are now predominantly asphalted, even in the interior of the country, so that movement of people and produce has been vastly speeded up. The most recent data provided by the Ministry of National Development allow us to follow growth in the decade 1959-1968, which show that the number of motor vehicles has been expanding about 20 percent per year, with the countryside keeping up with the metropolis in the latter half of the decade. Compare this with Singapore, where growth was 3 to 7 percent per year and accompanied by strong complaints concerning congestion. Bangkok has reached a stage where there is one four-wheel vehicle for every 7 to 8 residents in the region while Singapore still has around one for each 10 to 11 persons. In Bangkok the congestion greatly reduces the quality of service provided by the buses, so that people will pay more and take the jitney-type baht-bus that can sometimes maneuver itself through the jams, or acquire a car themselves in the hope of beating the traffic tie-ups.

It has been obvious for some time that something has to be done about the population explosion in autos. More than three-quarters of the new models on the streets are of Japanese origin, so that vehicle manufacture control will have a selective impact. The idea of making automobile production a local industry has occurred to many; therefore first Ford and then General Motors were invited to look over the market. However, the proportion of components imported will remain high unless Thai consumers are willing to discipline themselves and accept an extremely standard vehicle, a situation no one expects at the moment. One must imagine some kind of political and administrative crisis in Bangkok before activities based on structures and land use, such as residence, retail sales, light manufacturing, and cinema attendance, and on networks, such as transport, water supply, electric power, and telephone, actually grind to a halt. The city can be directed to a path of steady development only with the aid of some new institutions that accumulate highly competent local talent and yet remain open to imported ideas that are carried into Bangkok from all parts of the world.

Cultural Values in the Modern Institutions

The new metropolitan institutions must be operated by middle-class Thai, products of the local educational system. They will be directed by Thai that have gone overseas – about 40 percent to the United States and almost an equal proportion to other English-speaking countries. The basic technology is transmitted either through the military, where the advisors are American, or through the multinational corporations where, out of 168 companies maintaining offices, 68 were from the United States, 21 from the United Kingdom, and two apiece from Australia and India. However, the 28 Japanese firms operate much more often in the English language than in Chinese. Thus the remarkable openness of the Thai society is seen as being open only to those who use

English; for the speakers of tongues other than Chinese it appears quite insulated. For the Chinese, if one gauges by the inscriptions on tombstones even in the villages peripheral to Bangkok where ancestor worship is still important, the absorption into Thai culture is largely completed, so the young people in particular think Thai, but learn English if they wish to rise in the world.

The Thai society is aware of the risks of alienation associated with the learning of English and therefore special care has been taken to counteract the evil to which the teenage youth are exposed. In Bangkok this is done by providing a "catechism" of Thai nationalism in the English language itself, so that fluency in English is reached by reviewing the dogma underlying one's own culture. This technique of teaching renders the subtle forms of English more understandable and therefore easier to learn. The textbook entitled 140 Essays and Letters for Advanced Students was found in a state publishing house display window; it had just such an approach. A highly condensed treatment of Thai values to be transmitted to incompletely socialized adolescents is thus made available to the outsider in his own language. Imagine the following principles, operating as part of the unspoken consensus in the modern sector of Thailand, much of it still in the early stages of institution building, and compare it with the sophistication in content of parallel materials in South Korea.

The first lesson asserts that Buddhism is the oldest of the great religions and based upon "Four Noble Truths" of "the Middle Way," one of which is the eightfold path. The message is laid out in 20 questions and answers with the following conclusion:

> Under its good influence the Thais have become a peace-loving nation, with unrivalled tolerance and hospitality to people of different races and creeds. It is not too much to say that, in the past, this admirable characteristic of our nation helped a great deal in preserving our national independence while the neighboring countries all around us were losing theirs.

The second lesson continues this theme by describing the operation of the wat, the Buddhist monastery-school-temple establishment. It commits the citizen to assist the priests in obtaining food, clothes, medicine, and shelter so as to perpetuate Buddhism "in our beloved country." The third exhorts them to "Uphold the moral standard in this corrupted world" by observing the days of the waxing and waning of the moon called Wan Pra. The fourth takes up the ordination ritual for young men at age 21 where they learn "how to curb their passions at an age when passions are strongest." The fifth discusses a new holiday declared especially for the onset of the twenty-sixth century of Buddhism. Asalaha Day commemorates the beginning of Buddha's teaching of the ascetics who became his disciples, a reminder of the "Triple Gems" principles.

Thereafter, the essays become more secular in character but no less serious. Essays cover nutrition, followed by traditional games, kite flying, and <u>takraw</u> – which uses a wicker ball. Then the famous Thai dramas, replete with dancing, are explained so that the popular version can be distinguished from the classical. The ritual of greeting, the <u>wai</u>, is justified on the basis that "it makes the Thai people look quite lovely and amiable. . . ." There is a great deal of attention paid throughout the text to the image the Thai national presents to the outsider.

Once the truly important lessons have been learned, the professor can relax somewhat and translate familiar aspects of life-style into English: transport means, modes of communication, influences of weather, and recreational opportunities which draw upon the 4-H principles so familiar to American farm youth. Then the role of education (which "makes a full man") and its two streams, intellectual and manual, is elaborated according to structure and function characteristics. This sets the stage for a discussion of the progress of science, which glorifies technological developments from James Watt's steam engine to the communication between earth satellites. A hope is expressed that science will be used for the welfare of the people, and it leads to a special essay that attempts to define the welfare of the people. The latter is particularly important because the extent to which a state provides for human welfare is seen as an index "of the efficiency and stability of the government." One sees in the argument a genuine recognition that the future elite can be secure only if it is based within an environment that it is able to improve through the use of modern technology.

In such a manner are the proprieties of participation in urban and social affairs laid down. As yet there seems to be very little disenchantment with education in Bangkok, so the text would not normally be labeled as "preachy" or hypocritical by the students, but merely of use for conforming to modern ways of life in official circles, just as English is of use.

Building Ultramodern Organizations

Students steeped in these Thai traditions must become participants in the most modern institutions with the strongest technologies. When the Koreans faced the same problems they stressed the traditions and popular culture of the English-speaking peoples, and thus prepared their overseas students much better for the shock of cosmopolitan living in the West. Thus, the Koreans found it quite possible to adapt and transfer loyalties to the host country, so the nation suffered a considerable brain drain, while the Thai got homesick and accepted even the unrewarding posts back in Bangkok. Nevertheless, the social and economic development of Seoul is far more rapid than that of Singapore, and even further ahead of Bangkok, in large part because Koreans have learned to take advantage of opportunities in new technology and marketing that originate overseas.

An example of the means by which modern institutions are built in Bangkok is provided by the Telecommunications Training Center and its spin-off, the Test and Development Center, at Nonthaburi and Pathon Thani on the Chao Phraya River a few miles north of the city. It was founded upon a general recognition among the overseas-trained members of the elite that telephones were an essential feature of the kind of modernization they thought appropriate for Thailand.   Telecommunications increase the capacity to govern because they speed up the response of government to local emergencies and they permit a much higher degree of coordination between departments, agencies, offices, and enterprises in both government and the private sector. The government could no longer depend upon foreign concessionaires to develop such an essential utility once Thai engineers and technicians were available. The program was expedited by the International Telecommunications Union (ITU) and the United Nations Development Program (UNDP).

The Training Centre had to start from the very beginning with translation of the training manuals used elsewhere in the world, establishment of dormitories, the acquisition of equipment, and formulation of a recruiting program for the various levels of trainees. Nevertheless, it now has 1,200 trainees per year, almost double the planned rate. The Test and Development Center provides a place for checking out new and existing telecommunications equipment, and a base from which improved operating procedures can be worked out as well as the plans for developing a system that fits the country's needs for communication. The extra push that was needed to overcome obstacles very often came from the armed forces of Thailand, but the military influence within the institution is difficult to isolate. The most effective technical assistance thus far has come from India, after a somewhat shaky beginning when the source of help originated in Australia.

From this base Bangkok is expected to link up the countries of Southeast Asia – Laos, Cambodia, Malaysia, Burma – tying them to the communications satellite already over the Indian Ocean. At present there is an impasse between the Telephone Organization of Thailand, which handles domestic telephones and the links across the boundaries, and the older Post and Telegraph Department which has the microwave relays transmitting television from Bangkok to the lesser cities of Thailand. Once the two systems are married to each other, the channels for modernization will be vastly amplified.

Ultramodern technology seems to be introduced into these societies much more rapidly and smoothly now than in the earlier era based upon the diesel engine, electric generator, and the printing press. The latter are now dependable, almost invisible mainstays in these metropolitan communities with mature, self-sustaining institutions to back them up.

The new contraceptives provide an opportunity for creating ultramodern organization aimed at achieving a greatly needed social adaption. The rate of population growth in Thailand is now estimated at 3.3 percent per year, which is among the highest in the world. Thai women average about 6.5 births over the reproductive period of life. All the concomitants of such growth are everywhere evident – a very youthful society, a housing shortage, schools that bring the population up to literacy but can take only about 2.5 percent of the age class to higher levels, and an expressed desire on the part of women for smaller families. In 1968 surveys showed that suburban women, who comprise a relatively educated population, were succeeding in reducing births by 15 percent over those in a rural district used as a control. Among the contraceptors, Thai women are distinctly underrepresented, while Chinese most frequently use the available services. In government, recognition at the policy level has been given to the forthcoming population crisis, but it has yet to be followed through with the provision of adequate funds. A family health project began in 1968 and became official in 1970; about 5,000 workers have been trained and 3,500 clinics organized. About 5 percent of the population in need is presently served.

The number of acceptors has roughly doubled each year, reaching 225,000 in 1970. The method of contraception now favored by more than half of the early adopters is the use of pills, while female sterilization is preferred by about a fifth. Now a five-year plan has been formulated with the aim of doubling the number of acceptors within that period and establishing an integrated family planning program capable of much more comprehensive services in the decades to come. The aims are still modest, particularly those for reaching 7.5 percent of the target population by 1976. The project received only $500,000 from the Thai government for 1972, a bit over a third of what was requested. However, four times that amount is expected from overseas sources, most of it in the form of pills and instruments with the major share of the aid coming from Germany.(24)

Thus family planning is at an earlier stage of institution building than telecommunications. The prospects of effecting a rapid demographic transition, the kind that has dramatically accelerated in South Korea and has gained great momentum in Taiwan, Hong Kong, and Singapore, does not seem likely in the Thai culture, even for Bangkok. The prospects are for the overall population to double in size over the next 20 to 25 years, and for Bangkok and environs to quadruple. This population pressure will spin off new urban settlements into the adjoining countryside at an increasing rate.

Potentials for the Future

There seems to be no barrier in sight that would prevent a continuation of the pacemaking function by both Singapore and Bangkok. Indeed, the overview of specific constraints experienced in these metropolises suggests that the pace may very well be stepped up over the next several years. Singapore in particular appears to be in a position to profit from the shifts in the world politicoeconomic system.

Many of the institutions that Bangkok needs have already evolved in Singapore and elsewhere. Thus the management techniques for the refining and petrochemicals complex, the telecommunications establishment, public housing management, family planning organization, and dozens of others can be learned and borrowed from Singapore, the next stages in transport organization can be adapted from Hong Kong, and industrial organization in export garments, appliances, and electronics from Taipei, Kaohsiung, and Seoul.

Interesting for the sociocultural analyst is the observation that each of the transfers of a technology, mode of management, institutional structure, or legal instrument needed for installing a given institution seems to require translation into the English language from the Japanese, Chinese, or Korean version and the Thai before decisions can be made or action taken. Therefore the review of the policy for English-language instruction provided earlier becomes exceedingly significant; the institutions for extending the standard training in reading and speaking, and the comprehensiveness of the English language periodicals, become important for future development involving regional inter-society transfer.

The institutional solutions that Singapore needs are most likely to be found in Tokyo or the United States. Due to Singapore's former colonial status the teaching of English has made much more progress there, and no longer represents the eye of the needle through which modernization must pass. The university, for example, must now set itself standards equivalent to those of the leaders, rather than developing country type compromises, for research as well as teaching.

Exchange of these complex organizational concepts for both these cities is increasingly expedited by the regional offices of the United Nations agencies clustered around the Economic Commission for Asia and the Far East (ECAFE) headquarters in Bangkok renamed later the Economic and Social Commission for Asia and the Pacific or ESCAP. A number of special projects have begun to spill over into the nearby hotels in their search for office space. The ECAFE-related activities needing economic research are assembling on or near the campus of Singapore University. Another kind of international institution, the Asian Institute of Technology in Bangkok, is a graduate school drawing students from all of the Far East as a substitute for training in Western countries, but because textbooks and source materials are predominantly in English the language of instruction must also be English. The problems under investigation, however, are either contributions to theory or relevant to Asian development. The growth in these coordinating, promoting, and educating activities is far more rapid than the rates of economic growth experienced in these countries, but progress still seems to be proceeding at a snail's pace as compared to the modernization gap that becomes increasingly visible to the participants in the process. They are discouraged much of the time, and feel reinforced only occasionally. Yet any objective measurement of achievement seems certain to reveal that the groups with a modern outlook indirectly affected by the coordinative work of the official and unofficial international institutions are rapidly expanding their influence. Moreover, careful questioning of some of the principals associated with a success reveals repeatedly a step or a stage in the ticklish process of promotion and reduction to practice that depended in a crucial manner upon the output of one of these international agencies or institutes. That kind of stimulus to development may be expected to increase as the colonial era recedes into history and more representative organizations struggle to be born.

KHON KAEN – URBAN CENTER FOR NORTHEAST THAILAND

August 1974

Sometimes the economic base for a metropolis lies outside its computer range. There will be more of these kinds of cities as modern refinements are introduced into agriculture.

Only five days were scheduled for this appraisal of a vigorous urban center in the Mekong Basin. The principal contact was through the university, which was closed. Therefore, this analysis had to depend a great deal upon visual cues.

This is the regional city for the frontier province of Thailand. The nearest parallel in America is the part of Texas that lies between "deep in the heart of" and the Rio Grande, east of the Pecos and more than a hundred miles from salt water. This part of Thailand is being settled the Asian way, with the surplus population going out to carve a farm for itself in the easily worked soil that collects runoff, producing one good crop a season with rain and enough water collected to outlast the drought. Like Texas, this soil either washes out in flood or blows away in drought. In only two or three years in ten are growing conditions reasonably good.

The Mekong River has cut its channel about a hundred miles to the east of Khon Kaen. It flows through this territory the way the Colorado cuts through the West, enriching very few until it reaches its delta, where the population is too numerous for many to get rich. It is a bigger river than either the Colorado or the Rio Grande and drops from China and upper Burma, where the mountains rise much higher than the Rockies. So the Mekong has potential energy that could enrich this part of Thailand and neighboring Laos. The principal difficulty is that the projects must be bigger than those that have been installed in Texas, bigger even than Hoover Dam and the tributary dams on the Colorado. The United Nations has become involved, due perhaps more to the vision and efforts of Gilbert White (now at the University of Colorado) than anyone else at the beginning stages. Thailand has to work its way up to this scale of operations, and it has designated Khon Kaen to be the administrative and development center for projects in the Northeast Region. Altogether four million people depend upon the city's services.

The American West was always urban in emphasis after 1865. Almost half the people lived in cities. Boomtowns were a fundamental feature of frontier life. The reasons were mining and railroads. The Thai settlement pattern is just the opposite. There are no large cities. This regional capital has less than 80,000 residents, and they are distributed very thinly. The roads are more important than railroads.

Though the signs are in an unreadable script, walking around Khon Kaen can be shocking to an American. Nowhere else in Asia do the urban patterns so much resemble those at home. The things that are important — hotels, motels, movie houses, bus stations, the string development along the highways — repair, filling stations, retail auto sales, missionary churches — are also here, but without extensive neon signs (they were nipped in the bud by the energy crisis). The wholesalers operate in force.

The prevailing building style next to the main streets is a stucco or concrete house over a ground-floor shop, almost all new, clean, and modern looking. The exceptions are from a bygone era — unpainted wood frame buildings adjacent to unpaved stretches of red soil, merchants' houses of wood perched on posts about head high, so that the vehicles and the kind of debris that normally collect in garages may be stored underneath. Inside the large blocks are more open houses of more ordinary people, smaller, unpainted, closer to the ground, with rusting corrugated iron roofs, and clean-swept sandy clay ground cover. The sidewalks themselves are generally protected from sun and rain by overhanging panels. Squatters' shacks are on the "other" side of the railroad tracks, but only a few hundred of them are to be found. The highest constructed elevations are the radio (microwave relay) and television towers, but several water towers follow after, and two factory chimneys for rice milling plants rise almost as high.

Roads enter the city from the four corners of the compass. The north road leads from a dam and reservoir (a German project, rejected by American AID because of the low cost-benefit ratio), passing the university and agriculture experiment station, and is then joined by the railroad line, which it parallels at a distance of one to two blocks all the way through and far beyond the city to the south. The airport road feeds into the fast highway passing several Buddhist monasteries — there are twenty-five of these wats in the vicinity — and a radio station before it enters the sparsely settled periphery, crossing the other highway and the railroad, then passing several missionary establishments and secondary schools before proceeding out to more country still green from the rains.

The hollows in the land are planted in rice, white plots of kenaf (a jute-like plant that will stand up well against moderate drought), manioc, and maize can be found among the stumps and crippled trees.

The town site itself is in the northwest sector of the crossing of the highways. It contains a remarkable number of cars — Toyotas, Fords, Isuzu pickup trucks, the baby Datsun, Volkswagens, Toyota Hiace minibuses, Hino light trucks, an occasional Lancia and Mercedes. A reasonable guess is that there must be upwards of 5,000 four-wheel automotive vehicles, almost all of them of very recent vintage. The regional bus station will park 100 buses and can launch 30 at a time. There are no stoplights as yet, but a dozen intersections have rails that keep pedestrians and dogs from wandering into them. There are perhaps 300 Lambretta three-wheel scooter-cabs operating as taxis and jitneys, and about the same number of samlor pedicabs. There are also 5,000 motorcycles, scooters and mopeds. Thus motoring has become, in the past few years, a way of life in Khon Kaen. The recent 60 to 70 percent rise in gasoline prices did not seem to inhibit the flow of traffic. About one out of five of the shops in town is involved in the sale of vehicles, their repair, or in the spare parts distribution business, indicating that the fraction of cash income in and around the regional city spent on automotives is very close to that of the Texas parallel before World War II.

The public buildings, whether offices or homes of officials, all show the hand of an architect who knows how to work within a tradition. The Chinese shops are simple, clean, orderly, and well lit. There is no junk lying around the countryside, nor any dilapidated houses, though some are reported to exist. The sides of the highways are not littered with bottles, cans, plastic, or paper. The Pepsi, Coca Cola, and Esso signs are limited to establishments selling the commodities themselves. Even the simple structures put up by barely literate house builders, or the owner himself with the help of neighbors, almost always retain their proportions – beams do not sag and the rotting timbers and boards are replaced before they become ugly. To find such a city in the back country of a Southeast Asian country is quite surprising. Many Americans would be glad to settle down here, and of course many Chinese, some Sikhs, and quite a few Lao have already decided to do so. All of the shop houses seem to be snapped up as soon as they are constructed.

Economic and Social Assessments

The economy that supports Khon Kaen is one that is moving away from subsistence into a middleman-sponsored cash market. Rice is the staple; it produces $15 per acre net in the hollows at ordinary prices but all crops are now two to three times higher. The middleman brings in a truckload of rice and stakes a farmer to a year of food for his family if he will raise corn or cotton. The Japanese have bid up the price of corn in this part of the world (it is higher than in the Midwest by 10 to 20 percent), and cotton is also selling at a premium. The gamble is to outwit the boll weevil. A corn crop is worth two to three times more than rice, and cotton five times (if there is a crop at all), so the returns are highly visible to the younger farmers willing to gamble. The drought is risky for the middleman also. Last year a number of them (called crop buyers) borrowed money from big-time operators to lend to the farmers they worked with, providing advice along with the rice and the insecticide. Their equity was wiped out when the farmers' crops failed and they could not repay. (As in American history, many farmers just picked up and moved on, leaving no trace. The middleman dropped back down to agent or salesman.)

The mobility of the Thai present is illustrated by the resettlement process. Whenever a dam is built, a fair amount of bottom land is flooded and people cultivating it are evicted. Some people are also scratching a living from the sloping hillside that gets covered. About 70 to 80 percent of the families take their compensation money (they now receive it almost on time rather than several years late or never) and resettle themselves. The remainder take up their home acre and five-acre allotment of cropland in a resettlement estate where they build houses for themselves and their families in the cutover forest; these families then go out in search of day labor (at 80 cents per day for men, less for women), farm a few patches of land (if it rains), or go over to the reservoir to fish, hoping to get enough to sell to the fish collector. Women set up crude looms to handicraft Thai cotton or silk patterns. Road maintenance once required a lot of human labor to keep in decent shape; unfortunately for this underclass, the Americans introduced big road-making machinery so that the present outlay is about 70 percent for machines, fuel, and parts, and 20 percent for supervision, with only 10 percent for labor.

One income alternative is to join the outlaws. This is not so much for family men as for the displaced sons who would risk anything to get a motorcycle of their own. Cattle rustling is a big-time business. Squatters run 5 to 20 head in the grassy patches of the forest tended by children and women; irrigated areas support cattle in the off season. Some bigger operators go semicommercial with 50 to 100 head and Santa Gertrudis or American Brahmin breeding bulls. Full-scale ranches, like those in Texas, have been shown by extension type studies not to pay in this environment. (If it was at all hopeful, generals would have settled down on retirement to be big ranchers.)

Another kind of outlaw is political. This is often the university student who begins to compare the differences in justice as meted out by the government. Such students may drop out and join a Communist party cell. The best of them are sent to training centers in Laos (the local dialect is closer to Laotian than Thai, although the language of education is Bangkok Thai); afterwards they work on the fringe of legitimate society until mobilized or else join a group that lives by plunder, protection rackets, and communal organization of production. The potential leaders are sent to Peking to become hard-core organizers.

A few months ago a whole train was held up and all the cash and valuables of the passengers taken by a gang recognized as non-ideological desperados. Even more recently an air-conditioned coach was hijacked, taken into the forest, the passengers cleaned out, and the coach burned. The rumor in that instance was that it was encouraged by the competing bus firms who apparently were paying the communists for protection.

As a result of the outlawry the authorities have marked off "secure areas" around major towns and close to all-weather roads. Much of the forest and the isolated valleys are considered insecure, particularly after dark. That is one of the reasons for putting so much effort into road building – it expands the area that can be covered by the big police stationwagons with blue overhead lights and the Land Rover troop carriers. It even provides a rationale for using the capital-intensive approach to road building; the machines cannot be subverted or threatened, so the job gets done.

On the whole northeast Thailand is probably safer than Texas. We saw only one man carrying a gun – a hunter with a night light. (The hunter moves his beam around the forest until he finds a pair of eyes, blinds the animal with the beam, then he shoots between them.) The most dangerous areas are those where the squatters are opening up new land to hoe culture. This is illegal but winked at once the clearing has been done. Accidents are more common than violence, and automotive accidents increasingly predominant. Crimes of passion are the most typical forms of violence, so one should fear friends more than strangers.

The future of this territory lies first in water, then in agricultural differentiation. For example, the only tree crop in the region is mango, but coffee, oil palm, avocados, nuts, and many others are suitable, not to mention pine. Along with the differentiation comes agro-industry – paper from kenaf, tapioca starch from manioc, chickens from the maize and rice bran, and canning factories for fruit preserves. That is where the development will occur when water is assured. Then the population will become more dense, the output bulkier, the trucks larger, and the roads wider. Cheaper power than diesel fuel should cause the railroad to electrify and specialize in moving containers to the big metropolises and the container ports. Khon Kaen would then attain a population of over one million, and be as complex as San Antonio, although it would retain its position as a regional city.

THE ENVIRONMENT COMES TO PENANG

April 1974

Historically Penang (George Town) has matured in the shadows of Singapore and Bangkok; now it is anticipating another kind of future. The local image of its destiny is undergoing rapid change. However, a well-informed outsider alert to the external forces converging upon this small metropolis is likely to see directions and outcomes not yet apparent to the island itself.

What follows is the product of a full application of the technique of observation for a single visit. When the conclusions hedge, reaching no clear-cut forecast, they indicate the degree of uncertainty felt by my sources of information. (As it happened, most of the major proposals for change described in this report were deferred for various reasons, mainly political.)

Only four years after Earth Day was launched in Ann Arbor, Michigan, ecological ideas, concepts and enthusiasms have penetrated the newly modernizing areas of the world. Here in Penang a similar assemblage of speakers has been assembled to discuss environmental issues.

Labeled "A Seminar on Modernization and the Environment," the conference was carefully staged to end with a declaration of policy regarding nature conservancy that would apply to the nation as a whole. Therefore, all the proprieties needed to be observed. In Malaysia an important meeting is held in the big community hall, and all salutations and introductions are in the official Malay language. But environmental issues cannot yet be expressed in Malay so each major speaker, including the authentic Malay at the head table, quickly regressed to English.

The opening speech was by the highest-status Malay, and it introduced some unexpected associations. Unconventional tourists were labeled "hippie pollution." The government had finally acted to clean up the situation by the enforced expulsion of 95 Australian, American, European and other ragtag types squatting on the beach. He was explaining the somewhat garbled news we had read in the morning newspapers.

Significantly, pollution remains an English rather than an Asian concept. The exhibits by high school students were in English although Malay is the medium of instruction. Their poster art attempted in an amateurish way to overstate in the manner of American cartoonists. Photographs showed some garbage dumped along creek banks, litter-strewn tidewater, and smelly drainage ditches. A senior investigator captured sights of some hillside erosion and misplaced "telephone booths," a local euphemism for privies, with his slides. The severe problems encountered elsewhere in Southeast Asia — stinking fish, dead jungle, sheet erosion that produces patches of desert — were not presented. Apparently, it is not to be found in this vicinity.

What are the felt threats? Asians take up subjects in order of priority for attention. The next speech listed industrialization, urbanization, alienation, population growth, pesticides, and ecosystem disequilibrium. When pressed, however, the speaker acknowledged present acceptance of all of these, because the alternative would mean a halt to the nationally accepted program of modernization. The political perspective was followed by the views of the professionals.

A Greek Turk, with a chair in a German university, illustrated hillside gardening with added proposals for improved terraces and reclamation of the spoil from tin mining. A Malay forestry department head clearly assigned national priorities — mining over agriculture, and food production over trees. So the wooded areas in the outer islands of Malaysia are being converted to commercial crops, especially palm oil, altogether a timely transformation. Replanting must be enforced in order to prevent massive erosion.

The best politician on the platform by far was an architect, the chief planner of urban redevelopment. San Francisco-style redevelopment and renewal is due to be introduced to George Town, the chief urban center (population 350,000). Lim Ching Keat is a leader of Architects Team 3, which is now possibly the largest firm of designers operating in Singapore, Kuala Lumpur, Penang, and hereabouts. He was vulnerable to public questioning because he was the youngest brother of the chief minister and his mother (according to an out-of-town graduate student in urban studies with ambitions of going to Berkeley) is the biggest speculator in suburban land. Lim revealed the process of identifying what needs to be preserved in George Town (38 churches and temples, and 10 open spaces) and noted that conservation of the avenues, traditional residential areas, and structures remains under discussion. Presumably the remainder would not be defended against demolition. To me this method seemed to overlook quite a potential that exists in Penang, because here one sees, in a tropical green setting, the richest aggregation of urban images in Asia. Perhaps what is essential and unique to this cityscape should be reported before it disappears.

The Penang We See and Feel

Pulau, Penang, was settled in 1786 by the East India Company. One of their freebooting captains had found a way of saving some petty sultanates from Thai invaders to the north and marauding Malays from the south. He took his reward in the form of an uninhabited jungle-covered island a couple of miles off the west coast of the Malay peninsula, with excellent anchorage in the straits. The town was named for George III, and General Cornwallis (once beleaguered at Yorktown) came in from India to supervise the construction of fortifications. Its control of the Malacca Straits quickly raised Penang to equal status in the Empire with Calcutta and Rangoon.

Having been a free port throughout its history, Penang collected the rootless people of the Orient, as indicated in the English cemetery that contains the remains of the founding father, Francis Light, and many successors. Gravestone inscriptions indicate that life was short and lusty in the old days. The Indians arrived as servants, and graduated to become the petty merchants; some hit a jackpot and postgraduated into big-time operators. The Chinese began to move here at the same time they shipped to California and Australia; in the Straits Settlements some made fortunes out of tin mining. Their family homes were in villages behind Amoy, Swatow, and Canton, with a contingent of Hainanese ship's cooks also staying. The Burmese came in as rice traders, the Tamils, many refugees from Ceylon, as lowly rubber tappers, but moved to town. There are little pockets of other types as well, such as Thai speakers (mostly Chinese), and a community of Christian missionaries spreading different interpretations of the Gospel but cooperating in the education of the children. Attempts are being made to preserve the best examples of the remaining dwellings.

Hindus bought education for their children with their savings, so the merchants' sons left business to become doctors, lawyers, and administrators. Chinese moved in behind them to take over at least 95 percent of the commercial sector. The Malay, vastly outmatched and, in this state, outnumbered, are found either near the top – in government and the military – or in their original kampungs.

Today there are close to a half million people on the island, all but a thousand or so on the flat land below the green hills that peak at about 2,600 feet. Pestilence is under control, the water is as trustworthy as any in Southeast Asia, and mosquitoes and flies have almost disappeared. The climate is equable, 76-87°F, though humid, and the beaches are comparatively clean. The level of living is high for Asia, far more pleasant than Hong Kong or Singapore, but incomes are not as high.

George Town is small enough to be seen on foot, but the trishaw with carriage-like appurtenances and a pedal man behind under a resplendent ribbed parasol is less exhausting. What strikes the newcomer is an incredible variety of institutional buildings – temples, mosques, churches, schools, family name associations, trade associations, public markets, hotels, cinemas, banks, burial grounds, godowns – each one unique. The street vendors are almost all on wheels, clean, and carry a good stock of what they sell. The Chinese shop houses are mostly in good repair despite their age. Most important, these are not preserved images, restored and dedicated to posterity, but vibrantly living traditions. People use these buildings and sites daily for their intended purposes. It is true that quite a few of the old mansions have been refitted into private schools, nursing homes, "moral uplift" societies, and clubs, but somehow these also fit the spacious plots under tall, hundred-year-old trees that skirt the avenues. The Malay kampungs – with their wood frame houses on posts, thatched roofs, shade trees, flowering shrubs – disdain all the kinds of communal order with which we are familiar. Their feel for the site and the development of these feelings with many modest touches imposed upon the structure and around the yard, cause the roving eye to stop for a minute. They are natural and forthright.

All of these sights tease the man with a camera – certainly it should be possible to capture these qualities – but failure is almost total. So much of what one perceives in Penang is a contrast with what one sees to the right, left, above and behind. The camera eye cannot transmit the context. So the great photographers on the island concentrate upon character portraits – old folks, children, social roles, exquisite flowers, the shape of a headland, old mansions, mosques, or the favorite flamboyan trees.

It is everywhere evident in Penang that many good men and women have devoted a significant share of their lives to creating communities. In doing so they have taken much of the turbulence out of urban life. One sees this in the way people board the bus, compete for the attention of a potential customer or drive their cars through cluttered roads – little things that show deference to the rights of others as an ingrained habit acquired from many early lessons. If one were to try to measure this quality, he would be forced to count the frequency of unspoken, almost intuitive, micro-accommodations occurring in public behavior.

In George Town, I could find perhaps three to five hundred sites so important to this sense of community that they would stand in the way of a land clearance approach to urban redevelopment. Each of them would have a constituency strongly concerned about displacement, and a true sense of loss should it occur, because the facility is part of their identity. Perhaps one example will suffice: in the course of rehousing people in a slab-type Singapore-style experiment, it was recognized that problems would occur which could only be settled through concurrence of neighbors. Two were serious: bicycle security, since they could not be kept in apartments given the elevator size and service, and funerals during which the head of the corpse should not be pointed toward living persons, or toward the door, an impossibility in many flats. The collective decision was to allocate part of the open space to a facility which protects parked bicycles from tropical rains and which serves as a communal funeral parlor. Customs prevent the choice of most of the available space, so again a unique facility with unexpected neighbors results from the living tradition.

Muslims have a problem with the centerpiece for the city. The Esplanade is an open space next to public buildings, part of the British tradition in harbor design and park development. The central mosque next to it is a dumpy, unprepossessing building, adequate for the few Moslems in the harbor area. However, now the cruise ships taking pilgrims to Mecca tie up at the quay. This is a gala occasion. George Town compares badly with all other harbors that are way stations on the pilgrimage. A committee of citizens, mostly Chinese Taoists and Buddhists, recommended that this prized open space should be given over to a grand, modern mosque in keeping with the image of a city in a nation where the official religion is Islam. People educated in Europe or America — especially those with design training — object to the loss of open space. Yet if Penang is to be an effective community there should be such a mosque, and no other site will do. Perhaps its designer may be able to resolve the conflicting interests in the site by creating a great mosque that keeps the grass and preserves the line of the sight to the further shore at Butterworth. (I suppose I would start with the idea of a crystal masjid, a gem by night and day, surrounded by a feathery wire work that, like a Steinberg pen, outlines in heroic proportions the visual elements of a mosque, but lets through more than 90 percent of the sun, the sea breeze, and the view of the far shore.)

The Future Centerpiece

Emblazoned in fresh red on a wooden fence along Penang Road in central George Town are the words: SITE OF THE URBAN CENTRE. This is the first large-scale urban redevelopment in the central area. It burst upon the public without warning on the first day of spring, 1974. Slick brochures were ready, and retouched bird's-eye-view photos with the development superimposed were distributed at the press conference. In the project two 18-story residential slabs are set down next to a 40-story cylindrical tower on a much larger 4-story podium that 1) houses the displaced urban settlers, 2) rationalizes the bus terminals, 3) provides parking downtown, 4) introduces roof-top open space for the public, and 5) provides a concourse for public gatherings with many convenient vendor stalls. The prime office space in the city will be in the tower. The design was finished, the developers had been chosen, and the pile drivers were moving in to prepare the foundations at the time of the announcement. About 80 percent of the land had been cleared and lay derelict behind crumbling plastered brick walls and all of the first phase was in city ownership. This fait accompli had been carried out in such great secrecy that it had not been preceded by the usual barrage of rumors. The reason, of course, was to prevent nearby speculative developers from projecting schemes which reduced the payout of the Urban Centre.

These were metropolitan tactics in a small-city environment. The reactions were foreseeable — within two weeks there was a call for an official commission of enquiry. This is one of the principal devices for delay in a society that operates under rules set up originally by the British. The syndicate of politicians, planners, and developers were obviously prepared for this ploy, but they have yet to reveal their countering tactic.

A walk around the site indicates that the preparations have been exceedingly thorough. All the area within two hundred yards was zoned for moderate density — no more than two floors on the average — to prevent congestion. Only one site is nonconforming — a major hotel owned by a leading group of property holders. The tail end of the strip of dry goods merchants on Penang Road will have to move, so the rest of the row must offer bargains competitive with the sellout prices that this handful is advertising. The others to be displaced are marginal — driving schools, parts salvage, old books, cheap coffee houses, etc. Most of them will probably not take up their options in the residential slab, but seek shop houses elsewhere in unpretentious neighborhoods. There are three cinemas, which should certainly refurbish and then prosper from the centralization of passenger traffic. The classic Chinese temple across the way, perfect in every detail, and glistening in red, gold, and green, will gain greater prominence. Only a few will be hurt directly, and they have little clout in public affairs. (Nevertheless, the bargaining power of the little men may be much greater than anticipated. I transmitted to Anwar Faizal, then director of investment and promotion for the Penang Development Corporation, a reference to the newest issue of Land Economics, which had just arrived on the island, where Hartman and Kessler summarize some analyses of the distribution of benefits from the Yerba Buena Project, a similar but larger proposal for San Francisco, and warned him that the legal briefs which virtually destroyed that project had recently been transmitted to bright young advocates in Southeast Asia.)

The real danger to the project lies in the property syndicates that are used to operating under cover. They may gang up on the Lim family, which runs perhaps the biggest syndicate in its own right, but cannot control the total situation. If this were a feud in the old Penang style, there would be stabbings and assassinations, even pitched battles in the streets, similar to 1867, by which grudges would get settled between the secret societies. However, as in Hong Kong, the secret societies were infiltrated by British intelligence operatives, and almost totally destroyed before Merdeka (Independence). This bare-knuckle competition would be parochial, an insular struggle under wraps, were it not for the discovery by world-scale operators that Penang is headed for the big time. Hot money has been funneled into the syndicates through Hong Kong and Singapore, because the action will be here as much as anywhere in Asia. In its own way Tokyo is also involved, as are Eurodollar commitments from London and Zurich. One clear indicator has been the fact that certain patches of real estate have doubled and trebled in value over the past couple of years (although land is still cheap as compared to competing Asian centers) so that all precedents for deciding a fair price are now obsolete, with no clear alternative at hand. A tightening of credit could postpone redevelopment.

The Urban Centre captures for itself the air rights at the future city center, stealing much of its eminence from several existing hubs. It constitutes a revolution in status within the propertied classes that use the planning law to protect themselves from competition. Chinese business groups are very jealous about status as indicated by physical symbols, so they seem likely to ally themselves with outsiders so as to control further development of Penang. They may also leave the battlefield to the Lims after a few skirmishes and concentrate their forces elsewhere. A struggle between adversaries who are not beneath a bit of gouging and other foul play is dramatic and persuasive but it too represents only one level of understanding. The actions of these coalitions represent the placing of only a few small moves in the vast game that is now being played in Asia by world forces. Penang over the past two years is a stage that is being set for a scene in a historic transformation of Asian peoples.

A Whole World Converges on Penang

Penang has always had to be sharp in the ways of the world. When London was the center of the Empire, Penang was a focus for free trade, continually responsive to supply and demand in commodities of interest to both the West and the Orient. It became a center for transshipment, a regional market for distinctive purchases and a reknowned receiver of smuggled goods. It provided places for entertainment and schooling, piety and personal security. Holidaying in Penang evolved into a tourism industry.

The principal change really came with the upgrading of the airport. Presumably it was intended to support the tourism industry, but the air freight component has turned out to have the most ramifications. The containers from the harbor are combined with regular shipments by air for the newly established factories along the south coast. The garments, microcircuits, and servomechanisms are shipped out mostly by air. For this reason the modern new factories are clustered around the road connecting the city with the airport.

Penang exports the products of its labor to the world by means of a system managed by multinational corporations. Malaysia had carefully structured its laws so as to encourage investment in manufacturing that would balance its heavy commitment to primary products. This policy began to work when full employment hit Singapore and Hong Kong, and wages in these places began to rise as rapidly as productivity. All the major Malaysian cities, and some towns as well, benefited from that squeeze, but Penang with its predominantly Chinese population and high level of services most resembled those other metropolises and has tended to get a high-quality assortment of factories. With them have come small to medium-sized tracts of modern middle-class housing, more automobiles and trucks, and an enlargement of the luxury services, such as private schools. The ferry to the mainland has become overloaded, and citizens fume as full buses refuse to stop and pick them up after they have stood at the roadside for a half hour. Hundreds of bicycles rush out of the factory gates to merge with the afternoon traffic. Interestingly, they are almost all women – young, earnest, and of all races and are the labor force in greatest demand.

Malaysia is beginning to discover that "modernization," that magic word that summed up their national ambitions, means jobs for women. Men are not wanted, except for casual labor in construction, while a few bright boys are invited to serve as operating engineers. Fortunately, the government can afford to hire many more of both sexes, and the extra paychecks mean that there are more niches for the self-employed. A larger fraction of the males are encouraged to continue at school.

Government must continue to extend the infrastructure. Thus a tall suspension bridge is scheduled to displace the ferry, although some desperate measures may be necessary before it is ready. The road to the airport will be made four, later perhaps six, lanes and the bridges widened to accommodate bicycle traffic alongside. The airport will be expanded, and later very likely abandoned in favor of a larger site on the mainland. A new town will grow up on its acreage that should quickly expand to the dimensions of George Town itself, particularly when the new airport site is fully developed.

The Science University of Malaysia (Universiti Sains Malaysia), lying between the old city and the prospective new town, will have to multiply its enrollment many times. The government is trying to reach the rest of the world, breaking out of the British mold set in the older University of Malaya. The new institution draws heavily upon Americans, Canadians, Australians, and Western Europeans. Its schools and teaching programs are heavily interdisciplinary. The library has been endowed by the World Bank, the Marine Institute by UNESCO, and it is hoped that some of the laboratories will be fitted out by the rubber producers and tin mining syndicates. In its university development Penang seems to be following about 15 years behind Hong Kong and Singapore, but is avoiding some of their mistakes.

For example, the Science University of Malaysia decided to create programs in urban studies and race relations, and a school of housing, building and planning. The graduate and undergraduate sections of this school have just begun to function and only about a third of the faculty has been assembled. The present faculty is temporary, since it is made up of young expatriates who will be asked to leave when Malaysian faculty has been trained. Much of the short-term consulting work in planning will be carried out by faculty assisted by students. Thus, with the aid of books, instruments, and personnel drawn from the world at large, they hope to cope with the problems created by the capital, management and technology that is settling up and down the road, and help the people who are attracted to Malaysian cities.

The Science University of Malaysia is a nest of environmentally conscious individuals who would gleefully frustrate the aims of speculative syndicates, if they knew how, but most of the fast money will be moving in and out of factories, hotels, tracts of land, recreational promotions, warehouse inventories of hoarded commodities and commercial services more quickly than can be followed by part-time investigators. The principal effect is that of bidding up the price of land until it rivals the costs in Bangkok, Singapore, and Japan. The cost of preservation then will have reached heights that should cause the public to rebel against the environments' proposals.

Alternative Futures

Some of the key decisions about the future of Penang will be made in places like the Santa Clara Valley of California, Nathan Road in Kowloon, Hong Kong, and a number of office blocks in Marunouchi in Tokyo. They will decide Penang's share in manufacturing a wide spectrum of products that those firms plan to market. Ultimately the decision rests with the consumers of computers, electronic appliances, and clothing made of synthetic fibers all over the world. If they snap up the products, the Penang factories will go on double and treble shifts – if workers and trouble shooters who manage quality control can be found. The stresses of the future will arise from the acceptance of Penang's new products.

Malaysia will find itself depending heavily upon those factories, because it is due for some severe shocks in the next two years for which it is not psychologically prepared. One of the consequences of the energy crisis has been a sharp downturn in the purchase of new automobiles and the tires that go with them. The reduction in speed has also reduced the consumption of tires and the drop-off in accidents has saved a bit more rubber. All of these factors will hit natural rubber consumption more strongly than synthetic, so for a year or two the price may well drop to half the present levels and be insufficient to pay the labor cost of collecting rubber for most of the plantations. Simultaneously, the increases in the production of coconut oil and soy bean oil will depress the market in palm oil. Moreover the market in tin is also likely to be weak. On top of this there is scheduled to be an election. The United Malays National Organization (UMNO) coalition has been increasingly combatting inflation with subsidies taken out of income from the exported commodities, so that the government would be forced into severe deficit financing which is inevitably followed by inflation only a few months later.

With the rural areas hit as hard as this, the farmers' daughters will be quite willing to come to the factory in the city. The farmers' sons will volunteer for the army, join an oil company crew, or even sign up on a ship, in order to get away from disaster at home. Thus the cities with reduced budgets may have to make room for an increased flow of in-migrants from the hills. Until now it has been the surplus population from the more densely settled paddy fields that supplied the most willing migrants, but in the next few years the rubber plantations should be the prime source.

The bumi putra policy in the universities will also have unexpected effects. At present the brown Malays are at the bottom economically but are everywhere given strong preference. This means that of a panel of a dozen students submitted for consideration for overseas training, the top ten may be passed over and the scholarship given to the best Malay. It also means that students staying in Malaysia are likely to be more energetic and better scholars than those going overseas. British academic administrators understand the distinction and can judge the likelihood of competence by surname. Most Malays, at least those who are not connected with the nobility (a different problem), will be steered to the lowest ranked institutions where they stand a better chance of earning passing marks. The situation is of course greatly resented by the high-performance students because Malaysia has become a society where academic achievement is compromised by the desire for racial equity. The situation could hardly worsen for the Chinese and Indians – unless Malays should again go amok.

Local civil servants worry about the stability of the UMNO coalition even without foreseeing the shocks transmitted from the outside world. If it does not survive, then what? Will the military seek to rule? This is almost certainly likely to work less well than in neighboring Indonesia, or even Burma. If the Federation of Malay States falls apart, Penang would be a fragment forced to imitate Singapore, but with 40 percent of its population and 30 percent of its resources. Sabah and Sarawak would also go their own way. The rest of the society would ordinarily not be classed as an economic cripple (on the books it should be better off than Thailand), but no one knows whether it could retain the confidence of its economically active Chinese minority. If they should flee, leaving their property behind, Penang, Singapore, and Australia would gain by the quality of the human resources in the refugee influx. Much of the liquid reserves of the firms in Malay would disappear and turn up later in Hong Kong, London, Singapore and elsewhere. Young men who felt the injustice to themselves keenly would join the insurgents in the mountains so conditions in the Malayan peninsula might come to resemble the disturbances in the southern Philippines where tens of thousands of rebellious settlers are in arms.

This future sounds very gloomy indeed, yet it must be remembered that straight-line projections of world trends have always suggested that Malaysia was headed for great trouble. Thus far, it has shown greater powers to recoup and advance than any of the neighboring nations. Administration, community development, applied agricultural technology, and a bit − not too much − of oil and gas have enabled Malaysia to put together a record for development that is surpassed only by Japan and Korea. Malaysia seems to have had many hidden institutional resources that are drawn upon in emergencies; now some are becoming visible to outsiders.(25)

The new Malaysia, based on factories and commerce rather than plantations, will be epitomized by its new towns. The British built Petaling Jaya before they left, just as they put together the high-rise complex called Queenstown in Singapore. Both projects challenged the local administrations, but the responses have been carried to excess. Singapore has been building huge complexes of flats ever since, and Kuala Lumpur is much too sure that the mistakes made by the British can be overcome in the new designs they have in mind and are now building.

The new town on the other side of Penang's airport will be an interesting determinant of the future. It will relegate to George Town and its suburbs those things that are traditional and seize upon an image which combines what is good in a palm tree setting with what is valued as shiny and modern.

The new environmentalism will rise to maximum relevance. The Chinese need to demonstrate achieved status and maintain their customary face and must come to terms with physical demands upon the environment that are backed up by Malay political power. Malays brought in by the factories will prefer the new town location. At the same time the kampung Malays are destroying the natural environment more rapidly than any other group. Just as those in shifting agriculture in the back country of the mainland burn up the forest, fishermen dynamite coral reefs off shore and destroy the habitat of the fish. Divers in search of colorful aquarium species are stripping the reefs and preventing the replenishment of these populations by leaving rocks upturned. The new marine biological station located there hopes it can guide the development of the land-sea interface toward a more harmonious future.

The hillsides require equally strict protection. The base rock is a large-grained acidic granite that decomposes into sand and yellow clay. Since the rainfall is high − about 120 inches per year − erosion is difficult to prevent and slides are quite common. The old-fashioned cogwheel and cable railway to the Peak needs competition depending upon some less scarring funicular system that permits entry into the upper park land and playgrounds. What kind of equivalent might there be to the 1,200 steps on the other side that the Chinese faithful ascend?

Materials of construction will have much to do with the appearance of a new town. The days of profligate use of wood by the Malays are now past; people will have to make do with varnished veneers. Some striking effects are still obtainable, especially in conjunction with traditional roof forms. Cement is now scarce, but new capacity is being built elsewhere in Malaysia. All studies show that in George Town itself people are most content in walk-up condominiums with community services based upon a series of stalls. If they can be made garden apartments as well, the satisfaction should increase further.

The automobile is the uncontrolled factor in this arrangement. People are beginning to take it for granted in Penang, and increased incomes will naturally produce one and two car families. The normal tendency in George Town is to imitate the good life in Europe, so the present inability of Europeans to come to terms with their cars seems likely to be transmitted to new settlements on Penang. The design compromises that sell condominiums will produce grave frustrations for everyone. Smog should be no problem, but traffic delays and noise and expense will be serious. The danger is that Penang will evolve into a second rate Florida.

It appears that Penang is fortunate in having a school for planners to meet its foreseeable problems and help save its heritage. Many other places in the world will be looking over their shoulders to see how well they do. Planners in Penang will have to work with the slim resources of a semideveloped region under steadily increasing pressure. They are more fortunate than fellow Asian planners in that they will be able to live in Penang as they propose its future transformations. They will at least have a more pleasurable present, even if the prospects are uncertain.

Further Developments

April 1977

A year of rapid changes in world affairs leaves Penang much less changed. The expected drop in rubber prices turned out to be very large indeed, but it began to recover due to the resurgence in the sale of automobiles. Palm oil prices also have been down seriously.

Those events reduced the income of the rubber tappers and others in the rural areas to levels below subsistence. Thus more have been forced to seek employment in the cities. Students in Kuala Lumpur, and later in Penang, demonstrated on behalf of the hard-pressed rural plantation workers and smallholders. One unexpected outcome has been the confrontation of Malay students (whose places in the university had been quite protected by national policy) with Malay police. Some observers believe that the ideological spectrum among the educated classes will be extended by the reconsideration resulting from that experience.

Meanwhile a shortage of capital caused postponement of the re-development of the center of Penang. Much of the part that has been cleared and walled off will no doubt grow a thorny thicket that progresses rapidly to jungle while the project awaits more propitious times.

Some of the industries in the industrial estate are encountering marketing problems, so there may be fewer jobs in assembly for a while. However, greater world competition in electronics and electro-mechanical products puts pressure on firms to cut production costs; the multinational firms with home offices in Japan, California, Switzerland, and Germany may decide to put the new growth in Penang rather than in high labor cost areas. These cross-cutting trends suggest that the Penang economy will experience uncertain times, but may not suffer any long-term injuries.

The uncertainties for investment and for employment seem likely to lead to extended postponement of the new town that has been planned. On the other hand, the bridge to the mainland should go through on time. The disturbances that its construction and the subsequent traffic redirection will have upon the bus system will keep it from achieving any readily apparent improvements in service. New hotels springing up along the beach may be forced to encourage a jitney system that would overcome bottlenecks in the road leading past their gates. The trishaws are robust enough to survive in and around George Town and will be less discouraged by authorities in the future.

The environment of Penang seems likely to survive but not prosper. It is continually being judged by ideas external to itself, much more than by its own long-standing cultural values. Challenged with the implications of a new export industry for the production of mushrooms, for example, will the threat of coastal pollution balance out the recycling possibilities for organic wastes? Or will the national employment crisis supersede all other considerations?

6 Delhi, Calcutta and Bombay*

Notes accumulated from visits to India during 1966-70 were tapped to prepare a comparative study to illuminate a principal function of metropolises – the support of institutions for control of territories and peoples. This first selection was presented at the Great Cities Symposium of the Society for General Systems Research and the American Association for the Advancement of Science in Chicago, December 1970. Updates, based upon findings of subsequent visits, follow the various sections of this analysis.

THE CONTROL OF INDIA FROM THE GREAT CITIES

November 1970

It has not been fashionable recently to analyze how <u>cities</u> control a territory. The standard explanations for the exercise of power start with the framework of a state as given, and then identify the specialized institutions – parties, corporations, dynasties – with a hand on the levers. The headquarters of these institutions must operate in an urban environment, but little attention has been given to the structuring of that environment so as to facilitate the governing of distant places. In India, where this kind of control has been mysteriously eroding away, much less understanding exists for designing capitals that can govern. Therefore the facts remain scattered; this discussion can only propound what I expect would be found if a careful probing were undertaken.

India has three effective capitals. Delhi rules because it houses a civil service with an acknowledged veto capability regarding any

*Estimated 1985 population: Calcutta – 12 million; Delhi – 7 million; Bombay – 10 million.

120

legitimate proposal coming to light in India as it acts upon the sheafs of forms and permits which legitimize transactions. Delhi pulls the strings that unleash the police forces and issues the orders to armed forces in cantonments and on the borders as needed to back up the police, so that legitimate coercion is monopolized there. Delhi operates a fair proportion of the nationalized industries and all the great banks; it is now attempting to gain control over the policies of the research centers. Being India's "window to the world," the one city with pretensions to grandeur, New Delhi has a virtual monopoly on negotiations with foreigners and the allocation of the plums of foreign aid. Calcutta's power depends upon the hold of the past upon the present, since the port, the railroads, the banks, the stock exchange, the basic manufacturing, and education for the professions are all efflorescences left over from a period when the British were devising institutions for exploiting the wealth of India. Bombay, the gateway that linked India directly to London through the Suez Canal sea lane, directs the growth of the economy through the creation of technology-based enterprise, the judicious supply of private-sector capital, and the production of a corps of top managers. Therefore Bombay promotions are to be found throughout the country in commerce, manufacturing, advertising, recreation, and even politics. Bombay has dash, an alertness to world trends, and a constructive concern for its own future.

Historically, Calcutta has been a city of palaces and Delhi a site for capitals. The palaces, with two exceptions, have been enveloped by slums, and the capitals – perhaps ten of them over a two-thousand-year period – also with two exceptions, have fallen into overgrown rubble from which a wall, a moat, sometimes a courtyard, has been reclaimed. Calcutta was the capital selected by the East India Company; it grew fat with the power of the British raj, attracting communities from all over Asia. New Delhi was a many splendored creation synthesized in the second decade of the twentieth century, a sparkling gem in the imperial crown. Calcutta has become dingy to excess, but retains many green patches imprisoned behind the walls of the nineteenth century villas. Delhi, aside from its asphalted avenues and crowded lanes, is sere and dusty. Bombay is tightly packed, almost fully paved, with a growing skyline on land reclaimed from the sea just outside of the mercantile district. The tall chimneys from its early textile mills smoke less vigorously now, and funds from their amortization have shifted to a wide range of modern factories out on the periphery.

The Machinery of Control

The new nations were right when they associated political control with an airport and an airline. A charismatic leader can amplify his impact if he can move from center to center by air. A calculating executive can maintain a credible threat to decentralized operations chiefs when he may appear in person at any time and demand an accounting of their stewardship. A ruling clique can disperse and reassemble to seek consensus on the issues in the hinterland. Calcutta has many hundreds of persons daily moving in and out of Dum Dum Airport, a converted military strip with a newly modernized hotel-resort for transients. Even at daily peaks it entertains no more than five planes. It welcomes technical specialists to a very large extent and politicians in season, and sends out sales officers or negotiators. Delhi has Palam, stopping point for dozens of globe-circling Boeings and DC-8's each day, and a terminus for several thousands of persons when the people that count are back from the hill stations. Delhi's traffic contains a fair number of short-term tourists, the diplomatic movement which circulates about 10,000 foreign sojourners, the provincial politicians and special pleaders who hope to make their pitch at the highest level, and the always deferential, but continuously pressing, India Administrative Service officers on trouble-shooting missions. Palam has not yet been made a symbol of modern India, so it looks as functional as a funnel. Santa Cruz Airport serves Bombay – the name being a holdover from Portuguese occupation in the sixteenth century – with a bustling businesslike expediting of flows to offices, hotels and apartments predominantly at the tip of the peninsula.

Face-to-face transactions undertaken once or twice can be repeated and extended by telephone and mail. Calcutta has the largest telephone system in India, but it is built to a prewar standard far more susceptible to overload, so the user is harassed by delays in getting a line at peak periods and by audible cross talk picked up from parallel circuits. However, the dish-faced tower of the Telephone Bhavan in the Dalhousie Square district has been in place for several years, and the microwave relays installed by the Japanese are coming into operation none too soon; orders sent by telegraph are knocked out for days at a stretch when thieves run off with lengths of cable containing semi-precious copper. Delhi's telecommunications center was carefully set in the midst of the most modern secretariats and only a mile from "tabloid row"; the serviceability of its local networks is quite tolerable. Bombay's telephones are more frequently overloaded than those in Delhi, but the system remains almost as dependable, so one can build organization around a dependency on the telephone with some degree of security.

A more universal means for control is the postal service. The volume is quite respectable for a developing country – about 250 units a year for each urban household and business address in India. The transmission of mail is largely devoid of advertising and greeting cards, so the content is more purposeful than in Japan or Western countries. Bags and bags of sleazy, brownish paper envelopes pour into Calcutta's huge, redbrick Victorian, Writers Building. They contain mimeographed – the word is "cyclostyled" here – forms on porous, unbleached paper, which move from pile to pile on desk after desk, yellowing along the way. Babus with their fountain pens write remarks on the margins, after checking and rechecking the additions and subtractions. Some forms are returned because they are improperly filled out, some get into a queue that progresses at a snail's pace, and others are tied with cord and stacked up on shelves where the exposed edges turn brown. A few merit replies, the typical response being one or two more forms requesting further details. Government mail gets through because postal employees cannot steal the stamps from a franked envelope, but the reverse flow encounters some hazards.

A registered factory with 20 employees will regularly fill out three such forms each month, with one or two extra for each legitimate purchase of raw materials, several more for the purchase of capital equipment; there are also quarterly reports on production, and several each year for the payment of taxes. The firm must make separate reports to the labor exchange on each new employee. Some forms are directed to the decentralized offices in the great cities, but most go to New Delhi. Calcutta has 200,000 clerks responsible for compiling information and making out the forms; Delhi has only about the same number to process the paper coming from an economy 20 times the size presently served by Calcutta. Described in this fashion, the apparatus for control seems quite puny for a country of well over a half billion persons. Considering that machinery more advanced than a light adding machine or an occasional typewriter is hardly to be found, and that the industry of the Scots bookkeeper-instructors was never transferred to the didactic Brahmin scribes, it is no surprise that productivity is low by whatever objective measures are used. Therefore, when affairs reach a critical point, the small manufacturer realizes that he must arrange for some influential person, perhaps a politician, to hop a train to Delhi and make a direct plea.

The Indian Railways are a source of strength. Their service has been steadily improving, so that the postal service frequently surpasses American standards for delivery schedules. Electrification of the lines proceeds only a year or two behind plan in all heavily trafficked zones. The railroads bring in a profit of from 8 to 10 percent in a normal year as compared to an average yield on all nationalized industries, including rails, of only 1 to 2 percent. Railway executives are given their head in Delhi. Their finances are autonomous except when an unusual spurt of electrification of dieselization is taken on. As a result is it exceedingly difficult for the planning commission to make a veto stick. A million employees work the railroads of India, and a special welfare state within the state has been constructed for their benefit.

The Indian Railways are too large not to have some weak spots. Its management ranks had been the preserve of the Anglo-Indians, but this contingent found itself orphaned after the British left and the Indian government appointees took over step by step. Disappointments with India's politics and plans caused them to "go home" to Britain by the thousands in the past few years. Among the skilled workers in the foundries and engineering works, dissatisfactions with working conditions have accumulated, so the Communist party of India (Marxist) has been able to penetrate the railways via its labor union congress. A number of train wrecks over the past three years have been attributed to sabotage. The railway administration was further compromised when one division (southern) buckled to political pressures during the October-November riots of 1966 in Andhra Pradesh, aimed at compelling the Centre to allocate a steel mill to the Vishakhapatnam area. The railways report they suffered $25 million in damage during this crisis. However, another section resisted such pressures, with the result that damage to it was minor, and perhaps a lesson was learned about the desirability of taking a decisive stand when the country drifts into chaos. (Note that this report is dated 1970. Telex, then employed only by a few multinational firms, has come to the great cities. Scores of organizations are using it for dealing in world markets and managing far-flung operations on the subcontinent. Banking was one of the earliest activities to make the leap toward modern management. Computer applications followed; they made major penetrations during the 1975-77 Emergency, when worker agitation was dealt with harshly.

(The railroads later fell into the slothfulness of other national industries, being further set back by strikes and a severe drought instigating extensive power cuts and industrial shutdowns, but almost all of them rebounded rapidly under new management to reach record levels of output in 1977. The fraction of industrial capacity utilized has begun to reach respectable levels. Roads have been improved and extended, so buses and fleets of trucks have become far more numerous. All the new growth in intercity passenger movement was taken over by Indian Airlines. Metropolitan bus services in all three of the metropolises have been noticeably rationalized during the emergency.)

Urban Fixtures for Administration

Every designer of control systems knows that response time is a critical specification. A general-purpose system, such as government of a headquarters organization, must maintain response times involving change in direction or quantity of effort ranging from the planning horizon (usually 5 to 15 years in India) to those involving instruction by telecommunications (same day or next day). Once messages have been received in one of these capitals, headquarters may distribute activities within a metropolitan area and an office block so that action can be taken, if necessary, in hours or minutes.

When Calcutta was the sole seat of government, the focus of the city was in the section north of the maidan (a local name for the patch of central land, common to all British colonial capitals, that served as parade ground, race course, cricket field, public park, and so forth). The godowns (warehouses) of the port were a stone's throw to the west, the banks an equal distance to the north, the mosques and missions to the east, and the villas to the south. A number of bazaars formed an arc to the north; industry, once it emerged from small shops back of the bazaar, moved still further out — the jute mills upriver, engineering around the Howrah Rail Station across the river, and consumer products at points around the rest of the fringe. Now, of course, the swollen population has spilled much further out into a number of suburban communities served by train, railway, and bus. The inner city was built around the needs of streetcars, cabs, and rickshaws, but rickety Ambassador taxis have replaced the horse-drawn cabriolets, which now are relegated to serving the gypsy-like communities camping in open places. Persons in the outer city formerly traveled by foot; now they use bicycles, pedicabs, skiff-ferries, and an occasional scooter to get around the periphery. The outer city is connected to the core by buses, electric trains, and a limited number of streetcar lines.

More than anything else, Calcutta needs another bridge to Howrah, on the south side of the maidan. The present structure was finished just at the beginning of World War II and presents almost a caricature of Oriental congestion — pedestrians in many kinds of local dress, hawkers, beggars, pavement sleepers, bicyclists, cartmen, rickshaws, three-wheelers, eight-ton trucks, jeeps for the back lanes of Howrah, small cars for the important people, cabs bound for Howrah Rail Station and points north and west, and big American cars for the Marwaris. Five hours a day the traffic crawls, but sometimes it stops. Calcutta has the manpower, the capital, and the organizational potential to do much better than this, but it remains paralyzed by special interests.

The 6,500 rickshaws in Calcutta should be replaced by taxis and scooter-jitneys. The public bus company, which is unable to collect many fares or maintain buses, should be dissolved. A number of intersections should be rationalized, and widened roads should be converted into freeways. Parking space must be created near the center, probably in special structures. Nothing happens, however, and by now people feel that nothing can happen. The nearest equivalent in civic hopelessness that I can recall is the Chicago of 35 years ago. Calcutta needs money to lubricate the construction process, but its income taxes, corporate surtaxes, and excises have been skimmed off by the center and were not permitted to return because the risks of waste are too great. Even now, when a special development corporation has been formed, the cash trickles back slowly. Calcutta is too impotent to collect taxes for itself.

Delhi has had what Calcutta lacks — a centre-sponsored development plan for the creation of a modern city backed up with cash. The old city within the remnants of the medieval walls has modernized mostly at the edges. It contains more than a half million persons and a conglomerate of small enterprises in about 1,000 acres — a style reminiscent of Calcutta. In contrast, there is the spacious new city of New Delhi, the planned "colonies," and the various unauthorized settlements. The gravest error made in postindependence Delhi was its overreaction to the congestion of old Delhi: densities of the new housing were purposely kept low, with the result that the costs of water, sewers, roads, and urban transport have been staggering. Law enforcement has broken down, so squatters have invaded some of the green belt and land speculators have violated zoning provisions out beyond.

Government in New Delhi puts on an architectural image that is rarely ponderous and actually carries off a number of nice touches that promise to wear well. That image is most important when it affects the impressions of visitors arriving from the airport, most of whom have planned quite brief stays. Thus New Delhi has become a gigantic "Potemkin village" calculated to convey to outsiders the idea that a new and dynamic India is being born. The further one penetrates behind the facade presented to the outsider – and thus closer to what the Indian professional encounters – the slower things become. Middle-rank administrators – the "gatekeepers" in the bureaucracy – are supposed to be on hand at 10 o'clock, but rarely can answer a telephone before eleven o'clock, leave well before five to beat the crush, and have a long lunch in between. This is not really as scandalous as it seems, because they are following a long British-cum-Brahmin tradition of sinecures that allowed management of family estates, the writing of scholarly monographs, or the direction of a rich variety of cultural productions on the side.

Altogether, however, it must be admitted that the physical framework for a quick mobilization of authority has been laid down. Health facilities are good enough to keep epidemics at a low level, water supplies are assured for a decade or so, and the police recently demonstrated their ability to control the cleverest demonstrators in the country – the left-wing students. The military presence, once banished from a pacifist, neutralist capital, by 1970, shows up discretely at many points around the Defence Colony and the airport. The Indian government has been learning the hard way. When the Chinese attacked in 1962, ministers muddled and vacillated, causing far more confusion than was warranted. Therefore when the Pakistanis invaded in 1965, the entire top echelon of the military submitted its resignation and could be induced to resume only if granted a free hand to meet the threat. The precedent is recalled by higher civil servants and business executives because the repeated crises in confidence and the present lack of strong leadership at the top is generating talk of the need for a military regime. The capital is now amenable to an effective authoritarian government which presumably would scrap the paper-choked planning and administrative controls and turn the government's attention to a limited number of priority projects. At the same time the system of public persuasion and self-criticism operates so that no military personalities are built up into national figures; as a result the communications institutions hold off what the administrative apparatus might facilitate.

The Urban Human Resources

Calcutta's population grows in a more unbalanced fashion, because of migrants, than any other million-population city. Most immigrants are temporary residents, men from Bihar, Orissa, and Uttar Pradesh looking for some kind of employment to help support their families in the village. They return home for annual visits and the conception of sons, leaving a slot for a neighbor. Perhaps only one in five brings his family; the remainder pay a few rupees a month for a few square meters of shelter where they put their belongings, so that a household may consist of six or eight single men, some of whom may sleep in the streets most nights elsewhere in the city.

Calcutta also possesses a number of entrepreneurial communities. A few Chinese deal in shoes, leather goods, plastics, and restaurants. The turbaned, bearded Sikhs are in taxis and auto servicing. Parsees are found in management and medicine. There are Sindhis also – perhaps 20,000 show up at festivals – but I never found out what their specialities are – beyond smuggling. The new refugees from East Pakistan (600,000 of them) are hawking and taking up jobs as servants, while the older ones are established as white-collar and skilled labor. Muslims (at least half a million remain) are in many of the manual trades and small shops. The handful of English are bitter and disconsolate, having lost first their power and then their money. Their managing agencies have been liquidated, to be replaced very often by shadowy Marwari syndicates.

The Marwari are not a new force in Calcutta – more than a century ago, they were an influential class of small traders, active in the Calcutta bazaars; today they are tabbed as the business elite of the next generation. Good vegetarian Hindus, they claim descent from the Rajput kings of the sixteenth century, but were influenced by the Jain sect, from which they obtained a strong sense of stewardship for property and wealth. Starting as petty moneylenders, their Vaisya castes had a strong sense of astrological destiny that matched the Scottish character in business in the same way that the Bengali Brahmins possessed qualities enabling them to rise to the top in an English-run organization. Marwaris come almost exclusively from the minor towns of Nawalgarh and Pilani in dusty Rajasthan. They moved into trading, particularly wholesaling, then into the managing agencies of the British. A decade ago, eight elite families held 565 company directorates. Of these, the Birla organization, now the largest in India, has the most prestige. The Marwari elite are heavy contributors to the Congress party (whereas the Parsees started the Swatantra party, the splinter-size conservative opposition) but are looking around for means of hedging. Generational changes among the Marwari are striking, the stereotype being the parsimonious great-grandfather in Barra Bazaar, the manager-grandfather going about the city in a rickshaw while others walked, the father driving a big American car and smoking cigars, and the son with an overseas degree and a professional patina superimposed upon the family-based business acumen. The Marwari are said to control the urban land market in Calcutta and to comprise the most potent vested interest with which urban planners must wrestle; yet, within the bureaucracy or the legislature, their existence, like that of the Mafia syndicate in Chicago, is unmentionable except in the most private conversations. Calcutta's comeback, nevertheless, depends upon the forging of a coalition between the new generation of Marwaris and the Madrassi and Bengali Brahmins in the civil service. No political analyst I talked to could imagine where the statesmanship will be found nor what might constitute the quid pro quo of such an agreement. However, the leading Marwari syndicate (Birla's) recently hired a Princeton-trained Bengali to handle its "community relations," and it has been hiring others at the top of the India Administrative Service

(IAS) exam list, presumably for their managerial potential. Thus a first step is being taken. (Calcutta has begun to turn around, and the strongest force for change, the Calcutta Metropolitan Development Authority (CMDA) is directed by a Madrassi IAS officer managing the investment of funds from the Center. He learned to cooperate with the various managerial elites in the industrial region on the Bihar-Bengal border before arriving to take up this post. However, the plan for the symbolic Second Bridge over the Hooghly has remained a continuing embarrassment.)

The Political Capital

Fortunately Delhi has been studied more quantitatively, so that the urbanization process is less subject to the cliches and overgeneralizations that provide the basis for much of the Calcutta portrait.(26) Altogether, the origin of new households in Delhi is almost equally divided among three groups: refugees, immigrants, and Delhi-born family units. The immigrant units are the most interesting because they reflect the attractiveness of Delhi as a metropolis – a full quarter of them were "transfers" brought in by government departments and therefore qualified for the new housing in the respective "colonies" or nagars. About 60 percent of all immigrants belonged to families still in the process of movement, the mean time involved being about seven years. Incomplete families visit together at least once annually, and the Delhi side sends out Rs 80 yearly, of which Rs 15 is in the form of postal remittance.

The services available to the new population are not out of line as compared to the old settlers. Housing for the refugees is lowest (36 square feet per capita) as compared to immigrants attracted to the city (52 square feet) and old residents (41 square feet). Forty-five percent of the housing is provided by landlords, 23 by government, 7 by private employers, 7 by evacuees to Pakistan, and 14 percent is built by the refugees themselves. The average dwelling unit houses 2.4 families, but 15 percent house five or more families. More than 70 percent of children in the 5-14 age group and about 25 percent in the 15-20 age group are enrolled in school. About 20 to 25 percent of the population see the cinema, but only about 1 percent attend political meetings.

Institutions for the development of human resources in Delhi are as highly capitalized as any in India. In contrast to Calcutta, where 80 percent of the secondary schools are private (but heavily subsidized with state funds), Delhi's secondary schools are mostly public, including some of the most prestigious. Delhi University is part of the new development beyond a green belt, and so is grievously affected by the "low-density syndrome" deficiencies common to new towns in India. The new Nehru University is still further out.

Sometimes the human resources are distributed through a national capital in such fashion as to make it possible for a street mob to bring down the government. In recent times Bagdad, Damascus, and Ankara come to mind; Saigon, Karachi, Kuala Lumpur, and Athens also feel the threat. Delhi's layout seems to foreclose a takeover from within the city; nevertheless, two attempts were made in 1966 to use mobs built up by countrywide agitation. The first of these used the huge, anti-cow-slaughter demonstration of the sadhus, which had brought perhaps 400,000 persons to Delhi, most of them camped in the desert and the urban open spaces. The fanatics converted the demonstrators into an auto-burning, brick-throwing army of zealots. On the second occasion, the professional students — those who take five or ten years to complete a three-year course — tried hard to get the 30,000 to 50,000 left-wing students into the capital, but they were thwarted by preventive police action in the suburbs and on the railways.

It is often said that India has overinvested in its human resources, educating too many for the number of available white-collar jobs, but a review of the statistics suggests that the disparity was caused more by weather than poor planning. The two-year pause in economic growth caused by the drought and famine in 1965-67 was not serious enough to affect university attendance, so a large share of those two classes are surplus.(27) The surplus of graduates is concentrated mainly in Kerala and Madras in the South, which has fewer job opportunities locally.

> About one million squatters, as estimated by journal-ists, were removed to the edge of the city by the Delhi Development Authority by drawing upon the extraordinary powers invested in the Government by the Emergency. Much of the space they occupied is now covered with weeds; until now there was little doubt that it would be covered by administrative or housing structures within the next two five-year plans. Projections were made for a variety of growing clusters in Delhi; they included blocks of business offices in New Delhi, an expanding inter-national district, and the huge brick complexes of offices and nagars which are steadily filling up the map.

> One of the most unexpected shifts in immigration pattern has been created by infusions of dark-pigmented South Indians. Most often they have been attracted by the shortage in farm labor in the Punjab to the north, but they drift back into construction and service around Delhi when the crops are in.

> Until 1979 the prospects for Delhi seemed increasingly suspicious, due to its political and bureaucratic domi-nance. However, with the future of both leading parties in jeopardy, and decentralization of authority in as-cendance, one expects employment buildup and land prices to drop off sharply, and vulnerability to riots may return.

The Bombay Style of Development

Everybody one meets in India exclaims that Bombay is different from ordinary South Asian cities. Why? Because, they say, it has public-spirited local leadership. All agree to this statement, but when informants are pressed further on this point by being asked to describe what these leaders actually do, the replies are excessively vague. The Parsee (Persian) families, especially Tata, are always mentioned, and very often also the Jains, who are another tiny religious minority, an offshoot of Hinduism. It is significant that they say <u>families</u> and not a clique in the Chamber of Commerce or an inner circle of the Rotarians. How do families, even special families, energize a city?

Much of the ecology of influence begins to spring into view when the addresses of the entries into the telephone directory are analyzed. The rich and powerful are better able to cluster together both in physical space and committee membership. With some knowledge of surnames associated with language group, region of origin, and caste, one can quickly discover the presence of specialized colonies. A few hours spent in reading current newspapers and books, reviewing recent history, will turn up a number of surnames that have been involved on the national scene and an overlapping group of great names that get publicity at home for their efforts toward collecting people and funds for pet public projects.

A brief inspection of the directory reveals the names of some of the great families of Bombay: Advani, Ashok, Bhagat, Birla, Dalal, Desai, Gandhi, Kamani, Mafatlal, Mehta, Menon, Modi, Patel, Premchand, Sarabhai, and Shah.

There are also some famous names of the past, such as Sassoon and Abraham. As independent cloth merchants their primary loyalties were directed to Lancashire, where their concerns for public enlightment showed great effect around the turn of the century. Also names like Rao, Chokshi, Joshi, and Shroff pop out from the pages. Interestingly, enough, these families have come to Bombay from the north, Gujerat, Rajasthan, and the Sind, even though Bombay as a whole is said to be a predominantly southern city.

In America, where a dynastic involvement with public welfare and service is limited to a select circle including Rockefellers, Tafts, Kennedys, Harrimans, and very few others, it is difficult to assign much weight to the influence of key families upon the development of a metropolis or the state that the metropolis dominates. However, in India the family leaves a man few choices of his own. It designates his education all the way through to professional training; it picks his wife, and it assigns him his job. As a man demonstrates competence his voice accumulates greater weight in the family counsels. The great families of India tend to be quite large, so that at least some of the sons demonstrate managerial competence. Thus family traditions and responsibilities for land, property, enterprises, charities, and rituals are absorbed, acted upon, and transmitted without question. If a father or grandfather had stimulated the building of a part of Bombay through the exertion of personal initiative and leadership it is quite natural for the scion to spark the addition of some complement to that contribution.

The Tata brothers stand far out ahead of the other family groups. They require three times as many lines in the telephone listings as their nearest competitors. Over the past three generations the family has moved from textiles, banking, and steel, in which it is still preeminent, into chemicals, vehicles, electronic instruments, and fundamental research.

Going into the 1970s however, the Tata group have experienced some setbacks. A government study initiated by suspicious socialists in the Parliament shows that the resources of the Tatas have not been growing, while at the same time resources of both the Birla and Mafatlal groups have. It should be noted that qualitatively the Tatas have advanced significantly in sophistication, a feature which is brought to mind repeatedly by the modern architecture they have sponsored for their headquarters and endowed institutions. In this respect they are surpassed only by the Sarabhais. The real competition in Bombay is provided by multinational enterprises such as Esso, Stanfac, Caltex, Unilever, Siemens, and Bank of America. (Alas, the head of the Sarabhai clan died in 1973, and the multinational firms have been swallowed up by national corporations; nevertheless, their executives remain some of the most effective community leaders to be found anywhere in Asia.)

Curiously, there seem to be no published accounts regarding how basic urban development decisions are made. The planning organizations in Bombay are built up of "working parties" with special interests and assignments. Members of the family firms participate with leading professionals, often from universities — who may themselves be members of these propertied families because other academics are forced to find outside jobs in order to live up to expectations for their status in life — and civil servants with relevant experience. Planning staff serves as secretaries to the working groups, researchers, and coordinators. Thus six or seven independent policies are threshed out in the working parties after some of the key issues have been resolved at the level of an overall board that meets every six weeks. This apparatus is new, having come into being around 1965, but it appears to exploit the older mechanism of development that began with the choice of a mission by a family which then promoted support from its own ethnic and religious community, and from professional associations and chambers of commerce, often by a subscription technique, whereupon civil servants bowed to the inevitable. The working parties serve as an integrating device for such promotion.

Planning Future Urban Development

Indians have never really thought through the implications of industrialization, modernization, and economic development. Congress Party politicians felt they understood "village India," and believed that large aggregations of people, as in multimillion-size cities, were highly undesirable.   During the 1960s scores of industrial townships were formed away from established population centers, but these new communities found it particularly difficult to introduce adequate commerce and transport; these "new towns" served the large industries very badly by fostering dissatisfactions that led to strikes and political unrest, as well as lower levels of operating efficiency. Those that functioned as state capitals have consistently failed to provide the communications infrastructure needed for organizing and integrating development. American, British, and other overseas economists and aid officials also disliked large cities, and argued with the aid of ad hoc models that a better alternative existed (e.g., expanding the well-located market towns and villages or decentralizing metropolises), without clearly recognizing that population growth must soon be so great that such new centers would coalesce in a matter of a few decades to become a continuous web of urbanization little differentiated from what is now happening.

It was not until 1966 that the Calcutta Metropolitan Planning Organization translated some of the implications of the prospective five-year plans into targets for metropolitan development, but then only for West Bengal.(28) Delhi has had a plan much longer but its targets for population growth and physical development were so unrealistic it soon became obsolete; very likely the existence of the plan and its forceful implementation reduces Delhi's capacity to govern more than it promotes vital functions. Greater Bombay's plan suffered from many deficiencies, including the fact that it did not cover the full metropolitan region into which most of the new growth would spill but merely proposed to export many of Bombay's problems to the periphery.

In 1970 development authorities were created in Bombay and Calcutta as vehicles for using Centre funds for projects of national interest. Delhi has undertaken a major study on the National Capital Region and is already addressing the traffic and utilities problems as well as landscaping its core area in order to prop up its international image. Bombay quickly set out on its ambitious twin city proposal – building a modern new metropolis on the hilly shores opposite the harbor area.(29) Calcutta is still trying to get assurance of a complete second bridge across the Hooghly River.

Although the reorganization of agriculture that presses India in the direction of the high-yielding intensive food production system of Taiwan or Japan has taken hold only in the past few years, a number of consequences for the great metropolises of India can already be identified which will intensify over the next several decades – if India continues to develop.

1. A new group of families will acquire sufficient wealth to move to the nearest city, invest in advanced education and political influence as well as a variety of enterprises, and in the process force a new link for controlling resources development in the hinterland. They will effectively "Indianize" technology borrowed from the West a decade or more earlier.

2. There will be an added flow of young college graduates into a pool of largely unemployed and underemployed white-collar and professional

workers. Thus salaries for engineers are likely to remain at the same level as for machinists.

3. Large numbers of literate poor will arrive in search of employment in manufacturing and service who expect to send a good share of their earnings back to the family in the village and later return to the village themselves. Nevertheless an important fraction of these will find secure niches in the metropolis and effect a transfer of at least part of the family.

4. Surges of distressed rural people will flee the countryside during droughts and squat upon the interior open spaces and the fringes of the growing metropolis, thus forcing a more enlightened policy upon the authorities for providing minimal self-help-type supports and eventually finding some employment.

Thus the green revolution postpones the neo-Malthusian day of reckoning but shifts much of the pressure from the inaccessible countryside to the highly visible metropolis. It exacerbates stresses in the metropolis among college graduates and among squatters, where conditions are already very close to the breaking point. The real test of the ability of these metropolises to govern will henceforth be in managing the accreted population growth over which they presently have very little control.

Governing Resource-Conserving Urbanism

The kind of urban settlement that fits into a feasible future for India is strikingly different from that which has evolved to date either within India or outside. Having to struggle against very low ratios for natural resources per capita will force a rather intensive recycling of wastes and cause the growth of a physical structure that is far more economical in energy consumption while still producing a full range of modern services.

A quantitative assessment of the inputs and outputs that presently seem to be required for such an approach was made in my Planning for an Urban World.(30) It appeared that such a city could reduce the consumption of fresh water, for example, to about 40 liters per capita per day, or about 4 percent of present American consumption, and still allow virtually full operation of all services and centers of employment. Energy use could similarly be reduced in tropical India to about seven or eight percent of present American levels. Other raw materials can be conserved almost to the same degree except for food commodities. Food is likely to be imported from the outside in roughly equal tonnages, but it would be reprocessed and improved in quality within the city itself. Human wastes can be economically recycled to help produce most of the perishable foods within the environs of the urbanized zone.

A principal reason such huge economies can be accomplished is that one major resource, the electromagnetic spectrum, remains almost completely uncommitted. Moreover the unit cost of transmitting information via these channels is expected to decline for at least the next several decades. This means that internal communication for the control of mechanical equipment and the guidance of routine activities, such as accounting and the operation of public markets, will become very voluminous. It could very easily become orders of magnitude greater than at present in the most developed countries.

A symbol of the telecommunications revolution is the communications satellite that has been operating over the subcontinent periodically since 1973. It will allow the capitals of India to talk to each other, and to the other cities, towns, and villages, perhaps without the repeater stations that have hitherto been needed. Mountains of slow-moving paper can be displaced with such channels. The Atomic Energy Commission is working hard on systems that would permit transmission to isolated points in sufficient volume to upgrade the quality of education as well.

The hardest working computing centers in India are in Bombay, Delhi, and Kanpur. Systems analysts, engineers, economic planners, meteorologists, census administrators, survey researchers, and many others fly into these cities with dispatch cases filled with problems and programs. The population of competent programmers is growing by 30 to 50 percent per year. Clerical workers are already parading through the streets demonstrating against the adoption of the computer. Labor union leaders are inventing slogans to be changed during the marches to come. Managers compromise and postpone some of the most productive uses of the computers, but still modern computation comes in through the back door to some of the offices most protected against agitation, such as the Atomic Energy Commission, the Indian Institutes of Technology, and the military, and even the government-owned Life Insurance Corporation of India has managed to install its own equipment. The greatest difficulty in 1970 seemed to be frequent electric power cuts that many cities experienced due to storms, defective equipment, and localized overloading.

The future government of India, the kind that will control the great cities it needs for development, must learn how to use this ultramodern machinery. It needs to overcome the tendency to "Indianize" the administration of the country, which isolates it from the world and the overall stock of knowledge that exists mostly outside the boundaries of India, and it must build the modern new institutions – the banks, distribution systems, agriculture with irrigation and fertilizer, airlines, and telecommunications – which can convert knowledge into income.(31)

The large interdisciplinary Calcutta Metropolitan Planning Organization was an attempt to cope with the future of India's greatest city. Ten years later there remains little hope that the powers granted it are sufficient to make any progress at all. The Delhi Development Authority was endowed with a strong executive having operating responsibilities, and with ten times the amount of capital investment, but it too has been floundering and needs thorough reorganization. Now Bombay is making its move with the City and Industrial Development Corporation of Maharashtra (CIDCO) which proposes to build a new city across the bay almost equal to the size of Bombay itself, with modern industries, residences, transport systems, communications equipment, schools, and other services. It is far more ambitious and thorough than anything that has preceded it.

If Bombay succeeds even partially the other capitals of India will be stimulated to innovate at planning-promotion-management to keep from being left in the dust.

But Bombay did fail most disastrously: for five years the program was held up by a curious coalition of villagers and landlords, who prevented construction of the roads and drains required for land development. Costs sky-rocketed.

Many strategic lessons for urban planners, from interim reports of succeeding visits, are presented in the next section.

"SAVE BOMBAY"

September 1974

The force of ideas in the city-building process can never be underestimated. Here we see a handful of environmentalists deflecting the normal evolution of a great city.

This essay is a product of my fourth visit to Bombay. It reflects long-standing familiarity with Bombay's problems and its workings; I had by then lost my sense of wonder at its unexpected competence. Instead I found myself tuning into the extraordinary amount of energy that keeps its inner machinery in motion. This selection has been drawn from a working paper.

New concepts of the environment are invading Bombay. Feelings regarding the proper image of a city and the appropriateness of urban design similar to those that engage San Francisco have become the focus for debate. Previously civic groups in Bombay were contentious, but almost always regarding alternatives for starting new services that become part of a future Bombay. However the new environmentalists stop the normal course of development in order to save something in the present community that is valued by a prominent minority.

The Save Bombay Committee is an ad hoc group of professionals allied to enterprising politicians. It sets up study groups, seminars, and thrives on special issues. It had stopped a high-rise at Bandra, an inner suburb, in order to save a small beach. There were three or four other localized projects in which they were active, gained publicity, and were reasonably effective. But then the State of Maharashtra presented them with front-page issues that will last for some time.   The first is reclamation of new land on the waterfront, which would fully Manhattanize Bombay. The second is a proposal for Metro government.

A public seminar organized by the Save Bombay Committee to ventilate these issues is very interesting to watch. The steering committee working behind the scenes is made up of young professionals (in their thirties). All but one of the six has arrived within the past three years from overseas education — accountancy and law from England, and economics, engineering, and business administration from the United States. Thus they are playing games which generate publicity about values they have heard expressed in the West. The steering committee creates situations in which they mobilize the technically competent do-gooders and the politicians who are still building their careers in the presence of the press. The reporters were eating out of the committee's hand, because this occasion seemed to be honest and spontaneous, while standard politics has become a series of dusty cliches. Although the preliminary reporting had been slipshod and erroneous the accounts of what happened on the spot were fair and favorable, and also threatening to the cabinet and the Chief Minister of the State of Maharashtra. These office holders felt that they had been doing a careful and, relative to the rest of India, very competent and progressive job in developing both Bombay and the State of Maharashtra. The Save Bombay agitations reached dimensions they had not expected.

The Public Managers

In order to understand what has been happening we must trace out the strategies of Governor Naik. He is a man wholly dedicated to Maharashtra, who repeatedly spurned enticements to play a major role on the national scene in New Delhi. Chief Minister for more than a dozen years now, he is totally secure in his post. His problem of balance is something like that which was faced by Rockefeller and his predecessors in New York State — the metropolis generates the revenue, but the hinterland has the votes. Thus ballot power must find a compromise with economic power. In Maharashtra, therefore, the top politicians must supply state services for a population that is more than 80 percent non-Bombay from revenues that are 84 percent supplied by organizations in the metropolis. It is definitely to the advantage of politicians to encourage further growth of the flock of geese with golden eggs and it should be done as much as possible through low-cost stimulations and promotions.

Bombay has long been extraordinarily overcrowded; it now has a density that approaches the level of Hong Kong. In order to be more productive it needs more space. So as to be sure that this would happen, two alternative approaches were developed. The first and largest was New Bombay — the development of open land across the "bay" — which is really a submerged estuary, called Thana Creek — while the second was further reclamation at the lower end of the patched together island containing old Bombay. Both promised to make possible new employment in offices along with luxury residences.

The New Bombay program has already stalled due to poor planning. It committed the usual mistake of planning too spaciously, so it priced itself out of the mass market. Added to this was a natural willingness to mobilize the black money (undeclared for income tax and often derived from underworld operations) for pushing the development. When gray investors (i.e. those who "wash" black money) learned a major drive was aimed at the sources of black money, they felt that a slowdown in New Bombay's expansion was inevitable. Therefore the other project for reclamation of new land was authorized, despite the protest of the city advisory body, after some back-of-the-scenes collusion with banks. The latter are now independent government corporations that have newly added functions and need to expand their physical facilities so as to obtain the floor space for extra white-collar employees.

The development of this reclaimed land would further delay the unfolding of New Bombay and diminish the return on investment already made in roads, drains, and utilities. Therefore the City and Industrial Development Corporation of Maharashtra (CIDCO), the state-organized promoter of New Bombay, must reinforce the group which wishes to keep the present skyline of Bombay by providing them with the technical expertise needed to make their points. Thus it is possible to demonstrate quite persuasively that the transport of workers to the new high-rise buildings at water's edge would be exceedingly expensive. This remains true despite the fact that the previous grandiose plans submitted to the World Bank costing over a billion dollars had been scaled down to $400 million for installing a new electrified rail line to the suburbs.

Members of the city council feel that they are nothing more than puppets, because they have no veto over State or Centre final decisions. Power of this kind allows the State to remain impervious to local opinion. The only redress is delay by means of litigation. Going to court is so expensive it is usually reserved for the defense of honor, family unity, and sacred duty.

The metro-Bombay proposal is another administrative device that is designed to ease the life of the administrator, eliminating some of the intolerable features of fractionated authority. The management of Bombay and its dependent area, along with its further development, will be assigned to five ministers chosen from, and backed by, Bombay's elected legislators. (This plan is similar to the solution for Scotland and Wales in the last British election, except that Scotland and Wales are minor troublesome appendages, while Bombay is the economic core.) Metro-Bombay offers no basis for increased self-government of urban communities, so it will be opposed by all vocal Bombay citizens. Alternative formulas with greater popular appeal are not being prepared.

Meanwhile the implementation of the plans for New Bombay is failing very badly. The first township, Belaput, is planned at Western standards (again!), which means that it will require large amounts of subsidy. Since it serves the upper middle class primarily, this use of public funds will become a scandal. The planners (led by Charles Correa) have formulated designs with standards that suit their professional critics rather than taking dead aim at the middle of the market. The idea of self-help site-and-services projects has yet to be worked out for this territory in sufficient detail to be ready to launch with real hopes for success. In India the tendency to plan communities made up of a single income class is very strong, even though it disregards the apparent demand for servants and service labor in the vicinity after the construction is completed. CIDCO has been too Western in outlook, even for India's most Westernized city.

Although the greatest single mobilizing force in Bombay is the realization by citizens that they must act to keep the city from quickly going the way of Calcutta, it appears that CIDCO cannot move with confidence because it has lost its bright young talent even more rapidly than the Calcutta Metropolitan Planning Organization. It has fallen prey to the same diseases, even though they are not as fully advanced. Both Calcutta and Bombay are now deeply into the land development business, and neither has the flair for promotion that is needed. In each instance they are constrained by a society which must mollify the ambitions of state politicians with steel mills, oil refineries, fertilizer plants, and government establishments rather than seek out the most economical sites. The political system similarly directs the location of new activity in the private sector, often away from the most economic sites based upon public, not private, values. Every single potential error in the planning of new towns that I could list in two lectures to CIDCO staff in 1971 has already been committed in a big way, and a few others in addition. I do not blame them because they were overcome by a force much bigger than themselves. It is called India.

This ominous outlook is not relieved when looking at the critical water supply situation. Although the World Bank has financed an expansion of Bombay's water supplies, the chances of running out of water — by their own calculations — have only been reduced from one year in 20 to one year in 35. This is based upon a common sense evaluation of the data, but it is suspect. Part of the reason for suspicion is that no statistician is at work evaluating the meteorological data for the hydraulic engineer's office. (Most statisticians in India seem to be Bengali, and just at this time a British detective story novelist was being politely chided for assigning Bombay's finest a Bengali surname — unthinkable!)

However even a statistician might err under the present circumstances, because climatic conditions since Indian independence seem to have been more favorable than for the long run. Year-to-year variation had markedly diminished over a period during which Bombay more than tripled its population, but this decade the typical variability of the monsoon seems to have been resumed. Worldwide forecasting models built up in 1974 from data acquired via the ERTS satellite suggest that there is about one chance in ten that Bombay will run out of water in 1976. In that case it would have to mobilize all the tankers and barges available in the Indian Ocean to transport water from whatever nearby river mouth has a flowing supply if the urban population is to survive; many offices and certainly all manufacturing would have to shut down. However, Bombay proceeds with little concern for the odds; long-term risks do not affect the value of property, the demand for industrial sites, or the pressure to immigrate.

Meanwhile in the Trombay laboratories the planning of the nuclear-powered agro-industrial complex that could feed Bombay during a drought has slowed to the pace of an ox cart.(32) Attention seems to have been focused upon achieving the explosion of the "peaceful nuclear device" set off in India earlier in the year. The nuclear site that was chosen to energize the unified program for obtaining extra production in the Indo-Gangetic plain has now been allocated to the Delhi-Agra power grid and agriculture will apparently be advanced along the more traditional lines for implementing the green revolution.

The proposal to use the arid coastline of the Gulf of Kutch about five hundred miles to the north has not been revived even though the new levels of food prices, both worldwide and in India, would seem to make the proposition rather attractive economically. Early in 1974 most of the west of India was very close to starvation; travelers to Delhi and elsewhere filled their suitcases with rice before returning home, because it had become virtually unobtainable, even in the black market.

Fortunately not too much time has been lost as yet on the food front because the test facility for advanced desalination techniques should be in operation in 1975 and design standards suited to Indian conditions may be forthcoming by 1977. Meanwhile the first fertilizer plant in the Gulf of Kutch was due to go on stream in December 1974 using the natural gas that has recently been developed in that region.   This ammonia production line at Kandla, the free port, is an outcome of collaboration with the agricultural producer cooperatives in the United States rather than a multi-national corporation. Top-grade management might still make the desert bloom by 1984.

Postscript – 1975

A few months later the sequel came through to this side of the Pacific. The cooperative and socialist engineers brought the fertilizer plant on stream on time. All the dubious equipment had been made to work. But then the power shortage caught up with them. The state utility required power cuts equivalent to other industries, but those on-again-off-again schemes will not allow a contin-uous-flow catalytic process to function, so the plant was forced to shut down while managers argued with bureau-crats in Gandhinagar, the new town capital of Gujarat. Everyone was somewhat less chagrined however when it was discovered that the tank cars for carrying away the fertilizer-grade ammonia had somehow been cancelled. The one trainload of cars available would allow the plant to operate a few weeks and then it would have to shut down for lack of place to store the product. Perhaps after a few years trouble shooters will bring this plant up to the capacity average for India – about 30 percent – but food for a future enlarged Bombay is not assured.

ON LIVING OUT THE EMERGENCY

Now that the Nehru dynasty has fallen, only to be resuscitated, the period leading up to the transition will be carefully scrutinized by historians. The notes that follow were taken during a 12-day visit a half year before the election was called. They demonstrate very clearly the difficulty of making projections in the political realm.

August 1976

Under the guise of the emergency a number of moves were made against potentially competing power blocs and potential sources of instability, some of which were calculated to be widely popular, while others were necessary, as for example family planning, but generated very little enthusiasm among the general public. Step by step the independent actions of the states of India were put under the thumb of the Centre. A method was devised for collecting undeclared income tax, allowing wealthy prior evaders to escape jail and legitimize their former gains if they paid up before a specific date, thus attacking the wealthy opposition in the pocketbook and the private safe-deposit box, where it hurt the most.

Winking at various smuggling practices ceased, so the black money in the cities dried up, thus crippling both film production and construction for the private sector, but also cutting off the flow of authentic Scotch whiskey. Student elections for the council and the chairmanship of the union, which had often become politically polarized and riotous, spilling over into the community outside the walls, ceased altogether. Similarly, all manner of strikes and street demonstrations were halted. If flash protests did occur, no mention was made in the newspapers, so much of the satisfaction of getting into print and thus publicly recognized can no longer be obtained by the instigators. Centralized controls over previously independent organizations such as non-Congress labor unions, cooperatives, and firms, are being devised, as are "apex" organizations for administering them fromthe Centre.

All the intellectuals and professionals with whom one can discuss current developments know personally of one or two tragic cases where some "relatively innocent" individual is held without trial, and greatly limited in the contacts he is allowed to have with visitors. These same leaders of the professionals also expect frequent police interrogations. Bureaucratic callousness is common, but torture is not reported.

It has not escaped the notice of Indians that the forces of nature have been extraordinarily propitious during the emergency up to this point. The monsoons have been adequate, and well distributed. Reservoirs are full, so electric power cuts have virtually ceased. Industrial production in most places is up 10 to 20 percent over the previous year, a marked improvement over 1974. The inflation of prices has ceased in almost all sectors of the economy; many restaurants have reduced prices 5 to 15 percent over the past half year. Moreover, the railroads run virtually on time; an older and mostly European generation remembers this as the first prominent success of fascism in the 1930s, so the parallel is almost always lost among contemporary Indians.

Nevertheless, there is consensus, even among those who have been harassed, that the emergency may have "done some good, because it brought discipline," an element all Indians recognize as lacking in their national character. The socialist labor unions, which are very much at odds with the government and the Congress-dominated unions, have agreed to participate in a study at the Indian Institute of Management (Ahemdabad) of the costs and benefits associated with the enforcement of the emergency. Everyone recognizes that daily life has become more orderly, and that it is easier to make personal plans and then be confident of being able to carry them out.

The New Bombay plans had been frustrated by the virulent resistance of key villagers who were over time able to mobilize the full population affected. Just before the emergency 10,000 villagers were preventing the installation of infrastructure, such as bridges and water lines, in the area, and agitating for the retraction of the New Bombay plan. A small amount of progress could be made on filled land for which no villagers could claim title. Immediately after the emergency, the program could start building in an orderly manner. The excessive costs experienced in prior years are now approaching the metropolitan average and housing may soon profit from economies of scale. A previously demoralized planning organization is now regaining its aplomb.

Similarly, the bus system of Bombay, one of the better urban transport services of India but still possessing a severe maldistribution of carrying capacity and an inadequate program for preventive maintenance, has now been able to reorganize and use its equipment to save the time of residents. Part of its success is due to the fact that the storm sewers were cleaned before the monsoon, so that surface drainage is better.

Evidences of "discipline" are found again around the squatter huts. Certain central hut communities have been displaced altogether, theoretically moved to the northern edge of Bombay. Others are being dismantled in stages. This means that some long-delayed urban development projects can now be implemented. The face of Bombay most often presented to visitors will quite noticeably improve in appearance. Acceleration of maintenance work on older buildings adds to that impression.

But is the lot of the poorer classes improved by this redirection? The best evidence I have is the cost of unskilled construction labor hired on a daily basis. The principal kinds of people now so employed are Adivasis, or tribals, from Madya Pradesh, who are very close to the bottom of the social pyramid. They are now getting 10 to 12 rupees as a beginning wage instead of 6 to 8 rupees in 1970, with a better chance now of advancing into the ranks of the semiskilled. Women are employed along with the men, and make whatever is the lower side of the wage range. Therefore, families can attain the salary of a civil servant for the first time, as long as the construction is not interrupted by strikes or demonstrations. People say the higher wage is due to the fact that many of the labor contractors who negotiate for their own people, living with them as they work, have signed up with engineer-builders in Kuwait, Dubai, and Iran. Actually it is the semiskilled carpenters, stonecutters, and metal benders from the same regions who have been attracted by the high pay, and Bombay is most affected because it gets news of the opportunities first. This relationship suggests that the improvement could well be localized to Bombay, its satellite cities, and the towns and cities tributary to them — perhaps 30 millions of people in all. One needs to look further to draw firm conclusions.

One other prominent sidelight is worth mentioning. The English-language bookshops feature Irving Wallace's novel The R Document. A number of Indians, ranging from a new engineering graduate to a university vice-chancellor, brought it to my attention with comments like, "It's a really significant book!" or, "It's sure to be banned very soon." So I paid Rs 12.50 ($1.38) for a copy and read it as if I were a citizen of India. To Americans it is merely a debunking of J. Edgar Hoover and the FBI myth, obviously a post-Watergate potboiler, but one curious "fact" (probably true) that crime is much lower in company towns in America strikes home in India. Here every major firm, whether publicly or privately owned, is already required to create a township for permanent employees. The major cities are crammed with townships like those of the Port Trust, for example. Therefore, a policy involving the deployment of the company-town model to create a fascist state in America after the Bill of Rights has been amended away, as imagined by Wallace, sounds all too real in India. After all, their bill of rights has already been subverted, so they see themselves ripe for the next step.

> (More turns of the screw were added over the next six months, but then called off for an election. The over-confident Indira and Sanjay Gandhi were decisively top-pled. After three years of increasing confusion at the Centre, they have been returned to start over.)

Progress in the Cities

This subtitle is the kind used by Indian publications. It represents a steady transformation of the central city to a Western image, although with middle-class Hindu trimmings, at the expense of the squatters and relocatees. Delhi has now forcibly moved out 150,000 squatters and relocatees, the product of about six years of effort. The last third of this removal has been accomplished since the emergency, so there has been some acceleration. Our students, together with a minority of those in planning and architecture in India, have agonized over the inherent injustice, but that does not change the course of "progress." The predecessors of those now in power had been too spineless, so they allowed the squatters to creep into the city and gain the protection of ambitious minor politicians. This cleanup of the cities is being pushed from the very top – the prime minister's office – so the small-fry politicians can be disregarded.

August 1976

Perhaps some good may come out of the squatter removal program. Communities of Muslims which had been forced to look inward for support, and demanded complete conformity regardless of costs in welfare, have markedly changed within a year. In the resettlement area young women no longer wear the burkah, the sign of submission to conservative tradition. Individual freedom and initiative can be noted, where previously it had been inhibited by the elders of the community. But it also means that in times of crisis the community supports will be much weaker and less adequate.

Simultaneously the DDA (Delhi Development Authority) has been forced belatedly to develop more adequate procedures for site-and-services settlement. What is being learned is now brought to the School of Architecture and Planning by Jaswant Rai. It is possible that, in its own fumbling way, Delhi is arriving at the same solution Seoul reached in the early 1970s – build an instant city on the periphery, provide good bus connections with the metropolitan market districts, and require new industries to settle alongside the self-help settlement. New immigrants from the villages, especially families, would be directed there, while educated people would arrive as individuals, find a room to share, and gradually work up to being able to marry and occupy an apartment in one or another of New Delhi's "colonies."

In May one of the communities in old Delhi was hit by two high-priority policies – compulsory sterilization for one of the parents (usually the father) of families with three or more children and compulsory relocation to a site where transport costs would eat up a quarter of their income. The sterilization camps are infamous among the respectable poor, since they are places where people expect to get drunk, often for the first time in their lives, and a flock of prostitutes work the periphery. The men are ordered about like new army recruits with the white-uniformed doctors serving as the officers shouting the commands; after a few days the men are vasectomized and then put on a bus, almost always without medical follow-up. Relocation was even more traumatic. This community next to Jama Masjid, the great mosque of Delhi, and the Thieves' Market, is different from others in that it is apparently made up of progeny of the rejects from other communities, so it contained Muslims, Hindus, and even some Sikhs, living together side by side. The resentments in the community exploded; men and boys started throwing stones at official vehicles and precinct police. The special police were moved in, and tear gas used to quell the riot. This action caused the government to back down somewhat from its compulsory sterilization stand. The responsibility for enforcement is being passed to the respective states, with Maharashtra and Bombay presently the most emphatic. The pressure for relocation continues, but more subtly.

One of the most far-reaching pieces of legislation passed during the emergency, the Urban Land Ceiling Act, has yet to make a significant impact. It was originally intended to control land speculation and to keep land prices from being inflated by black money. It required land to be put to use within a relatively short time, otherwise this land would be taken over by government and used for public purposes. As passed, the law sounds appropriate, and is a means of redressing some defects in the application of eminent domain in India which allows the process to be extended over seven years or more in most states before a public project can be started. However, zealous administrators have interpreted the act to include urban land with structures on it and activities under way, so that it can be used to expropriate property of any firm or family, even if the land is not vacant. These rulings are admitted, even by staunch Congress adherents, to be based upon "ideology." As a result, the private sector is up in the air; the managing directors do not know what part of their operations will be expropriated under the Urban Land Ceiling Act. They hope clarifications will result from Supreme Court decisions over the next few years, even though the courts have revealed themselves to be supine in the face of the ideologists of the Congress party. The strategy is much more that of patience, since they and others think that this enthusiasm, like others before it, will wane over time.

This weak parallel action was taken to control the private organizations and individuals engaged in social welfare and cultural activities. Thousands of Indian voluntary groups, ranging from churches to wildlife preservation associations, and tens of thousands of individuals, have been able to gain support through donations and tied grants for their independent purposes. The capability of many such individuals to gain support from overseas, enabling them to fly off to Europe or America, or to continue on the urban scene without local financial backing, angered the strategists of the Congress party. So a new law was concocted which requires anyone getting a grant or a stipend to obtain approval from the government in advance of acceptance, even when living overseas. This especially applies to the standard devices of Third World and refugee assistance – visiting professorships, fellowships, teaching assistantships. Presumably the law will stop the exodus of top talent from Delhi that has been noted over the past few months without arbitrary removal of passports – a measure taken in Iran.

Expected Sequels

What expectation does all this (and much more that has not been reported) generate for the future? At one time, only a decade ago, the destiny of Calcutta seemed isolated from that of any other Indian metropolitan region, and much the same conclusions were reached in places like Bangalore, Hyderabad and Varanasi. In large part this was because the states were launched upon independent trajectories, and offered or withheld their food surpluses and other resources according to those objectives. Some were Congress party (what later became Old and New), some Communist party, and others a confusion of contending factions. However, exploitation of the victory over Pakistan led to what is effectively a one-party nation, with all the states harnessed to obey directions transmitted from the Centre. The cities are pulled along so that they too share what seems to be a common destiny.

The improvements in infrastructure have reinforced the appearances of parallel development. Indian Airlines, which carries mainly top bureaucrats and "millionaires" (since tourism in India remains a trickle through the vastnesses of its social system), must have expanded its capacity at least tenfold. The Indian railways are laying on more express trains, and have just finished electrifying the Delhi-Howrah line, preliminary to completion of all the main trunk lines over the next two decades. The road network has been improved, and the buses and trucks have quickly followed each widening from one lane to two lanes, thus creating a transport shed around every city. On the whole city-city visits, and the communications that follow up after them, have multiplied many times, and rural-rural contacts have also noticeably expanded (the crowd of southern peoples in the rural areas of the Punjab and the buildup of migratory laborers in all the higher income states with export crops), while the rural-urban interaction has expanded much less.

Migration to the largest metropolises appears to be maintained at a rate equal to, or occasionally somewhat less than, the trend over the previous two decades. Perhaps because the crops have been excellent over the past two years, migration seems to add only 30 to 100 percent to the natural growth of cities. As compared to elsewhere in the developing world this pressure is not extraordinary.

The city-city exchanges equalize the destiny of cities. Thus, in Bombay, the Calcutta region is viewed as catching up. Similarly, the climates of action and opinion of the interior cities – Bangalore, Hyderabad, Nagpur, and even Durgapur and Bhilai, the steel and heavy engineering centers, are more equivalent to those on the coast which look outward to the world. Perhaps I am influenced by the homogenization of the newspapers which in turn tend to produce comments based upon events elsewhere and this talk covers up underlying divergent trends. But I believe this equalization is because the basic investments in urbanization are governed by standards decided upon at the Centre, which is jealous to maintain uniformity.

A continuation of the present developmental path may be possible if the good weather continues. Climatologists believe, however, almost unanimously, that weather in India over the past 30 years has been exceedingly "quiet." More typical meteorological variation will induce greater stress, with the rural areas suffering more than the cities, major transfers required for foodstuffs and materials of reconstruction from one part of the country to others, and overseas help slow to become involved. Out of the chaos a new order must be forced; it could still be different in Calcutta and Madras from Bombay or Delhi, but less likely as time goes by. My guess is that the huge investment in education will make itself felt, but the new direction remains unpredictable.

India has so much inertia – which becomes momentum when it moves – that the triggers for change depend most heavily upon a single dominating force, the weather, and its impact upon food production. The art of monsoon forecasting is far behind that for earthquakes.

AHMEDABAD: ENTERPRISING EXPERIMENTS IN COMMUNITY SELF-HELP

Among the lesser metropolises of India two stand out as innovators. Madras has repeatedly shown the way to higher standards of performance in urban administration, but Ahmedabad, Mahatma Gandhi's home city and center for the cooperative movement, has exhibited a leadership in practical morality. Neither has a monopoly in the innovations for which they have gained a reputation, because interesting developments can be found by the dozens across the sub-continent, but at any given time one or more interesting projects will be found in these cities that reinforce their reputations.

Ahmedabad lies halfway between Bombay and Delhi. It is the cultural and industrial center of the state of Gujerat, and its satellite city is the political capital. Therefore Ahmedabad is directly in the path laid out by most visitors to India, and is increasingly visited by those who are interested in the future of the society. The population living in the metropolitan area is expected to approach three million at the time of the 1981 census, so it might possibly qualify as the fourth city in the nation. Except for its Indian Institute of Management, Schools of

Architecture and Planning, and miscellaneous buildings by Le Corbusier, the city is determinedly Indian in its vegetarianism, abstention from alcohol, and its appearance.

The report that follows is from the third trip to Ahmedabad.

August 1976

Advances in community organization in India are still possible. Many who lived in Chicago in the 1950s wondered whether there was anything left of the attempted transfer to India of American experience in community development, evolved from an introduction of academic social research into the art of promoting community organization. Because the Hyde Park-Kenwood program had been widely reviewed, and admired enough to be imitated in many places, the Abrahamsons, Julia and her husband, were picked by the American Friends Service Committee for their Indian action program beginning about two decades ago. After a very careful search for possible places to locate, they chose Baroda. The decisive criteria were that it was a city (perhaps with a population of 300,000 at the time), and it possessed a good-quality university without an elitist image. Moreover, it was off the trunk routes, so that their efforts would not trigger premature publicity. Then they set to work stimulating self-organization. A few stories drifted back to America, borne by a scattering of short-term participants, but concrete results were impossible to estimate. The Friends said farewell almost a decade ago, so the question was whether the effort had ignited something worthwhile – a post-Gandhian wave of collective self-help – or whether it had sunk into the quagmire of India. The pioneers hoped that the ideas, themes, methods, and especially the names would become totally Hindu, so researching the phenomenon might take more delving than my wife and I could do if this speculation of ours were to be followed through.

However, when stopping in Ahmedabad to see the Vasna project which had been brought to the attention of world professionals at HABITAT-1976, one of the people meeting us was a Dr. S.C. Jain, who was a trainee of the first ill-fated community development program in the 1950s, organized by Albert Mayer for Nehru and also a participant in the Friends Service Committee project in Baroda. Moreover, he had recently completed an evaluation, including a cost-benefit study, of a follow-up community development program based upon extensive use of professionals, volunteers, "barefoot technicians" of many kinds, and local leaders. His conclusions showed that within a few years at least 20 to 30 percent of the bottom third of households had been significantly helped and very few had been hurt by an integrated program. The cost-benefit calculation assumed a social entity that invested effort and reaped all the rewards and losses received by the participating families that could be traced to the efforts applied. The result was three rupees of welfare for each rupee expended on welfare infrastructure and research. Our social-policy planning theorists would have many qualms about the meaningfulness of the appraisal method employed, but if I adopted their most immediate criticisms, making estimates based upon my knowledge of India, the more thorough evaluation should show a considerably greater payoff than three to one. The difficulty I could see was that the supply of competent professionals would be exhausted long before a significant dent could be made in the number of poor living in India. What has been found is a more efficient procedure for utilizing talent in social welfare organization on a larger scale than case work.

The Vasna project is in many ways a great-grandchild of the Baroda experiment. A pair of architects who had extensive experience with the rehabilitation of flood victims in villages had discovered the importance of social research for getting houses built by self-help approaches. They created Ahemdabad Study Action Group (ASAG) as a multidisciplinary, multipurpose voluntary group working for the poor. They received study grants but no action money and were ready to dissolve due to frustration when the Saburmati River washed out thousands of families from among the groups they surveyed. By application of extraordinary energy, money was rounded up from a variety of sources; land was found immediately beyond the city limits of Ahmedabad and "substandard" houses were designed. By this it is meant that the houses were 248 square feet and had earthen floors. But the cost was less than Rs 3,000 ($340) apiece.

The most important feature of the project, and one that can be traced directly to the Friends' work in Baroda, followed from the recognition that of these 9,000 people about half were Moslem and half Hindu. Political scientists recognize that this is an explosive mixture, particularly in a city like Ahmedabad, which has a long history of religious riots. Thus, a whole year of negotiation was engaged in so as to discover who would share with whom a) a toilet for two families, b) a courtyard for four families, and c) a frontage for eight. It was found that people preferred to reestablish as neighborhoods some of the mixed precincts that had existed before the flood. A collection of 40 helpless families asked to be assigned sites by authorities, but were told they could get no house until they chose their neighboring relations.

Less than a year after people moved in, the Vasna project gave the appearance of an orderly life. The external features of about a quarter of the houses have been improved by the residents themselves, and a much larger share of them have been modified internally in a constructive fashion. The greatest single failure was the standard Indian stove – it consumed too much fuel for the really poor families and was replaced by a "three-stick fire" maintained inside by three half-bricks. There were, of course, hundreds of children in evidence, and only a half dozen were so poor they had no clothing. Of course, the city was slow to do its part, so that the streetlights are not on, most of the buses have not arrived, and the school has to be improvised.   But, the training programs and workshops which aim to raise income are well underway. In short, this seems to be a community that is advancing to a new and higher standard of living.

Yet it is in the midst of a crisis which threatened its usefulness as a model for further urban social development in India. The state is in turmoil politically due to its strong resistance to Delhi and the dominant New Congress party. A new Assembly is being elected and three candidates are competing strongly for votes. They argue, in different ways, that the government owes poor people a living, so they need not pay Rs 20 month to amortize the loan on their dwelling. (About 40 percent of the cost was subsidy of various kinds, including a donation from OXFAM.) About 70 percent of the residents were withholding their monthly payment, hoping that the candidate who made the most extravagant promises would get into office. If he did, Vasna would revert to a squatter settlement, and the Housing and Urban Development Corporation's loan would go into default. The story of public housing in Calcutta and elsewhere in previous years would have been repeated.

Thus is revealed a flaw in ASAG's makeup – it contained no well-trained lawyers who understand indirect methods of social development which encourage people to honor the obligations which they have undertaken. However, such lawyers were known in Ahemdabad and were sympathetic, so the defect might be rectified with dispatch. A cursory analysis suggests that the acceptance of flood relief funds with their various provisions makes the houses nontransferable (unless successor squatters move onto the river banks and are also flooded out, thus providing an eligible, but dubious, population of buyers). Thus Vasna settlers have walked into a trap: when an opportunity to improve themselves in their home villages or in the city opens up, they must reject it because they cannot sell their equity in the house. Under those circumstances there is also little incentive for the families to invest in further improvements, or even repairs.

There is hope only because ASAG is better organized and connected in Ahmedabad than the politicians. It also has continuous, well-informed contacts with the residents. It has yet to work out a strategy which uses its strengths. I could suggest how such a crisis would be met in Chinese, Korean, and other cultures, but good counsel is likely to suggest an Indian solution.

Vasna has been an example of planning from the bottom-up. Kerala has just announced its solution for similar minimal situations when planning and designing from the top-down. A prefabricated house has been designed using pillars with 3.5-centimeter slabs slid in between. Coconut fiber and bamboo matting are used as well as steel for reinforcement. The cost for the same size house, on equivalent land, would be Rs 7,000, or almost four times as much, but still cheaper than the typical expenditure in India. The advantage is speed-components can be produced in three weeks and the assembly can be completed within one day.

URBAN-SPONSORED VILLAGE DEVELOPMENT

September 1978

The new Janata government, though never unified in outlook, did manage to transmit the message from Delhi that research institutes and universities needed to become "meaningful" to rural India. So the brightest and most energetic young people are foreswearing theoretical papers; instead they are attempting to put their technical skills to work in villages. Their elders, with an eye on the budget and maneuvers in Delhi, approve the new tack being taken, while at the same time they worry about some of the consequences. Village programs competently carried forward lead in unexpected directions.

One recent example under way near Madras will suffice. The investigator, Rotanda Nath Roy, is an engineer, but he has also been trained as a health planner in the United States. He focused upon dysentery, the chief scourge of the villages. There he discovered that the preventive – boiling the water – was known, but the shortage of fuel prevented the poorest people from taking the obvious preventive step. At first it was thought that the answer was to be found in a chula with greater efficiency of combustion – 30 percent instead of 8 to 10 percent – so the extra heat could boil the water. However, the new stove design costs 30 to 50 rupees, and it requires quite a bit of change in behavior in and around the household. Therefore the rate of introduction would be slow. An alternative is to produce more wood. The best opportunities are presented by fast-growing leguminous trees (Leucaena) that grow well in virtually any kind of soil. The Forestry Department has demonstration stands in almost every district by now. Woodcutting is a man's job, while wood gathering is taken on by children and women; therefore it is possible to introduce simple management techniques. Steady yields can be obtained after four years.

A good supply of wood is not only salable in town, but will displace cow dung at home as the basis for cooking. The use of the cow dung as fertilizer should significantly increase income. Sale of the wood makes possible the purchase of the appropriate stove, adding new efficiencies. The new method of cooperation to be learned is that of tree plantation management on barren land, supplemented by new procedures for preparing firewood for delivery and domestic use. The boiling of water will add significantly to the human resources available from the same amount of food (dysentery is a major drain on nutrition) so a number of new opportunities present themselves. How shall the newly available effort best be used for generating additional welfare in that particular environment? Cottage industries? Multiple cropping? Education?

Architects focus their thinking upon house building, so in a very similar way they discover conditions standing in the way of producing a needed house and must address themselves to a series of hurdles quite a bit more complex than those undertaken by the health planner and his engineering colleagues in the foregoing instance. There the domestic capital hurdle was only about Rs 50 ($6.30), while for architects it is

Rs 3,000 which is the cost incurred after government has taken to heart the decades of sermons by economists and social planners. They preach that the "standards" should be reduced to minimal shelter and the task itself assigned to the lowest bidder.

Kirtee Shah and his colleagues in the Ahmedabad Study and Action Group (ASAG) are now demonstrating the production of permanent housing in villages by the people themselves at just about half the cost incurred by the government. Moreover, when compared side by side, the self-help houses contain features that are significant improvements, from the point of view of harijan ("untouchables") weavers and basket makers, who are otherwise employed as landless farm laborers. This achievement has required an investment of two years of organizational work, preceded by a half dozen years of experience acquired while inducing the construction of settlements for refugees displaced by floods, as at Vasna. Only now is the payoff evident.

Rather than recount the trials and struggles which enabled them to reach the present stage – the drama and the suspense involved would be sufficient to provide several soap operas with story lines for years – it is better at this time to describe the streamlined process.

Fair-minded people approved of the legislation which required: 1) the village panchayats (council of five persons) to find some land suitable for housing for the poorest people in their midst, 2) the banks to provide loans at reduced interest to people who had never before had a credit rating, and 3) the district, state, and centre to provide small subsidies from their welfare funds. In 1972, Gujarat started this program of housing the landless workers with family incomes less than Rs 200 ($27) a month, well before the rest of India. A huge amount of committee work was required, but the designations of plots was ostensibly complete by the end of 1975. But after that progress halted, although the housing was scheduled to be completed in four years. The production of houses needed to be set in motion, but no one knew how to mobilize the bureaucracy for the task. Socialist bureaucracies must engage in top-down kinds of implementation to fit their ideologies regarding welfare planning. However, the bottom-up approach of ASAG had become quite well known and respected among some office holders. Because ASAG was nonprofit, yet operating in the cooperative and private sectors, it was invited to take on 39 villages.

Yet the first village that chose progress was not on the official list. The harijans of Rajoda had applied to authorities seeking action on the houses. They were promptly referred to ASAG. The recorded list of eligibles had to be reinvestigated, and the suitability of the site reassessed, not only for Rajoda, but for all others. As expected, the lists had been packed in quite a few instances. The final lists were running about 70 percent harijans, the remainder being carpenters, potters and other lower castes, mainly in the very large villages – really towns, often with factories.

A number of internal committees were set up within the village. They had a common secretary. Each had to become informed about the possibilities. For example, the hygiene committee was shown a demonstration unit where a shared flush toilet (minimal water requirement) could replace two much cruder private privies. Their eyes were opened by a visit to a Gujarati factory making many varieties of toilets.

Finance for the house was aided by grants of Rs 650 per household and a loan of Rs 1,000 at 4 percent. The remainder (Rs 200 or more) had to be worked for in some form of sweat equity. Twenty-five-page detailed family histories had to be obtained at the early stages, after a social worker had spent two weeks or so getting acquainted with the village as a whole. Within a year, a string of houses had already been raised, and a few that still required roofs and floors.

Other villages followed these early routines. When questions were raised about ways of overcoming one hurdle or another, deputations were sent to Rajoda or its early imitators. There they would listen to an account from those who had organized themselves; settle on an appropriate design after seeing sketches and models illustrating possibilities as prepared by architects; plan an appropriate common space and the drainage pattern for the neighborhood; and develop a dependable water source with the aid of ASAG engineers. They would do all this while managing their own financial accounts.

So far the detailed surveys have been obtained by social workers in order to provide a baseline for determining welfare improvement over time. Very likely this process will have to evolve into a self-survey of a kind that will reinforce the organizing process. It will pay attention to income requirements, employment, education, and other services.

From this record the livelihood of the very poorest must be analyzed. Is there some way in which the efficiency of their efforts can be increased so as to release the time required for self-organization and construction? From the first village they will hear the story of the basket weavers who once bought their bamboo canes independently and carried them home from the supplier at the market, but have now learned to pool their resources, borrow money for the short term, buy them wholesale, and bring them in by truck. A more complicated story of income supplementation would be told by the weavers. Later villages have found still other devices. For the very poor this income supplementation is an absolute necessity – the prospect of obtaining a house is a strong incentive for changing habitual and traditional behavior. Even more important, however, is the experience with new forms of organization, inside and outside the village. The more complicated designs for handicrafts, for example, require close consultation with the Gujerat Handicraft Industries – a State Corporation that serves as middleman and marketer – and coordination of households.

At an appropriate time of the year a youth camp is to be organized. Young people are the most flexible individuals and will contribute a large share of the construction effort later. Important provisions for welfare, such as the new standards for hygiene, can be transmitted to them along with a set of expectations regarding changing tasks as houses are raised.

On the matter of preferred house design, spokesmen from the pioneer villages will warn that it is best to make up one's mind early about the kinds of crafts and home industries to be engaged in when the houses are complete. The breaking of walls already laid and rebuilding them on enlarged foundations cost months of discussion and weeks of labor. The economies possible from a nonloadbearing thin wall need to be understood.

The team from ASAG must present alternative models for houses. This will take several meetings because women sit on the fringe of the presentation and are not expected to participate publicly. There will follow a period of discussion in the home during which each husband will be coached to seek further information. At least three full evening meetings are required to gain consensus on design. The ASAG team members get back to Ahmedabad in the small hours of the morning, but they are nevertheless expected to be in the office for a planning and coordination meeting at 8 o'clock the next morning. Recently they have acquired a van — with the assistance of Dutch backers — so the task is much safer than on scooters.

The ASAG team then takes over to map out drainage, foundations, piping, roads, the quality of local materials, possible fire hazards, and the like. On all points there is a great deal of local wisdom to be drawn upon, so more village councils must be called.

In the process it is almost certain that some kind of dispute, or a gap in essential services, will be identified. In Rajoda it was the school that was the problem. The number of children vastly exceeded the numbers of rooms available, so that some teachers were forced to hold their classes on the porch or out in the open. The problem had been present for five years or more, and growing worse, but with no basis for cooperative effort nothing was done. In a town called Bavla, the hidden private interests of the secretary of the cooperative obtruded. The director sensed the true intention behind putting the edge of settlement in the drainage path of a national highway, because of an interest in getting sites for a few shops. A private confrontation resulted and the man was shamed into putting public duties first. The discovery of a law requiring a 100-yard right-of-way for a national highway kept him from reneging at a later date. So Bavla is on schedule and progressing with even fewer hitches. At the councils, the cooperative participation of the harijans increases greatly. Even the prospect of houses, and an accumulation of experience at achieving consensus, gives the lowest status members of the community a stronger voice. Moreover, new leaders are found and young people often become spokesmen. These matters are rarely talked about locally because they are accepted by the local power structure, but they are quickly noted by visiting delegations.

The recommended organization of the work is to rotate the jobs, including those of management, in whatever way seems possible. That way each family should become technically competent to repair its own houses, and it would even learn how to keep a bank account.

The genius of ASAG shows up in the handling of the allocation of the sites to families. If a neighborhood is grouped around a central shaded plaza, some orientations will be preferred over others. Who should get the preferred sites? In most self-help communities, the inequities are resolved by lottery. Fate and chance are a part of the way of life of very poor people. In Rajoda itself, however, the cooperators were told that they had come so far by the dint of their joint efforts, could they not resolve a simple allocation problem on other criteria than to place it upon the laps of the gods? The basis for consensus that subsequently is found becomes a new precedent for managing later collective effort.

Moving in must, of necessity, be a big occasion. The village must show off to public officials and their neighbors what they have achieved. But it should be used to achieve some other desired ends as well. This pace-making village has had trouble getting the state to improve the country road connecting it with the highway. So the harijan deputation threatens to get ASAG to invite the prime minister. The road would then be hastily improved, they believe. State officials privately admit that ploys of this kind are likely to succeed in the long run. (Letters received later describe the eventful political history of the first dedication. In outline it came out as forecast here.)

Keeping the Chain Reaction Going

A visitor notes that Rajoda is "cattle rich." To an agricultural technician this means that veterinarian services would be appreciated. The returns are immediate. Certified insemination would add another 50 percent to the output from the cattle, but it requires cooperation and sophistication. Well-organized villages can do it.

The firewood option is already under way. Barren land is readily available. The Forestry Department has planted thousands of trees along the highway for the demonstration effect, so anyone can observe on his way to work in the fields or to the market which species appear more promising in what soils. If an arrangement can be made to establish and maintain a plantation, as well as distributing the output, the Forestry Department would be able to provide seedlings. Moreover, a new house probably deserves one of the more efficient stoves that also boil the water. Rajoda has two trees for every house and several hundred more in the gochar (commons).

Family planning must come in at about this stage. After all, it will be difficult to add new rooms to the existing school. Very likely a few families have already very privately arranged for sterilizations, but now the shortage of field work suggests that birth control is a village issue.

Family planning is a political issue, and divisive in its implications, but a series of prior achievements may give local leaders and urban professionals confidence that it can be faced collectively. India has now merged family planning into Family Welfare Administration to remove the taint of earlier authoritarian excesses.

In the near future, the village will have an opportunity to obtain battery-powered solid-state television. Gujarat is leading the way. The Lok Sabha (Parliament) is passing a law which will unfetter the broadcasting service, allowing it to be completely free in presenting programs, with the challenge to become as interesting as the BBC. Should a television be placed in a shrine in the middle of the plaza? That debate may either have an instant solution or it may rage for years. The Indian communications satellite is due to return in a year, and India will be mass-producing its own battery-powered solid-state television sets, so the village need not wait for electrification. Regardless of the predilections of the community organizers regarding the value of television, the issue cannot be postponed very long.

Meanwhile, the engineers and social workers find a number of villages on the assigned list and others as well are ready to go. Already they are working in eight. In favorable locations the average cost per unit might be shaved a notch. Only in the past few weeks have they become confident that they could meet the targets originally set. The ideas affecting cooperative house building are beginning to diffuse through the territory without extraordinary effort originating from Ahmedabad.

Soon the leading villages will tire of telling their story to the curious neighbors. Their own progress will also be visibly slowed. Simultaneously ASAG will be swamped. It will have to develop the role of "barefoot community organizer." A few of those who are involved in the whole process are already hired part time for Rs 100 a month. Some of them may acquire the knack of identifying the sources of organizational difficulty and using one's own personality and commitment to overcome them. A "barefoot" organizer would parallel the paramedics already selected and trained. From among the harijans in the first community there seem to be three that have the potential.

The pressure is felt from the outside world that some of the more romantic forms of appropriate technology should be introduced. What about windmills for pumping water off the fields during the wettest periods and onto them during the drought? And the challenge of biogas – could it become a device for learning how to become a community? All the technologies mentioned previously are indubitably "appropriate," but a few are considered more appropriate than others in the eyes of the outsiders lending their capital and prestige. The very poor must obtain capital and employment opportunity wherever it can be found. Such experiments must be tried.

From multivillage and multiprogram contacts the barefoot doctors and the village-developed community organizers develop a diversity of friends and acquaintances. Sufficient popularity could be generated for at least one or two of them to become a member of the Legislative Assembly. Success in community organization requires charisma, and ASAG must seek out and train the people that have it. Kirtee Shah's capacities are extraordinary but they cannot be stretched over all these villages and a half dozen other major tasks as well. Kirtee himself has no political ambitions, but those who learn to promote the development process might find the career of politician a natural outlet for the charisma with which they are endowed.

A number of other consequences of igniting such a chain reaction can be foreseen. Regional development potentials are already recognized, and the health, educational, transport, and leadership training programs are moving in that direction – even though one whole district has not yet been touched.

The limitations on time and personnel are only one of the reasons the furthest taluka (large township) has not been reached for action. Everyone thinks that the failings of India will be compounded there. All the infrastructure exists on paper and in promises, but not in reality. Inspections from the state capital (Gandhinagar) have almost always been skipped or faked. Thus all the problems that are encountered within range of Ahmedabad will be compounded. The real heroics in the drama of development will be played out there. My prosaic report cannot do justice to the tensions and responses that have already been encountered, but even those pale before what lies ahead.

One of the future problems can also be introduced. Within a few years it will be noted that a sizable fraction of the villages are impervious to this formula, which is based on the desire for housing as a driving force. The social workers will need to study the situation carefully. Are there more projects which must precede housing? What are the sources of recalcitrance? It will be noted that a major movement of village development that swept through central China in the 1920s and 1930s, stimulated by James K. Yen (who is still alive and active in the Philippines), did not depend heavily upon housing as a stimulator for development. Rural development formulae in Bangla Desh and Indonesia should also be reviewed, because house building has lower priority in those cultures.

Report from Ahmedabad

January 1979

The reference to "soap opera cliff-hangers" made above seems to be an understatement. Berkeley students working with ASAG have been corresponding with me.

The Vasna Project, now fully completed, erupted in scandal. As a community of very poor people, some of them naturally resort to illegitimate activities, such as bootlegging and goonda-type "enforcing." Corrupt civil servants, noting that families scheduled to move into the remaining houses had little power or influence, combined forces with the dadas (gangster leaders) and the goondas to sell "rights" to these houses at up to Rs 1,000 apiece, with the occupants' security to reside guaranteed by the gangs. This last addition was 90 percent Muslim, and other Hindu residents had been pressured to leave who were also replaced by Muslims. This integrated mixed community was "tipping," a normal course of events elsewhere in the world.

The ASAG board fought back by denouncing the civil servants involved. The inquiry lasted for more than a year, lapsed, was revived by ASAG action, and the details gradually leaked to the newspapers. The defendants counterattacked and denounced the director, Kirtee

Shah, since he signed the project manager's reports, leading to his arrest. He was due to go to Indonesia for a conference in three days, so his passport was confiscated. A rich friend went bail for Rs 10,000, so Kirtee took off anyway, postponing the legal action for a month or so.

Meanwhile trouble erupted in the field. The son of the new leader among harijans of Rajoda was beaten. Rumor has it that the village leader (sarpanch) wished to restore the political equilibrium that existed before the houses were built. Still more surprising, none of the 40 completed houses has been occupied. That prevents recycling of funds needed to meet the payroll.

The Bank of Baroda was stalling on its payments. The district was Rs 50,000 behind. The 17 employees of ASAG were overcommitted. Most are young professionals getting their first experience, which qualifies them for secure jobs in the bureaucracies, so their record-keeping is poor and their tenure is uncertain. Therefore, in December the ASAG trustees stopped further construction until 50 percent of the houses were occupied.

Yet everyone in Ahmedabad involved in public service feels sure that ASAG will "overcome" (in its civil rights movement meaning) and learn how to take on larger tasks. That kind of optimism is rare in a country known for its cynics. How instructive Indian television could be if it were allowed to tell true stories of urban involvement in village development.

7 Katmandu and its Backcountry*

I went to Nepal to take a holiday from intensive urban studies; my wife and I intended to trek in the high country as far from cities as possible. Yet it was in the back areas that I found, quite unexpectedly, the clues to an efficient strategy that might be utilized by the Nepali elite in Katmandu.

This visit coincided with that of a United Nations panel on erosion whose overall analysis enhances an understanding of the magnitude of the problems present, but offers few levers of a kind that can be employed by those who must continuously cope with the conditions of the environment. Enhanced erosion is a consequence of city building and the provision of food and fuel for urban markets; it is a product of socioeconomic pressure upon the land and a cause of enhanced stress in the future. The society seems to be locked into a vicious circle.(33) Nevertheless the successes of a modernizer, applied anthropologist Jiro Kawakita, added to my own observations, illustrate a constructive approach to finding a future for Nepal's many millions in their homeland. While trekking through the back country I discovered keys to the future of Katmandu.

NEPAL'S WAY OUT OF MEDIEVALISM

In an underdeveloped country a road acts as a strong modernizing stimulus; it is the cutting edge of urban influence. In Trisuli, and later in Sundarijal, we could see the special effects that even minimal roads introduced into subtropical mountainous territory. Already at the end of

*Estimated 1985 population – 700,000.

158

the line the trucks and buses that collapsed in the effort of building or in subsequent load carrying had begun to accumulate. Bicycles, which allow the city-bred man to get around on the valley floor or the plateau for a few miles beyond the road, but seldom further, appear on the scene. The horse, once used as a means of governing and managing the realm, has been displaced by airplane – even short takeoff and landing (STOL), temporarily – and helicopter, so very few remain. Police stations in outlying parts of the country are in daily communication with Katmandu by military telex systems, therefore the need for couriers has also been greatly reduced. This progress leaves almost ten million people in the countryside with no other means of transport than their bare feet and a headstrap.

All transitions are quite sharp. The metropolitan core of Katmandu contains not only the international airport and the several first-class hotels, but a bus system, and a variety of trucks and delivery vans. Most cars are yellow-topped Datsun taxis. Scooter-cabs work around the fringes, while perhaps a thousand cycle rickshaws and a few hundred handcarts busy themselves around the center, with some large Indian-made bicycles weaving in between. Yet even Katmandu has tens of thousands of people plodding in every morning with produce, wood, and rice – 30 to 50 kilograms at a time – on their backs. About a third of the Katmandu residents continue to live as villagers with their cattle, their gardens, and their traditional means of transport. Beyond the few roads leading into Katmandu, the pedestrian system of transport is an intrinsic part of the traditional life-style. The oxcart is a means of transportation existing close to the Indian border, but nowhere else. Donkeys appear not to be known here, although some are reported in the eastern parts of the country.

Wherever any soil is present, the mountainsides are terraced up to about 8,000 feet. The lower areas produce paddy rice, sugar, and legumes with some bananas and root crops, the intermediate areas maize and millet, and the upper areas potatoes, wheat, some apples, and grass for livestock. The surplus must be brought down by packing it on someone's back, trading it for such present-day necessities as cooking oil, kerosene, paraffin candles, coarse salt, tea, sugar, biscuits, cigarettes, matches, cooking utensils, ironware, and cloth, and then packing this reduced load back to the village or local market.

On a normal day a trail leading away from the road will be used by many hundreds of load carriers whose sole occupation, for that day at least, is the transport of goods. During periods of good weather this number increases several times. An even larger numer of people use the trail as a pedestrian thoroughfare. Once or twice a day one sees a "caravan," a group of 5 to 20 people, including coolies, who are transporting all their earthly goods, much of them accumulated from having "worked in India." At other times it may be a party conducting a sick person to the hospital.

The trails themselves are maintained by local villages, and are in quite good repair where the population is dense. Elsewhere washouts, erosion, and cattle movements have reduced them to fair passibility.

Most outsiders would regard the transport system at equilibrium with the subsistence agriculture that is practiced, but a look at the family size — the survivors of bad water, no dental service, and little epidemic control — suggests a 2 percent growth rate. Moreover drought in the West has brought many thousands of destitute families into the Terai, a lowland that has some jungle forest remaining, and into the central plateau. The idiosyncrasies of weather combined with construction project opportunities bring about quite large interchanges of population in the rural areas. The net effect of both growth and migration is intensification of land use. The yield per unit area can be increased if extra investments are made and new inputs brought up from the road. The division of labor and allocation of extra produce are handled in an equalitarian rather than a caste-based manner.

A new kind of benefit-cost calculation must be fitted to Nepali transport. The extra energy cost expended by labor for portage is about 1,000 calories per man per 25-kilometer day when carrying out 40 kilograms and the laborer demands rice as his fuel. Allowing for the backhaul at 30 percent of the prime cargo, one gets an energy cost per ton-kilometer of cargo moved of about 1,500 calories above and beyond human maintenance cost (about 400 grams of rice). Our Land Rover could match that performance if it carried 1.5 tons, a load that exceeds the recommended duty level, but the calories would be supplied by petrol at four rupees per liter. Even at that price ($1.35 per gallon) a rupee's worth of petrol contains three times the energy that a rupee would buy in the form of rice. Therefore the substitution of petrol energy for rice energy will allow further intensification of development.

Actually the best solution is to introduce as many examples of efficient levers and flow-regulators as possible at the points where physical work by humans must be done — hand pumps, barrows, pulleys, treadles, better implements and tools, valves, pipe, etc. Many of these pieces of equipment are already known, but not used because of the inconvenience or cost of delivery. Then, at crucial stages, where one Calorie of hydrocarbon fuel will save several of food, powered equipment should be introduced. The transport choices must parallel those that enhance the amount of food produced on the soils available, always trying to achieve an energy profit by the modification. Any improvement in the level of living beyond subsistence (which means allocating less time to physical productive effort and more to services such as education, health measures, family planning, and community organization) will depend upon achieving substantial energy profits of this kind.

The logic of arriving at a design solution takes too long to defend. I will jump to the description of a development by stages, starting from a mere expansion of techniques already employed and progressing to those that allow a tenfold increase in freight and passenger movement with no more than a doubling of manpower, covering the same terrain but with land trebling its yield.

1. Use all the means presently known to enhance movement on the trails — erosion control, prompt maintenance, small bridges, staging

services at rest points, ropeways, blasting out shortcuts from rock faces, short tunnels, reduced maximum grades, etc. Although this would cut the cost of most transport by only 10 to 20 percent, it would make possible the gang transport of heavier items, ranging up to a ton per item. Thus small sawmills, grinding units, hydroelectric equipment, pumps, steel beams, and similar equipment could go up the trail even during the monsoon season. The energy-expensive helicopter alternative for direct delivery is then less needed.

2. Along the main trails set up a smooth half meter-wide track, without steps, for express service via a light motorcycle, such as a cross-country Honda or a scooter, depending on the territory. This could also be used for freight-carrying bicycles, so that a man could double or treble his cargo capacity, even if he spent most of his time walking alongside rather than pedaling.

3. Improve many of these routes for Land Rover and minibus service as the traffic increases. The introduction of a greater range of human services to towns and villages — schools, clinics, and community facilities — requires much more passenger movement by both clients and administrators. Inevitably the increased population will settle along the improved paths, thus adding many short-range trips to their normal traffic, and requiring even further development of the road, such as widening, fencing, and surfacing.

4. Weatherproof the roads for bus and truck traffic. They should be kept separate from the scooter, bicycle, and pedestrian flows that connect all major market towns. Personal transport can be provided by introducing for-rent or for-hire services. The inns and teahouses should be graded according to the level of services they aspire to provide, and the list made available to the touring public. This last stage is relatively capital intensive and may require the collection of tolls at bridges and other key points, but it might then also be financed by the World Bank.

The proposed program sounds quite prosaic and unexciting. None of the romance of funicula or (VSTOL) (Very Short Takeoff or Landing Aircraft) and very few headlining "firsts" to go along with the biggest mountains of the world. It deemphasizes the place of automobiles in favor of a labor-intensive community-oriented process of development coordinated from the capital of the country by the host of new technicians and graduates being produced through expanded tertiary education. It ignores the politically potent Americanophile automobile-oriented group that has survived the energy crisis. Although reasonable in approach, it may not be able to attract the organizing genius that is needed for its implementation. Perhaps, in addition, it should be given its own telecommunications system, independent of the police, allowing it to give daily reports on road conditions and prospects, similar to meteorological forecasts. That kind of publicity might generate the support to keep the program going. With microwave-relay and satellite communications channels going at cut-rate prices, this technique is not too expensive.

Making a Livelihood

Evidence of recent agricultural improvement was everywhere. The cheese factory was making a Swiss-type cheese, with a bureaucratic definition of a cooperative and an oversimplified price structure, in facilities of European design. Apple trees were recently planted in the sunny portions of the potato patch, perhaps the second generation of imported stock. The rooster was of breeding stock that produced 15-rupee chickens instead of the typical five. The bull was from India, of a strain that has now been thoroughly interbred with Texan Santa Gertrudis. The Tibetan refugees cultivated the yaks, the most valuable animal on the hoof, excepting some horses. The vegetable seeds – cauliflower, cabbage, kale, beans, turnips, and others – came from England and America. Six years ago, it is said, they were not known in this region. The maize that hung from the rafters was a variety that had come from America from the days before the hybrids were developed; it contained a few kernels that were throwbacks to multi-colored Indian corn. The best ears of corn were being held for seed time very soon.

Foreign aid was already having an effect in the up-country by adding to the range of possibilities. It did not significantly change the way of life, but made it possible for more people to live on the land as they learned how to optimize. Trees are felled, land cleared, terraces built, huts away from the village transformed into houses, and other huts put up closer to the new plots. More animals are ranged in a territory where desperate mountaineers had once tried to grow some wheat, but must have failed to recover their seed half the time.

This is one of the frontiers being pushed at the expense of the forest. Another, already mentioned, is in the lowland. Elsewhere, as water comes under control – in the Helembu area, among others – terraces once assigned to maize and millet are converted to rice. Insect infestations follow upon this conversion, and so there are calls to Katmandu for advice. Now the knowledgeable advice is there, so that peasants are less fatalistic.

The forest that remains has been saved until now by the crudity of the tools – short axes, adzes, and heavy knives, but very few handsaws, no chain pulleys, no oxen, and obviously no bulldozers. Much of the wood is split off from the trunk in slabs two to four inches thick and two to four feet long, as wide as the trunk itself. Pieces with the best grain go into woodworking (window frames, etc.), the next best into shingles, and the knottiest into kindling for cooking. The children collect the chips. In that manner a log is reduced on site to a size a single man can transport on his back. To create a beam takes a small gang, which means cooperation between families, or entrepreneurial coordination of a kind not common on a frontier.

Potential Settlement Arrangements

Nepali planners are already alert to an incipient crisis, which starts from energy sources, but involves traditional building methods, and changes even the housekeeping and city-building patterns. The charcoal for both village and city comes from wood and the wood is disappearing at an accelerating rate. Government services in the back country require brick buildings (near the road) and corrugated iron roofs. The roof tile for lowland houses comes from rice straw, which is at least as efficient energywise as using the straw for thatch, and recognizably safer. Quarried stone requires trucks and roads for its transport, so it can be fitted to only a fraction of the needs for pukka buildings. The expanding population is working against a declining supply of fuel and building materials.

Cement prices are almost unutterable; like fertilizer, it may come all the way from Japan. Lime requires wood, but less of it. Aluminum sheet, even when backpacked, may soon be the cheapest roofing available. The demand for urban construction and the various local manufactures, mostly metal working and food processing, pushes the price of fuel in towns and cities, and along most roads, sky high.

Domestic use of the wood is not very efficient. Neither a formed clay stove, or an iron ring in an open hearth, both without chimneys, utilizes much of the heat. There are no hibachi in Nepal. Wood smoke hovers under the low ceilings, and the accumulated tar on rafters and mats glistens blackly in the candlelight. Any attempts to change provisions for cooking get at the very foundations of family organization and division of duties. Less fuel wood means more cold meals, less boiled water, and less family participation as well as more discomfort in winter and a greater need for clothes and blankets.

Add to this a closer cutting of brush for faggots, enhanced erosion, and loss of productive terraces. Maintenance work on roads and trails increases. Just to stay even takes rapidly increasing organization and effort, yet Nepali are still poorer and less educated than the average Indian or Pakistani, so there is very little margin separating them from repeated famine. The stress will increase.

Nepal badly needs an oil strike, but geologists hold out little hope. The geophysical history of the area did not provide convenient swamps during the carboniferous era that allowed the deposits to accumulate. Nuclear energy is no help, because the total demand for power in its largest grid is far too small to be economic.

The major potential source of energy is hydroelectric; the major source of foreign exchange and accumulated capital is tourism. Somehow these two assets must be fitted into a reformulated settlement pattern that is more energy efficient for the kinds of energy that can be made available. Have the technologies been invested elsewhere in the world which, when fitted together and adapted to local circumstances, would enable the Nepali to escape from these vicious circles?

One idea comes from the rice-eating societies of Japan and Taiwan of more than two decades ago — the electric rice cooker. Until now, even in Trisuli, more than 90 percent of the dwellings remain unconnected to the power line. Perhaps a teahouse or shop can be persuaded to cook people's rice for them for a fee less than the cost of wood. (There are considerable economies of scale here, even before assuming electrical energy to be more inexpensive than the portion in the wood that is applied to the boiling of water.) People with houses along the trail or road could then pick up their hot rice just before meal time. The solution is not automatically acceptable, but certainly a rice cooker can be modified to produce the proper stickiness. After that the acquisitive property-oriented families may see merit in purchasing one of their own along with a hot plate for cooking dal, and making tea. Then it will be noted that the cost of a light is no greater than that of a candle or a kerosene lamp, and allows the school-age son to study at night. Such reinforcing incentives might accelerate the rural electrification program presently stalled by the inmate conservatism of the rural people. This is likely to work only in those places where the wood supply must be purchased and is no longer dependent upon vigilant foraging.

Another wood substitute must be found in roofing and building materials. Aluminum has been mentioned, but any ingots reduced in Nepal with hydroelectric power would require imported alumina (or caustic soda, if a proper bauxite or clay was found), and would need to be sent out of Nepal for rolling. Transport costs involved suggest no reduction from present prices based upon imports.

Similarly bricks have a heavy transport cost (liquid fuel is involved here) before they are put into place. Electric firing of clay for brick making is feasible, but generally can be justified only for highest quality construction — luxury level rather than mass-produced pucca. Cement and reinforcing rods, despite the recent rise in price, have already displaced wooden beams in areas served by road, and should continue to do so in the future.

An intensive search for novel possibilities reveals one now being introduced through tourism. Polyurethane foam, first in its flexible form and later in its rigid structural formulation, is being adopted by the mountaineering equipment industry for many purposes. In cold areas its superlative insulating qualities save body heat to an extent that fires are often unnecessary. For cushions the material surpasses rugs, mats, or blankets. For roofing, a sandwich panel can be made that resembles the traditional housing but protects from thermal extremes much better. For walls a similar material requires less expensive framing than wattle and daub, or stones and mud. More important of all — for either mountaineering or ordinary human transport — the weight per unit of structure is only 5 to 10 percent of the materials for which it substitutes. Of course other foam materials can also compete, but none comes so close to being a general-purpose material. The ultimate raw materials are such that no further price rises of the bulk are expected, while competing traditional materials may double or treble. There are quite large economies of scale inherent in production and fabrication. Panels can be tied down in the old-fashioned manner of construction, nailed down in the international manner, or held by adhesives according to aerospace techniques.

The principal difficulty is that the working of this material is known to only a handful of Katmandu artisans. The task is to make it familiar. Cooperation is needed among urban artisans, the university scientists and designers, and the highly sophisticated Himalayan supply organizations with connections in Germany (which originated the product), the United States (which elaborated the applications to construction in the past few years), and Japan (where the material has been ingeniously orientalized and incorporated into special performance equipment).

After noting how rural people prefer to live, when they have a choice, and how they adapt to city ways, one strategy stands out. Bamboo grows mostly below 4,000 feet, but the mats have been carried up to Gosainkund and beyond for temporary shelter. I would waterproof and insulate the shelter by using thinner, more flexible mats with a centimeter of flexible foam as sandwich filler. For roofing on existing walls I would make a rigid sandwich with woven bamboo on the inner side and thin aluminum sheet on the outer side, with 3 to 5 centimeters of solidified foam in between. Walls might be the same, but with paper inside and jute outside. The natural color of jute would hardly differ in its appearance from a mud-covered house, while the interior paper surface invites printing and embossed figuring, so that designers and artists could have a great time inventing stylish murals, all at a cost much less than of the carved windows and panels found in Sherpa and Tamang country.

But even with economy and esthetic interest, I doubt that these innovations would sell rapidly enough to evade the crisis that is foreseen. Government intervention is also necessary. Already one can note that the strongest – and most unimaginative – deviations from traditional building are found in government structures for police, post offices, schools, cooperatives, clinics, power plants, and official residences. Government agencies can design standard, portable structures to be assembled on the sites where extra human services are to be added. Most developing countries have evolved a standard structures approach to the expansion of services. Local people then learn how to use the materials, and have the option of fitting them to their own needs.

But government needs to go further. It must experiment with new settlement patterns for the expansion of cities, towns and villages that combine the economies of light transport, electrification, and light construction. Some kind of civic order should evolve that can be varied according to altitude, culture, and relative wealth. Fortunately, it does not have to be achieved immediately, but should be improved upon project by project over the period of one to two decades.

Nepal is much, much more complex than can be comprehended from a 16-day stay, with 12 days on foot in the country. We contacted only a minor fraction of the cultural variety that is present. But the dilemmas of energy conservation appear to be universal, so that partial solutions identified in this small region should have equivalents elsewhere. There seems to be an interesting future here that propels Nepal in the direction of a much more variegated mountain state than Switzerland,

and in three or four generations, perhaps, it could be as prosperous. But the population growth would have to be brought under control long before then, because intensification and diversification have their limits. Energy problem solving is much simpler than social problem solving. The latter requires a totally different kind of reconnaissance.

POSTSCRIPT FROM TOKYO

Delayed by the same extended monsoon, was a project that confirmed and extended the insights about development reported upon here. Indeed, had the weather been better, we might have trekked in along with the head-carried loads of polyvinylchloride pipe and cable that Professor Kawakita, anthropologist from the Tokyo Institute of Technology, had flown in for a trial in Sikha Valley on the flanks of Annapurna.(34)

The Sikha Valley ranges from 1,100 to 4,800 meters in altitude, and the villages are located at the upper limit of rice cultivation – 1800 to 2200 meters. As elsewhere, the population – now 300 households, or perhaps 1,800 people – has outstripped the resources accessible with presently known technology. The acquisition of fuel and hay from the upper mountain requires a huge amount of effort; at the same time there is often insufficient water for the terraces growing paddy rice. Kawakita had been there earlier studying upland rice culture, and had concluded that the lack of transport was a major source of poverty, and that transport offered an appropriate means for intervening.

His solution for this valley was 1) ropeways, 2) pipelines, and 3) a special kind of hydraulic (nonelectrical) pump that would push water uphill 400 feet. It appeared that the people would be able to understand these technologies and use them. They made some trial runs between 1971 and 1974, working out such details as foundations built out of the rock rather than depending upon imported concrete. Then eight tons of fabricated materials were flown into Pokhara, and 5,000 man/days of village labor moved it to the installation sites; at least an equal amount of time was spent in planning meetings and in the actual installation of the equipment.

The polyvinylchloride pipelines were accepted as soon as they were demonstrated. The news spread rapidly and a number of other villages had installed them even before the Japanese project came to fruition in 1975. The ropeways of Japanese scale was not used, because its labor-saving usefulness was negligible in the much larger mountains of Nepal. When appropriate sizes were introduced in 1975 it became evident that cableways could pay for themselves 15 times within the first year of operation. However, Kawakita was counting only the villagers' investment plus the actual cost of the equipment. The value of the Japanese time and attention must have been at least ten times that of the cost assigned (their airfares alone were probably twice). Even so, this must be gauged a successful project and it led to many changes.

These villagers were Magans, who were originally forest people. They were using the extra time saved to range further around the mountain, thereby reducing overcutting and overgrazing along with the attendant erosion. They also invested more time in household industries and spent extra days in school. The Japanese professor thought that the next development should be a hydroelectric plant, but the villagers' choice went in another, equally logical direction. They wanted to create a university that would attract more professors like Kawakita. With thousands of college-educated trekkers in the vicinity each year and their number rapidly growing, their vision of a mountain college is not at all absurd.

Kawakita's approach is to allow natural cultural expression with a few crucial new tools. He recognizes the need for continuity, but does not realize that the enhanced education will lead to urbanization. My suggestions attempted to span that phase of the development and solve initial problems as well.

8 Jakarta*

How does one portray the special problems that the low-income metropolis presents to the architect-designer? Ordinary people cannot afford his services, because they must take whatever spaces and structures that are left after the rich and powerful have made their choices, and the poor build their dwelling out of whatever materials come to hand. Yet they respond to the public images that are created or selected by architect-designers for the main thoroughfares.

Jakarta revealed a unique chance to bring together and pinpoint what I had learned about its total system in the course of a stay of less than eight weeks, much of which was spent out of the city gaining environmental perspective. I found a situation where the highest skills of a designer could significantly advance national progress.

These assessments of the cultural and economic imperatives were transmitted to stay-at-home architects in America. They were not impressed. Words are not enough for them; slide-produced images and personal contacts are needed to sense the reality. However all who knew Indonesia could appreciate the importance of creating a setting that merged East with West constructively. Institutions like the Wisma Indra offer an unobtrusive gateway for the entry of complicated concepts that would otherwise be inadvertently excluded.

Many of the ideas significant for Indonesia take the form of appropriate technology. Grinding poverty is generally observed in Jakarta, but the resources available to the government are insufficient as yet to reduce very much of it, therefore many hopes ride on the bootstrap-

---

*Estimated 1985 population – 8 million.

ping capabilities of the kampong improvement program observed in a number of locales.

BUILDING AN INDONESIAN ENTERPRISE

March 1974

From the time of the Dutch before World War II up to the present, one repeated comment heard about the Indonesians is their almost universal retreat from the marketplace and their unwillingness to concentrate upon the management aspects of production, combined with their preference for a variety of social contests other than those calculated to promote complex organization. Statistically this shows up in a higher-than-normal rate of bankruptcies among Indonesian-owned and-managed enterprises, and a low-level participation in the management of manufacturing and medium-scale services. This was more true of the Balinese and the Javanese majority than of the Bataks and the Meningkebau populations from Sumatra; but in the home territory of these Sumatran ethnic groups, one hears much the same sort of self-criticism. Yet, as one might expect, there are quite a large number of exceptions. These successes can be much more illuminating for what they tell us than a recounting of mistakes and instances of failure, because the analysis of a success is likely to reveal the minimum prerequisite conditions for survival and growth; it allows one to identify the innovations needed to overcome a common cultural characteristic.

In the successful Indonesian enterprise one expects to find all the familiar functions, supplemented perhaps by some unusual features that enhance trust among the principal figures and reduce the risk of catastrophic loss. These features may take the form of unexpected decision rules, a restructuring of job definitions, a different approach to record keeping, a novel technique of marketing, or something else unspecifiable in advance. Such an enterprise is best studied if it provides a product or a service familiar to the rest of the world, describable in English, and very public in its operations. (The Americans would say that it operates in a fish bowl.) These reasons suggest a private hotel with a clientele drawn heavily from professionals working for the United Nations and similar international organizations (the Population Council, Ford Foundation, Japanese Export Promotion, etc.) as a good candidate for a case study.

Institution and Environment

The Hotel Wisma Indra (its real name) is located on a moderately busy street on the periphery of the "uptown" area of Jakarta. It has fewer than 30 rooms, and charges upper-middle standard rates that vary only a little in price from its competition in central Jakarta. Yet, while the other hotels in its class run 20 to 50 percent occupancy, with short periods in which they approach capacity, the Wisma Indra usually has a waiting list; some potential clients are deterred by the fact that a wait of a month or more may be required before they become eligible. Everyone in the hotel business knows that a continually full house at standard rates without any special commitments to advertising and promotion should be a highly profitable enterprise. Among a sample of a hundred hotels only two or three will come close to achieving this level of popularity.

The name itself requires explanation; it is too Indonesian to be readily understood by its largely English-speaking clientele. The word wisma means house, and in the context of hotel it means "guest house." Indra is a moderately common Javanese given name for a boy; in this case the enterprise was named after the first grandson of the founding Jamin family. Indonesians pay a great deal of attention to luck; therefore, the occasion for one lucky event, such as a male first born, should be linked so as to bring luck to a series of future events. The naming ceremony is an obvious transfer technique.

The street it is on, the Jalan Wahid Hasyim, is named after a revolutionary war hero. The road was built to serve the villas in late Dutch times; most of them had a front garden made up of ornamental shrubs according to the taste of the vrouw of the house. The original plots had a frontage of 25 meters and a depth that ranged up to 80 meters, as for the eventual location of the Wisma Indra. Deep ditches on both sides of the road served as canals, sewers, and storm drains simultaneously. Two or three of the houses with tile roofs and iron spiked fences still remain family residences, but most have been converted into enterprises that range from consulting firms to an ice cream factory, motorcycle repair shop, and a middle-class brothel. There is a sidewalk on the other side of the road, but the south side is due to have a water main laid – a task designed as a make-work project and therefore slow to progress. A telephone cable-laying project follows behind. Perhaps by 1975 it will be possible to build the sidewalk and cover the open sewer that now accommodates ten times the population for which it was designed. A great deal of attention must be paid to this feature because about four times a decade the houses are flooded on the Wisma Indra side and even more often on the other side where clogging due to litter is quite common. The nuisance of having to walk through diluted sewage, not to mention cleaning it up, is responsible for some of the maintenance of the front that would otherwise be inexplicable.

On the west of the Wisma Indra is one of the old villas, hidden behind ornamentals, its entrance obscured by a young clump of bamboo. To the east is an empty plot bearing the skeleton of a house that was indubitably Dutch. Now a side has been sliced off to allow a sleek new house to be built in villa style – a doctor's residence according to the sign and to the appearance of the car parked there.

The Hotel Wisma Indra is not alone on its own plot. The family and its associates operate several other enterprises on the site. At the end of the driveway, next to the wall on the right, are P.T. Prabu Setia and

P.T. Idamanta, while on the left with its own drive is P.T. Pamukan
Jaya. (P.T. indicates a private, profit-making firm, while the names
themselves have classical references.) They do not advertise their
functions. One of their principal reasons for being here, no doubt, is
that they can share the telephone, which, at more than a million rupiah
($2,400, or the cost of a cheap house) is an extraordinarily expensive
service to possess.

The Role of the Investigator

When research has to be done inside a system, the investigator must
consider what kind of role will get him closest to a set of informative
truths. I had already played the role of paying guest, but five years of
experience probably had confirmed the staff in a series of easy answers
that satisfied guests but revealed little about the culture or the way the
enterprise worked. So it was necessary to break out of the guest
relationship when asking questions. Sometimes sociologists invent an
interest in cooking, or the life experience of an individual, or in history,
to get at the facts needed to test their hypotheses.

The problem for curious Americans, especially anthropologists, is
that they are suspected of being agents of the sinister and extraordinarily influential agency called the CIA. Only a rumor needs to
move through the society one contacts, and a freeze in personal
relations sets in. They retreat to formal politeness with trivial
questions: "When did you come to Indonesia? How long have you been
here? Have you gone to Bali? How do you like Indonesia? What do you
think of the environment?" even if they already know the answers from
previous contacts. (Since the weather is not an important variable for
living in Indonesia, the Western equivalent of the polite exchange,
discussing the change in weather, is not a common subject here.)

In this instance the honest role of the interrogator can be highly
successful. I am able to explain my questioning by referring to my
architecture students. Locals can immediately understand why I should
ask questions about appearances of an organization and the reasons for
its existence. Also architects are beyond suspicion. People in Indonesia
have developed a stereotype for architects which makes them out to be
naive, other-worldly types, interested in form and materials and knowledgeable about modern presentation techniques, but incapable of serious political involvement. Architects obviously will not become competitors of a business organization, and they are presumed to be ethical
enough not to give away embarrassing secrets. Also, quite obviously,
they need to learn about hotels, so people are open and relatively
unsuspicious as long as questions relate to public information or the
conduct of the enterprise. Indeed, they enjoy talking about these
important facets of their life; responding to questions is a very
interesting way of spending time that would otherwise be devoted to
routine. People have sympathy for benighted, confused architects who
are trying to improve their craft.

Cast of Characters

The Hotel Wisma Indra was founded by Jamin Sukardjo, from Yogyakarta, a secretary of state in a former administration — a position
that combined the duties of assistant secretary in charge of administrative affairs and those of an under-secretary in America. In that role
he had an opportunity to be a guest in many of the capitals of the world
and was able to differentiate and respective qualities of a service
afforded. Specifically he had to deal with United Nations agencies until
Indonesia temporarily withdrew. When governments change, such a post
is sensitive and will be given to someone felt to be wholly loyal to the
new regime. So Jamin Sukardjo in 1967-68 found himself out in the cold
with one career apparently ended and a need to support his family. He
then refitted the family house and put air conditioners in every room.
There is an apocryphal story that it was once occupied by one of
Sukarno's concubines, but of course Jakarta has scores of houses with a
"Sukarno-slept-here" attribution.

A staff had to be assembled, and one of the first, who is still on
hand, is Tugino who provides room service and bar service. He had come
to Jakarta from an upper village near the Borobudur ruins of ancient
Hindu temples in Central Java because he had a soldier brother working
as a guard in the president's palace, who apparently also had contacts.
A few months later his brother Miskun came to join the staff, and three
years later a nephew, Mohammed Wahid, was added. All are, or have
been, attending hotel school, and have been learning about the way a
hotel ought to be run.

Old hands from the Ministry of State who had fallen on hard times
were added more recently. First Sukarto from Purakarta, Central Java,
and then Tukumin from West Java. They handle housekeeping and food
and beverage management, respectively. They have cooks and room
boys working under them who speak little English. The front desk and
the precious telephones are handled by the family with the assistance of
an alert young man from Yogyakarta, Sumandri, who often serves as
night clerk. The telephone requires patience and bilinguality.

The gardeners are important. They keep a hundred pots blooming
and presentable, an orchid nook, and a fish pond. Flowers are almost
always available for the dinner tables. The front yard is kept trim and
spare, in the shade of a tall clump of bamboo. Far back in the shadows
are the unexpected forms of birds and nymphs or a gargoyle from Bali.
The hotel has hired a specialist to come in once a week. He is quite an
old man for Indonesia. He has one or two barefooted, youthful assistants, but final decisions on pruning are left to the old master.

Resolutions of the Management Problems

Jamin is forced to make most of the basic decisions regarding the
interface between Indonesia and the largely international clientele.
(We counted 12 foreign countries represented among the people we met,
as well as Indonesians from most of the outer islands.)

Thus, to him is attributed the emplacement of four coach lanterns with strong white candle power, and the hotel name in a logo form in neon lights at the summit of the steeply pitched orange tile roof. This was a part of a refurbishment and expansion program finished last year. There is a heavy tax by the city put upon lighting of an unlit street by an enterprise, because the kota (traditional city) people know that light brings in the customers at night. Jamin is getting favorable publicity out of the necessity to pay taxes.

Lights are not dependable in Jakarta because the power plants often break down or the distribution system becomes overloaded, causing a transformer to become overtaxed and explode. So Jamin installed a small back-up generator which provides light in the halls and a twinkling beam at the front to guide those lost in the dark street.

Part of the proper image is to keep four to ten shiny new cars parked out in front and to the side. Due to the Indonesians' use of drivers, whose duty it is to shine the car while waiting, and sometimes doing minor adjustments also, the cars remain clean and slick regardless of rain or dust. Some belong to the family and the hotel, others to guests and friends. A new car is a powerful indicator of prosperity and luck in the Indonesian society, so the proper place for a car is in front where it serves as a superior decorative substitute for flowering shrubs.

Attention is paid to the little bridges over the canal, which are flanked by built-up solid walls about half a meter high, plastered and whitewashed. They seem to suck the cars in off the road, but their purpose was to reduce the likelihood of the canal overflowing into the yard. Jamin also obtained a sump pump to transfer the collected downpour from the yard into the canal. As this is being written, a faucet has been added to the front which will allow it to be irrigated during a dry season without depending upon the increasingly polluted water from the open sewer. (The greatest danger is from lubricating oil additives washed into the canal.)

Inside the lobby are two large aquaria, both well lit, containing a colorful display of lazy tropical fish, and very interesting for people to watch while waiting for guests or for business to be transacted by companions. The lobby, dining room, and terrace furnishings show a taste for the semiformal lived-in look. The acoustics are good, although occasionally when only Indonesians are looking at television, the decibels may be allowed to intrude upon the diners around the corner. (They are almost all much less sensitive to high noise levels than Western Europeans and New Zealanders.)

This is the kind of place, more than any other in Jakarta, where the international civil servants on short-term assignment can feel at home. The start of the day, at breakfast, is a close approximation to home, and the menu allows just enough choice to have something different every day of the week. The steaks are comparatively cheap and carefully prepared.

The Wisma Indra prospers in part because several international agencies are granting all possible help to Indonesia. This means a steady stream of short-term troubleshooters and evaluators. International

Labor Office consultants are given desks in the Departmen Trans-migrasi about a hundred meters down the street. The World Health Organization and UNESCO are at the United Nations offices about 250 meters away. The Ford Foundation is about 400 meters off, and the United States Embassy, with USAID, about the same distance. There are a dozen restaurants within the last-named distance – Padang, Malang, Balinese, Madurese, and West Javan cuisines from Indonesia with Chinese, Korean, and Western as well. One of the rare department stores, a public corporation, in Jakarta is also nearby for those who do not appreciate bargaining in the pesar.

Indonesia may soon lose its priority for attention by international agencies, due to its oil prosperity. But the increase in activity should bring more scholars and private consultants whose tastes would fit the hotel. Although many large tourist hotels are opening, none appears to compete effectively for these professional guests. The demand for lodgings at the Wisma Indra seems likely to be maintained even though the clientele shifts; eventually an enlarged flow should justify the prospective expansion. The relative flexibility of the staff is due to the existence of informal organization, the use of shortcuts instead of blind routine, and to the fact that a few new people are trained each year to replace those who return to the villages or manage to connect with a still better job.

We had an opportunity to compare the Wisma Indra with a compet-ing hotel which charged 10 percent more. It had all the characteristics one expects in a developing country: service people that comprehend only a few English phrases and are thus unable to accommodate personal preferences, a gloomy dining area too dark to read a morning newspaper, mosquitoes rising from the grass in the courtyard a month after the rainy season begins, unrepaired light switches that promise an electric shock if touched in the dark the wrong way, a noisy parrot that overwhelms conversations carried out at normal voice levels, furniture that is uncomfortable for Western body sizes, and many other petty inconveniences.   The important feature of the environment of the Wisma Indra was that much of it was negotiable, the staff tried hard to help, and no rigid hierarchy or caste system, as in South Asia, got in the way.

Potentials for the Future

All that has gone before suggests that the time will be right, perhaps by the end of 1975, to consider the expansion of the Wisma Indra. How can the appeal to the internationals, this unusual face to the outside world of high-level professionalism, he maintained despite the increased dimensions? Is it possible to enhance the pulling power of the image it presents to the demanding professional, since the very first impression remains important for those considering the alternatives?

For the architect these questions imply the formulation of a design program. It must be compatible with the future international relations of Indonesia, the prospective changes in the street, and the increased density of vehicles. By 1976, for example, there will be four new buildings with three times the office space of the existing buildings, all within a tolerable 400-meter walking distance. Vehicle density would normally treble, but the capacity of intersections and traffic circles will not tolerate such an increase, so pedestrian traffic will expand and very likely the new Tokyo "executive" minibus will be adopted as a substitute for the private car with agency-provided driver.   The mounted helitjak and three-wheel bemo will be displaced by a four-wheel vehicle, not necessarily the experimental versions with bicycle wheels now being tried in central Jakarta, but more likely the zippy little Honda vans equipped to carry up to six people – Indonesians, not Westerners. There will be less patience with the traffic-blocking maneuvers now required in front of the hotel, so prime attention must be given to expediting off-street circulation and on-site parking. Given the rates of change in Jakarta the handling of vehicles in a flexible manner is a serious challenge to the designer and landscaper.   Very likely the front half, or even more, of the empty plot next door will have to be given over to vehicles.

The strikingly increased value of land should, by that time, lead to the construction of two or three floors above the vehicles. That would provide 1,600 square meters of floor space, roughly doubling the present space given over to rooms. The kitchen, now very clean and remarkably modern in appearance, will have to be expanded to accommodate three or four cooks at a time, the menu enlarged, and the bar displaced by the dining space to occupy a new focal site. Relating the bar to the color television set for resident viewing will also require some very carefully considered relationships.

The design of the furnishings is already defined in part by the exquisite Dutch colonial cupboards that Jamin has acquired and maintained in top condition. They are the antitheses of the plastic fronts and the cluttered, dust-catching native arts decor affected by competing hostelries.

Perhaps the designer will be inspired enough to recognize that the guests are highly literate. A carefully organized library, separate from the television, but suited to the service of coffee or tea, would be welcomed. Indonesians rarely read for pleasure, but an active library with current English, American and Japanese books would be a powerful attraction for the most desirable kinds of local guests. The design of such a library lies more in the titles of the books and their open presentation to the reader, supplemented perhaps by foreign newspapers, than upon the furnishings themselves.

Finally there remains the trickiest problem of all. With the installation of a sidewalk and the contribution of added overhead light to the street at night, together with a doubling or trebling of pedestrian movement, the hotel locale will attract parasites. Peddlers of magazines and sculptures will stand by the gates, art sellers will unroll and expose to view their oil paintings and flip the stiff-backed panels with gilded etchings, hoping to catch a wandering eye. The kaki-lima selling cigarettes and morsels of hot food ("snacks") will camp on the sidewalk at dusk. Youthful idlers will lean on any available support or engage in horseplay. Worse yet, when the beggars begin to show up at moments of maximum flow, the general sympathy for their plight results in attempts to escape from their sight, and therefore could cause a retreat from the Wisma Indra to more protected competitors.

The authoritarian means of dealing with the new unintended urban niches created usually leads to a uniformed gate man, resembling a military guard, who depends upon police cooperation. But that results in a sterilized section of frontage.

The most appropriate means of controlling these undesirable elements is to make a deal with the kampong within whose turf the hotel operates. In return for some jobs for its members and donations for its celebrations, the leaders will usually cooperate in keeping the approach to the hotel attractive to the clients. As new threats to the image arise, new consultations are in order. Possibly the design of the fence and landscaping in the front may be negotiated with the kampong. The population served by the narrow pathway opening into the street immediately across from the Wisma Indra is very dense and, although the income is higher than average, it suffers from great insecurity. These are the people whose sympathy and cooperation is needed over the long run. They represent the real Jakarta, not the interface with the international professionals, yet here both are bound up in the same community. The neighbors across the road are more excitable than the fatalistic poor, and therefore present a greater source of long-term risk. An expanded Wisma Indra assured of survival will need roots in the local community as well as favorable word-of-mouth reports in the international community – a fascinating implication for a hostelry.

Although Jamin had a chance to read these suggestions, he took a very different tack. He found land in a kampong on the airport side of the central business district and built a new, more spacious facility with swimming pool. Members of the family and retainers from the Wisma Indra took charge. The design depended upon the status symbols of internationalized Indonesian society, especially its upper middle class, expecting to serve families much more than solitary technical assistance specialists from elsewhere in the world. Thus he promotes another kind of mixing. In 1978 the original Wisma Indra was only slightly refurbished, but still overflowing.

HUMAN SETTLEMENTS AND NEW LIVELIHOODS

September 1976

This visit to Java was made two and a half years later. Indonesia was now at the midway point in its five-year plan. The progress in central Jakarta was evident; colored photos on postcards could make the avenues look quite modern. Twice as many modern office buildings and hotels were functioning and more were under way despite the credit squeeze caused by the failure of Pertamina, the national oil company. Many more three-wheel taxis were buzzing about the streets, several of totally new design. Because the talk in the English-speaking circles always came back to the issue of corruption in the bureaucracy, my wife Gitta and I wondered whether the common people were benefiting. Replicating a long walk through the countryside up through the forested side of a volcano to its rim assured us that they were. The evidence lay not only in the houses and village centers, but in the observation that the young trees in the replanted forest were no longer being poached for firewood.

The kampong improvement program had its origins about 15 years ago. In its present form the residents of a community, with the aid of engineers, architects, or urban planners, decide on a system of paths to be paved, drains or ditches to be lined, bridges to be built, or badminton courts to be installed. Forty percent or more of the cost of the materials is paid for by the government, the other half by subscription among the households. The labor is provided by gotong royong, a kind of indigenous cooperation that is often reduced to "being volunteered" in the military sense. Within the last five years in the new kampongs we visited, there have been substantial improvements to the houses. Woven bamboo walls have been whitewashed or replaced by brick or stucco, various kinds of windows replaced by shutters, decorative plants installed and protected from the chickens and the interiors painted. Within ten years this improvement process reached about 95 percent of all buildings, with a number of houses achieving full middle-class standards of refinement, even though water lines have yet to be installed and methods of disposing of sewage and garbage are as primitive as in the villages, although much less convenient. A few roofs are raised to allow two-story living, and partial electrification has occurred.

Other urban developments become necessary as the edges of the city grow still further beyond the developing kampong. Roads must be widened, pipelines run through, the main trunks of the storm drains dug, and official buildings sited. The displaced families must start over again nearer the growing edge, endowed this time with more capital, thus allowing better dwellings.

This is a natural way for a metropolis to grow when it serves a village-dominated society in the tropics. The residents learn as they live, accumulating resources during good times, and helping each other during hard times. The difficulty is that the face-to-face community does not foresee obstacles to development, so that further advancement is halted, since the community is unable to assemble the political influence or capital to overcome an obstacle once it is encountered. The welfare of the masses may require urban land redevelopment of many such communities only 20 to 40 years old. Sympathetic help from urban planners will not prevent all these instances of displacement and dissolution, but it can reduce the losses. That sympathy has been slow in coming, because most planners and architects found employment with the Ministry of Public Works or with the metropolitan governments and their duty was to expedite the big projects. While their number was scarce, architects and planners produced at prestige institutions had little choice, but now, we are told, there are nine teaching programs training relevant professionals, so that a more sophisticated version of kampong improvement programming is due to evolve. The exchange of ideas at international meetings between proponents of similar programs is beginning to have an effect in Java; presumably it will be seen elsewhere in the archipelago in a few years.

Evidence is at hand at the Institute of Technology, Bandung. A reorganized Regional Housing Centre of the United Nations that also serves as a Directorate of Building Research for Indonesia is undertaking the design of 1) small community sewage-disposal systems, 2) solid waste recycling systems, 3) better rain water collectors, 4) recycling of household waste water, 5) water cooperatives, 6) solar water heaters, 7) energy-conserving designs focusing on health, nutrition, and family planning, 8) land tenure and development, 9) recreation through mass media, 10) intensive gardening, 11) small animal raising, 12) solar refrigerators, 13) small-scale credit, and 14) community workshops. It is the most integrated program suited to this stage of urban development to be seen anywhere in Asia. Work has already begun, even though the promised United Nations Environment Program (UNEP) support has not yet come through. The scale of effort is quite sizable — more than a million dollars over a three-year span — so alternative approaches can be devised and compared. National programs based upon self-help using these concepts and devices can be superimposed upon the existing kampong improvement program, so the means of diffusion already exists.

One of the cooperating groups is the Development Technology Center, on the opposite side of the Institute of Technology Bandung (ITB) campus. It implements the appropriate technology and backs entrepreneurs with advice and recommendations for credit. Filino Harahap, the director, has obtained enthusiastic backing from the Dutch; while American AID money has already been allocated, he finds too many restrictive second thoughts introduced at all the various levels through which the grant money passes. Appropriate technology requires as much investment in troubleshooting and marketing as any other kind, and the Development Technology Center is concentrating upon this previously neglected interface with a growing population of users. Thus the direction they have laid out for themselves, employing a learning-by-doing — including the chance to make mistakes — method to back up an ever-increasing scale of operations, makes good sense. From this point forward the development of appropriate technology will require management rather than planning. Management skill is perhaps the scarcest resource of all in Java, so the Development Technology Center hopes to fill the gap by stimulating small entrepreneurs, and is now casting about for methods of generating competent management for cooperatives.

The management gap is painfully visible in Depok, a middle-class settlement served by a newly established suburban station on the Jakarta-Bogor rail line. The planning concepts are not bad – they come directly out of European textbooks – and the pace of implementation is a considerable improvement over the past, but the detailed considerations modern societies have come to expect are not evident. For example, a 200-meter grid was chosen for roads, sewers, water, electric power, and subsequent services such as telephone and gas, but the plot of land had uneven boundaries, so that a number of odd-shaped, difficult-to-serve parcels remain. The roads were not adjusted to fit the contours or the boundaries. Similarly, the location of the market for the community seems to have been decided upon by designer's whim rather than a careful analysis of middle-class shopping patterns in Jakarta, so it is necessary either to change the site at the last moment, thus forcing a hasty replanning of the residential area, or accept the continuing friction. This is predominantly an Indonesian-managed project, but there were Japanese land-planning inputs, so the community will have to learn to live with the Japanese style of remaking land forms from paddy fields. The finishes of the houses and the assignment of private yard space are clumsy, but fortunately the demand is so great, the most painful administrative problem is that of choosing which families will gain the opportunity to occupy these terrace apartments. At least the Depok managers were successful in obtaining electric power – no mean task since the new Hilton is still waiting, six months after completion.

Radinal Mochtar, director of PERUMNAS (the national housing agency), is fortunate to have acquired a PADCO (Planning and Development Collaborative) team with experience in Africa and Latin America. As consultants to this national housing agency, they will assist in the policy planning and evaluation. Their skills will become crucial as the site-and-services projects for the low-income sector of the various metropolises open up for settlement. Pushed by the World Bank, but encountering many doubts on the part of the military, many of whom play the role of politicians in this society, and the top bureaucrats, the site-and-service projects are lagging due to familiar difficulties. In Surabaya, the shallow wells for water supply onsite run dry while another ministry's irrigation canals flow through the area brim full. Economical transport services cannot be guaranteed while the roads are so poor. Finally, there is resistance from the present squatters to the new subdivision of the land. Other problems will appear shortly. Few administrators recognize as yet the necessity for heavy investment in social survey among expected settlers and for social welfare work during the early stages of the settlement process. Poor families in Java tend to be at least as unstable as those in Latin America, and a large share of them seem to lurch from crisis to crisis for years on end due to illness, unemployment, difficulties with the law, desertion, natural catastrophes, mental breakdowns, and feuds. Housing remains only one of many critical problems for the poor.

Distribution, Transport, and Communications

The poor are kaki lima (hawkers, peddlers), betjak (pedicab and pedicart operators), unskilled workers in the market, and servants. The poorest of all are the scavengers who pick up cigarette butts and pick out bottles, paper, metal, and some kinds of plastic from the waste, while they burn bamboo containers as fuel. The poor are spurned in Jakarta, particularly if they do not have official approval for residence. (A recent arrival from Bali reported that his kartu penduduk (residency permit) cost $24 in payments to officials — about three weeks' earnings at the subsistence level.) The betjak are being forced out of an ever-expanding ring in central Jakarta, and the kaki lima are pushed off the roads and the avenues into the kampongs, where with a kerosene lantern they serve the other poor, lighting the lanes until nine o'clock at night, even later for cigarette vendors. The poor are made to feel unwanted in Jakarta.

Bandung has taken an altogether different tack over the past several years. The results of an empirical study of hawkers in various cities of Southeast Asia were shown to authorities in Bandung shortly after the raw data had been collected. Terry McGee had started these investigations in Hong Kong seven or eight years ago, after marveling that prosperity did not seem to diminish their numbers.(35) Later a comparative study was launched which included both Jakarta and Bandung. It showed that this low-capitalization, low-overhead approach to distribution provides a delivery service as well as a source of opportunity for making a livelihood; without this service at slightly reduced prices, the welfare of the bottom half of the population would decline significantly.

Thus Bandung has tried to find an appropriate place for each kind of retailing and transport. At night the kaki lima are grouped, so that a laborer can get his rice and vegetables with soup from one stand; get martabak (egg with cassava flour made into an omelette-like sandwich with sliced chili peppers on the inside) from another nearby as a rare treat; buy a new pair of sandals down the line; and pick up a pack of cigarettes in a single short trip. The organization of mobile vending is still a long way from the advanced form seen in Singapore, Penang, or even the small regional cities of Thailand, but congestion has been reduced even while people's incomes have risen and they are buying more.

A segregated traffic pattern in Bandung has developed from the original plan. Some streets are reserved for the three-wheel bemo, a six-to-eight-passenger vehicle with a scooter engine that is assigned routes with minimal slopes. Moderate slopes are granted to oplets, mostly 30-year-old Chevrolet vans with wooden bodies carrying up to 18 people with some produce, while the most increasingly used vehicle, serving more distant settlements, is the small Honda half-ton truck fitted for either produce or passengers, for which a special loading circuit has been devised. A two-drivers-and-a-boy system has evolved, with one man pulling in the customers in advance and then delivering the vehicle to a driver who takes it to the end of the line and back. The boy spots customers along the road and handles the change. Thus the two drivers have time for coffee while the vehicle keeps running full time. Major traffic flows between towns and to some suburbs are handled by buses operated in the private sector also, but these are increasingly regulated. The Honda, which resembles the "jeepney" of the Philippines in function, is a quite recent phenomenon, and is now the subject of a comparative study organized in Indonesia at Jogjakarta, and in Thailand at Chieng Mai. It seems to be a particularly efficient way of connecting a countryside engaged in multicropping with the markets of nearby cities; the vehicles serve as urban transport when villagers sell their produce, or they provide mobility for the lower-density, peripheral metropolitan neighborhoods. Betjak are particularly suited for cheap taxis for women and children of the middle classes and for interconnections between these other transport services.

While Bandung has been going the route of integrating an indigenous service system, Jakarta has been experimenting with new vehicles. In the last two years it has added the Italindo super-helicak, a relatively stable, well-sprung, three-passenger, three-wheel cab based upon the Greek Mevea chassis; the Bajaj three-wheeler from Delhi; and the Minicar three-wheeler, whose antecedents have not yet been tracked down. These are added to the earlier existing bemo, and the helicak. Some oplet routes remain, and the Honda, also a four-wheeler, is expanding its territory, although far from the degree observed in Bandung. Jakarta's bus system has been reorganized so that intercity buses are halted on the periphery. Traffic flow has been speeded up as a consequence, and less smoke is spewed into the atmosphere along the main routes. Jakarta has also added some new principal roads so that the most fearsome jam-ups are now a rarity, even though the number of automotive vehicles in the city may have increased 30 percent or more, due to a partial unplugging of bottlenecks at Tandjung Priok, the principal harbor.

A New Source of Livelihood

The first glimmer of an ultramodern technological revolution appeared in Java in 1976. The source of this up-to-the-minute know-how is the Santa Clara Valley a hundred kilometers south of San Francisco. In the special jargon of the sophisticated electronics industry the valley has come to be called "Silicon Valley," because a large share of its advanced developments are printed, engraved, or stored on pure silicon chips assembled into information-processing circuitry.

Recently the firms in this region have been challenged to produce control systems for automotive engines, "smart" instruments for monitoring the environment, and electric motors linked to a power supply unable to maintain constant voltage. Since 1974 the preferred solutions have depended upon microprocessors. In engines they save fuel and prevent pollution; in instruments they collect refined data needed for human health, record completion of social transactions, and monitor subtle transitions in the environment. Everywhere the design engineers look they see that economizing on the expenditure of scarce resources must be entrusted to circuitry as soon as human organizations have found a formula for conservation.

The first firm to establish itself in Java, Fairchild Semiconductor, is the same one that broke the quality-control bottleneck in Hong Kong in 1965, and solved the problems of high-technology production in the Korean society less than two years later. Once this multinational firm had demonstrated that low-cost – but carefully selected and trained – female labor could assemble the highest quality electronic circuits if given the right opportunity to learn, all the competing world producers were forced to follow. The emphasis upon women is a necessary one, since in all the cultures tested women make far fewer mistakes, and this is an industry that insists upon error-free hardware and software.

The program in Indonesia was triggered by approaching full employment in Korea, Taiwan, and Hong Kong. Roughly a million new jobs have been created in this part of the world, extending from Singapore to Seoul, and more than 80 percent of them are held by literate women willing to pay close attention to the prevention of errors. When the industry was much smaller, and dedicated to the production of transistors or other precise, yet simple, components, these jobs were held by Japanese women who were graduates of middle school. However, that supply of factory labor dried up because so many of the girls began going on to senior high school and college in the 1960s, thus qualifying for higher status jobs.

The origins of the first enterprise in Java can be traced back to 1973 when a Fairchild engineer – one of the ubiquitous Smiths – who was also a kind of specialist in applied anthropology, identified a locale not far from the new international airport which possessed a labor supply of at least 10,000 literate women. Other executives then flew to Jakarta to find the appropriate paths through the customs, since the machinery would come from Hong Kong by air, and the raw materials would be flown in from California or Singapore, while the output would, initially at least, be sent to Singapore for final processing steps and worldwide distribution. An application to establish a factory was prepared, but it was held up by the government while it pondered the significance of the Malari incident (riots following student demonstrations against Japanese penetration) early in 1974. Later in the year both Fairchild and National Semiconductor (a major competitor in Silicon Valley) were encouraged to proceed. The Fairchild site is at 28.5 kilometers on Old Bogor Road in a territory designated by Jakarta planners for enterprises that might otherwise generate intolerable congestion. A temporary building was found while ten hectares of land were acquired – a considerable achievement in a crowded countryside made up of small farms – and a windowless two-story concrete box of a building was constructed.

The factory manager in a developing country plays an even more important role than at home, because his personal style is infused throughout the growing organization among people without prior industrial experience. The ideal man was found when the Fairchild plant on the Navajo reservation in Arizona was shut down by the young braves seeking a showdown with the council of chiefs. While settling into the suburban edge of Jakarta with five children and supervising the import of machinery, he roamed the halls of the Institute of Technology, Bandung, in search of engineers with personal characteristics fitting the Fairchild image and the requirements of the industry – persistent when troubleshooting, willing and able to undertake preventive maintenance, sensitive to the dignity of the workers, and capable of rapid personal growth, more rapid than the growth in the complexity of the operations.

By the beginning of January 1976 the number of employees on the payroll passed a hundred. Word was put out in the community that women would be hired, so they began appearing at the gate for interviews. They were tried out on the ten or so hand operations required to construct an integrated circuit, and a fair fraction were asked to return for work. The principal criterion for success on the part of the worker is the learning curve. The manager had to know very soon how the Javanese learning curves compared with those in America and other high producing societies, such as Korea. Since no difficulties were experienced, attempts have not been made to discover which home backgrounds or ethnic origins were associated with the best learning curves.

Without advertisement the factory labor force reached 1,700 persons, 80 percent women, on the payroll by August. The absenteeism encountered was at the phenomenally low level of 2 percent, while the turnover rate was held at 10 to 20 percent – a very good rate for the first plant in a developing region – despite the inconvenient hours set by triple shifts. Personal security for the workers was assured by hiring a bus firm to move them between their homes and the plant. This is very important because the age range of the women is from 19 to 26 and there are no streetlights. The target work force is 6,000 employees, and it is to be reached by the end of 1977.

Everything must be done to the environment in this plant to enhance precision and accuracy; mistakes are far more expensive than raw materials. Therefore the working lines are well lit, dust free, and moderately air-conditioned. Noisy operations are segregated. The precious pure silicon is flown in from Taiwan or America in a sliced form; the women break it into small chips a few millimeters on a side. With the aid of microscope eyepieces, circuits are inscribed upon them adding tiny components flown in from the United States and linking them with fine gold wire and film obtainable in Jakarta; finally the units are enclosed in black thermosetting plastic with connectors showing.

Welfare of the workers is equally important for error reduction. Because women in underdeveloped societies tend to starve themselves in order to assure that there is enough food for the small children in the family, they are offered a snack shortly after arriving, and a full meal several hours later, and another snack to overcome fatigue in the latter part of a six-and-a-half-hour day. The pay is presently on an hourly basis and is set at levels that do not significantly exceed the going cash wage.

It is the aim of the management of this plant to make it the most effective of its kind in the world. The physical productivity of high-quality components per worker-day should be higher than any other. That means it will surpass a pace-making factory in Korea, perhaps some time in 1978. At the moment the learning curves and responses to incentives are all equal to or ahead of those recorded by the Korean plant, and the assistant manager, a Korean, is confident that Javanese workers can do at least as well. A crucial step will be reached next year when the women go on piecework rates, competing head-on with facilities elsewhere in the world at international rates. Then it is likely that most of these women will be able to make two, even three, times as much as the wages paid to men in their community.

The Fairchild managers have not yet begun to worry about the impact of the factory on the community. The firm contributes to the festival celebrations, encourages the employees to play soccer (Indonesian women are enthusiastic players), volleyball, and badminton, and it opens up some of the unused land behind the plant for the kampong headman to organize community sports. Pregnancy so far has not interfered with production, so no special instruction in family planning is planned. Nor does there seem to be any reason to teach nutrition, hygiene, or community organization on the side; perhaps setting an example of new standards is enough. Neither dormitories nor company housing seems to be needed, since the transport service allows women to live at home or board with relatives.

Such matters may have to be attended to by the managers of the plants to follow. Already the commercial counselor of the American Embassy reports several electronics firms per month are dropping in to discuss setting up factories in Indonesia. National Semiconductor was reported to be up to 1,100 employees in Bandung, and only two months behind Fairchild. The 1975 recession, severest of any experienced by the industry, was definitely over. Business Week now runs stories about every six weeks that emphasize the strength and variety of demand for microprocessors.

Every firm overseas must consider how it will handle the local corruption, a condition that can very easily slow down or halt the development of an installation. Recent disclosures of Lockheed, Gulf, Mobil, and other American payoff scandals have been rocking the Japanese, Iranian, and Malaysian governments for the last year. Some elements of the Jakarta bureaucracy have been demanding and getting large rakeoffs from the Chinese and Japanese enterprises. Fairchild's strategy is to avoid making any payments at all.

When the company's general counsel arrived last year to supervise the necessary contracts he decided that the best strategy was to hire a local lawyer famous in the society for being a successful advocate of the little man against corrupt government. He had even gone to jail for two years for his principles. The top manager was instructed to make sure that each demand for a bribe or payoff was to be clarified and sharpened so that the company knew who was to get what for which service for which period. Then the manager should state that of course he would have to consult his lawyer, mentioning his name. The last time a shakedown was attempted (a frame-up smuggling charge that was to be conveniently buried), the proposers suddenly realized after the meeting how vulnerable to public exposure by this attorney they had left themselves; they were back within a few days to call everything off. The reputation of the local lawyer made the difference.

The total number of jobs in this industry for Indonesia could easily reach 50,000 by 1980. Many hundreds of thousands more could be employed during the next decade. The Fairchild plans are to move the Singapore operations to Jakarta after a full range of skills has been developed. Then Singapore might become a regional headquarters for manufacturing and distribution in Southeast Asia, and Jakarta would receive manufacturing instructions directly from the California home plant. The Jakarta facility might then be refitted with new machines, while the existing, useful, third-hand equipment could be installed in some less central Javanese location. Meanwhile, if the history of the industry elsewhere is recapitulated, many engineer-managers may resign and set up production units of their own, manufacturing integrated circuits to the specifications of the big computer and instrument firms. Indonesian engineers who had already learned the business would join them, quickly rising to top management. Unprecedented amounts of money would flow to the professors in the engineering and business schools for consulting and research. The principal bottleneck in Indonesian industry and commerce is in accountancy, where the limited supply is already overextended. Availability of dependable telex lines would have been another bottleneck, but the existence of the new communication satellite (Palapa) will give Indonesia a competitive advantage for a while over nearby countries.

With high world demand, and with Palapa on hand to connect with California and Texas, perhaps also Tokyo, it appears that the newly skilled hands of the Indonesian women make make it possible for the country to pick up hundreds of millions of dollars of foreign exchange per year in the 1980s — the decade when oil production in this part of the world is expected to peak. This new industry could push the society into many unexplored directions that are favorable for the environment as well as the economy and the educational system. The social impacts do not seem to be undesirable, since opportunities for some of the most exploited components of the population would be advanced.(36) Accountants may have to be imported from other Moslem countries, such as Pakistan or Bangladesh.

The sophisticated electronics industry promises to raise many novel issues in the metropolitan regions of Java, later also Sumatra and Bali, over the next few years. Not the least of these is an infusion of features of Californian and cosmopolitan Asian life-styles, with their schools, clothing, books, recreations, television programs, and popular music, into a society that still insists upon censorship of the media by religious authorities. Nevertheless, if industrialization is to be implemented as set forth in general terms in the five-year plan (Repelita II), a nation could not pick a more promising category of manufacturing.

9 Cairo*

Although physically situated in Africa, Cairo is one of the
most influential metropolises in the Asian Third World. It
directs armies occupying an edge of Asia, and has exported well over a million of its residents to Asian
countries requiring skilled and professional labor. Any
high culture to be financed by Arab OPEC funds will
inevitably acquire a Cairene patina. Whatever political
unity is forged among Arab states will emerge from Cairo
headquarters. It is the city that should permanently have
displaced Beirut as the business center of the eastern
Mediterranean during the latter's time of troubles (1975-
78), but appears to have lost out to Athens due to the
abysmal communications services it offers. Politically it
is a quiescent volcano, stoked by a continuing influx of
very poor _fellahin_, spilling out of overcrowded villages. It
almost boiled over six months after this account was
prepared when the subsidies on bread and essential services were reduced to help control inflation. Order was
restored only by rescinding most increases, thus leaving
the economy even more precarious than before. Also,
according to surveys revealed later, the population that
has already arrived from the villages is now believed to be
about 10 percent denser than given in the reports drawn
upon in the description that follows.

---

*Estimated 1985 population – 16 million.

186

PRIMARY CITY OF THE ARAB WORLD

July 1976

Cairo has recently become a supermetropolis. The presence and the activities of its eight and three-quarters million residents puts it in the same league with Buenos Aires, Sao Paulo, and Mexico City in Latin America, Osaka and Seoul in East Asia, Bombay and Calcutta in South Asia, Shanghai and Leningrad in the communist world, while it has no peer in Africa or the Mediterranean as an urbanizing force. At the moment it is transforming almost a half million people per year into functioning flat-dwelling urbanites, 60 percent of whom are immigrants from the cottages and mud huts of the countryside. Yet even that is not enough; the task ahead requires stepped-up efforts because this is a society that has used up most of the safety margins that normally exist elsewhere.

Cairo is a difficult city to understand, and one which is very easy to get lost in when traveling by foot, yet that is the only way to begin. Fits of nationalism in the 1960s erased most of the bilingual street signs, and caused merchants to convert to Arabic in self-defense. Fortunately for the traveler there are many great mosques, which with the midans (open spaces) in their forecourts, a dozen tall office slabs for the important ministries, and a half dozen luxury-class hotels that rise up into the skyline in a scattered fashion, soon come to serve as landmarks.

As we left San Francisco we read a special feature on Cairo in Harper's magazine.(37) It was well written, and covered a multitude of features. It appeared to be substantive, yet our contact with the grit and din of the real city proved it to be mere froth, evocative of the moods of some local intellectuals; it had not gauged the momentum of this gathering tide of humanity for which Cairo is the vortex.

The planners' guess as to the current population of Egypt is 38 million, but they must combine every scrap of evidence to arrive at any figure at all because no census has been conducted since 1960. Demographers advise them that the growth rate is around three percent per year (lesser rates appear in newspapers), which is one of the highest in the world. Agricultural densities are already at, or are approaching, the highest ever recorded — over 1,000 persons per square kilometer in some places, but still growing. The crude death rate has been declining rapidly since World War II but still has a way to go before it touches bottom — a trend some Latin American and Southeast Asian societies are experiencing already — and starts a slow steady rise over the course of several generations. The reproductive momentum in the society suggests that the population growth rate is likely to remain virtually constant for the next decade or longer, even if the adoption rate for family planning is trebled over the present levels. The conclusion forced upon the planners is that the population of the nation must double over the next 25 years, and could not level off short of 120 million people — without the onset of a catastrophe unparalleled in the twentieth century. Thus rural areas will acquire densities equivalent to American cities if the people can be supported.

Family planning does exist in Egypt, and is gaining accelerated acceptance. Religious barriers are no longer raised in principle, although the interpretations of Koranic scholars in Cairo's preeminent El Azhar University are still diffusing too slowly through Egypt and the Muslim world, confounding the ad hoc judgments of local chief <u>mullahs,</u> who must render opinions in courtlike situations. The aggregate reports of a relatively new and loosely coordinated family planning program are expected to contain overstatements of coverage until proper auditing techniques have been devised, but even if they are taken at almost face value and converted into estimates of births prevented, it appears that the birth rate has been reduced by no more than 6 percent from the levels of natural fertility in a society with equivalent ages at marriage, divorce rate, illegitimacy levels, and traditions for weaning infants. Actually, the differences between recorded births and recorded deaths, which are now fairly good indications of reality, suggest a <u>growing</u> birth rate. The optimists in this society attribute the added fertility to the aftermath of the war with Israel; if they are right the birth rate should peak in 1976 and decline significantly in 1977, since the baby booms associated with prior wars were timed in this way.(38) Abortion is illegal, but not prosecuted, and its rate is apparently growing rapidly.

The Future Dimensions of Cairo

The population produced above replacement levels two decades ago — the fourth, fifth, and succeeding children, since three were then required for replacements — had no land available to them, unless tiny farms were further subdivided. About half of these "surplus" people are now finding niches in Cairo, and most of the others are accommodated in lesser cities. The remainder are either discovering ways to emigrate or are occupying new land opened for settlement. But henceforth the numbers accommodated will have to be doubled to provide for this year's crop of infants when they look for places to live.

Quantitatively inclined national planners are faced with the brutal necessity of finding ways of producing more goods and services from ever more marginal resources. Once they extrapolate the trends in population, resource availability, and productivity beyond the next five-year plan, they find huge shortfalls. Something new, resembling magic, must be added before a way out of the predicament can be found; otherwise no future exists at all.

But Egypt has become accustomed to political magic to overcome economic shortfalls. It acquired a friend in the North that not only provided external funds needed to tame the Nile River with a big dam and associated projects but also introduced additional support, material and financial, for the wars with Israel. Then, when that liaison became sticky, Egypt switched its line so as to gain grants, at a rate of billions of dollars per year, from OPEC members with surplus funds. It also bargained with the "peace broker" so that within two years it has become, second to Israel, the largest recipient of American foreign aid. At the same time it retained its position among leaders of the Third World bloc in the United Nations, which assures it a favored position for UNDP assistance and soft money loans. Estimates today suggest that 40 percent of the Egyptians are living on the largess of outsiders, since the differences between production and consumption seem to be running more than six billion dollars a year. Next year seems likely to be more magical than this because cotton prices are headed for all-time highs (high-quality cotton is Egypt's top export), tourism is coming back strongly, and individual Arab oilmen are buying property fast enough to double the rents for luxury flats, perhaps, because the prices are unstable, triggering a building boom in the private sector. Finally, new fields of natural gas and petroleum are being discovered, so that Egypt may be able to join OPEC in the 1980s. One has to search world history for centuries to find parallel instances of combined diplomatic finesse and good fortune.

This happy mirage could collapse totally within a matter of months, but such a reverse is likely to happen through a combination of circumstances other than military attack, because that would attract even more resources to Egypt. So the 38 million people will probably all survive, and Cairo will continue to stand; both will be seeking a long-range destiny that is more stable than the outlook at present and in the near future. In the meantime we must take account of the fact that Egyptians are depending upon a mirage, and are doing well enough to believe it can continue. Cairo's talk and imagination feed upon these fantasies come true, but physical life goes on as in other cities. What are the hard realities?

In a recent article I took up the fate of metropolitan areas at the brink of Malthusian disaster.(39) What path of future development most distinguished the risk of catastrophe? That article named the members of the class of cities for which the recommended solution seemed to apply, and one of them was Cairo, although the illustration taken up in many-sided detail was for the long run development of Jakarta. The same manner of thinking, using scientific and technological as well as economic justifications already provided in that article, can be applied to Cairo.

Most of the food required by 120 million or more people can be produced by carefully husbanding the water of the Nile, manufacturing huge amounts of fertilizer, and engaging in a high-precision, labor intensive horticulture. Enough fancy food products can be exported to pay for wheat, legumes, and cooking oil. This can be accomplished with 20 to 30 million people, so the remainder must find homes in the urban settlements. Thus the cities need to grow six or sevenfold in the three generations or so needed to reach an approximately stable population. Long before this process is finished the environs of Cairo would link up with Alexandria; eventually this ribbon of urbanism would contain 50 to 70 million people, about the number living in the Tokaido megalopolis of Japan in the 1970s.

It appears that the Nile will have to become an ever more managed river and Egyptian diplomacy recognizes this inevitability, since it is actively backing cooperative regimes in the Sudan. Extra food could be produced if evaporation close to the source in southern Sudan and countries neighboring on the south could be prevented. The extra food could be produced in Egypt, where the extra water could be transported to the relatively fertile dry soils behind El Arish, a Sinai settlement on the Mediterranean coast, and to land to the west of Alexandria, also near the Mediterranean. The so-called northwest regional plan, which channels surplus water to the west of the Delta seems likely to go ahead even though estimates of the cost of new land suited for irrigation exceeds $3,000 per acre.

The recently reclaimed land in this area has been handed over to Arab versions of the kibbutz. The population is made up of men who have served their terms in the army, gone back to the villages to marry, and are starting their families on the new land. The operation is highly disciplined, since almost everyone rises at the same time, does a half hour of gymnastic exercises, eats a morning meal, forms ranks for field assignments and other duties, and carries on through indoctrination meetings in the evening to lights out at 10 o'clock. Their farming is more mechanized than the norm, and should be adoptable to the most modern innovations in vegetable cultivation – their specialty – and pest control. The Cairo sociologists are amazed because there has never been anything like this before in Arab societies, so they wonder what will happen to children growing up in such settlements.

The alternative to Nile management is desalination of sea water in coastal districts using the surplus natural gas available there. Such projects will require extraordinary planning and discipline along with international marketing. Nuclear plants could handle the energy requirements after the gas has been depleted. Food production projects like these will determine the eventual locus of megalopolitan settlement.

The elongation of Cairo to form an Egyptian megalopolis was already evident to Janet Abu-Lughod in 1965 when she was writing her magnum opus.(40) At that time it was impossible to arrive at even a guess as to the extent of success of family planning programs elsewhere in the Third World, much less in Egypt, so there was no way of reaching crude quantitative estimates. That an Egyptian megalopolis could rival Japan in size hardly seemed possible when she was writing, but now it seems quite probable.

Given such expectations for the long-run future, it is worth exploring the more lasting transitions under way in the Cairo of the present. Also, how would such a megalopolis be different from those taking shape elsewhere in the world? What institutions is Cairo developing that could be pace makers over the next several decades? Can they take advantage of the opportunities offered by world trade? Over the long run Cairo must become economically independent, contributing aid to cities well behind it in the development process.

Social Progress

We are fortunate to have high-quality benchmarks for social conditions in Cairo for 1947, 1960, and some descriptive adjustments up to 1967. Since then the society has gone through two wars and has come to depend upon the bounty of the Arab states with surplus revenues. Janet Abu-Lughod adapted the Shevky-Bell technique of social area analysis, a method of washing out most of the unreliable census data, enabling her to identify "thirteen cities that make up Cairo," tracing their origins, and following their growth and transformation up to at least 1965. It is possible to pick up from that comprehensive assessment and update a number of her principal points.

First, why is Cairo located where it is? Are there changes in the society that cause the settlement to move in a direction more suited to present conditions?

A city of some sort frequently forms at the head of a delta that has been subjected to cultivation, and Cairo is one of these. (Compare with New Orleans, Sacramento, London, or Bangkok.) The reason is that crossing the quiet stream is usually easier than the frequently flooded delta. Memphis (5000-2500 B.C.) was the first such city, and it was reestablished in Greek times. Other walled settlements called Babylon and Heliopolis thrived here at various times in the classical period for Mediterranean societies, until Fustad was built by the conquering Arabs in 640 A.D. on the slopes overlooking the Nile. In 940 A.D. the Shi'ites swept in from the West, overwhelming the defenses, moved on to create an empire, and chose the site that was relatively unencumbered with prior settlement for their dynastic (Fatimid) capital. Once the heavy walls had been raised, the city acquired the retinue of a court, and then appropriated for itself a principal stage in the reoriented spice trade from China to Venice. In that period it became one of the largest cities in the world, eclipsing anything found in Europe. Under Turkish rule after the Crusades, the spice trade shifted again, much of it going to Portugal and Spain who circumvented Africa so that Cairo went into decline.

The Napoleonic invasion touched a nerve in its becalmed feudal society, so that most of the additions to the city on land created by the retreat of the Nile were laid down in the French tradition of that time as was Washington, D.C. That has become the modern commercial center of Cairo, while the bazaar, or suq, organized along traditional lines, carries on within the walls of the Fatimid city. Its old river port, well defended during the spice trade and still called Bulaq, is a densely populated slum engaged in many artisan trades ranging from rope goods to iron castings and forgings. Its recent changes seem to be associated with the rise of truck traffic, since it had already been accommodated to the railroad.

Control over the waters of the Nile was made possible by the first Aswan dam upstream in the nineteenth century and bridges to the newly stabilized islands in the river and to the other side. Such property on the banks was always claimed first by royalty and the top nobility and converted into gardens, then sold off by succeeding generations either to clubs or to promoters of luxury apartments.   On such land a predominantly British enclave was started according to "garden city" principles of the kind applied to Welwyn at the turn of the century, but the villas have now either been taken up by embassies or been displaced by six-to-eight-floor apartment blocks. Its shaded pavements remain quite well maintained, except for an occasional open manhole in the stream of foot traffic. It has been relatively free of commerce, but now Citibank of New York has invaded with a tall office-cum-apartment tower. The Semiramis Hotel on the nile side is in the last stage of reduction to rubble and salvage and will no doubt be replaced by several towers or slabs very soon. At the other boundary, the Garden City is being walled in by tall office blocks for the respective ministries. British style, the enclave was connected to a garden suburb, Maadi, just beyond the rubble-filled southern fringe of old Cairo, and on to Helwan which is now a rapidly expanding center of heavy industry adding thousands of barrack-like five-story walk-up apartments for the trained labor force in steel, cement, tile, pipe, and military manufactures.

Heliopolis, a half hour to the northeast, is an upper-middle-to upper-class new town of about 100,000 population started by a Belgian entrepreneur on a classical site at the turn of the century according to principles set up for the "streetcar suburb," so it resembles the parts of Boston, Philadelphia, and San Francisco built in the same era. Next to it is Nasser City, whose great square apartment blocks show clearly the strong Moscow influence. At the conjunction of roads serving these two settlements is the National Computing Center, an American contribution to the elitism of the present era superimposed upon that of earlier times. Enclaves of luxury are also forming on the banks of the Nile both to the north and the south of the main city. We heard of seven towers 120 meters high (about 40 stories) designed by local architects to be constructed by French engineering groups.

On the east the growth of Cairo is cut off by the "cities of the dead" on a 150-meter escarpment. Within these precincts a large expanse of sand and rocky soil is covered by a street grid of predominantly one-story, roofless housing containing tombstones within the walls. This area has been inhabited by the homeless of Cairo, including itinerant "Brethren in the Faith" consulting the savants in El Azhar University and elsewhere in old Cairo. Many refugees from Suez settled there, but they are now returning to their homes.

The physical change in the interior of Cairo is proceeding at just about the normal renewal and replacement rate; upgrading is rare except at the foot of the new Nile bridges. Most of the investment in physical facilities is being carried out in the peripheral industrial areas, where the rents appear to be subsidized 50 to 80 percent. Costs of construction are relatively high despite the scale of projects and the repetitiveness of the designs. My guess is that the uniformity of conditions of life for the trained industrial workers will lead to strong labor unions which may later assume political positions, as in present-day Poland after Gierek abruptly raised prices to put them in line with world market levels. Thus far I have not had reports of the existence of such social forces beyond the assertion that "some unions are strong." Such unions already manage a number of social services financed by government.

The most significant changes over the past decade have been caused by the accelerated influx of rural population. The social task of contemporary Cairo, as noted earlier, is the urbanization of immigrants. The Ministries of Education, Health, and Manpower are heavily involved, providing classrooms, clinics, and public works projects with on-the-job training.

The Egyptian urban-bound migrant is quite different from his counterparts elsewhere in the world — his savings are used to bring his family to the city as quickly as possible. The family tries to get a room, but it may even share one with strangers. Therefore the male-female ratio in the census never rose above 1.03 except in one troubled district of the city. Nevertheless in parts of upper Egypt 30 to 40 percent of young males are missing from the villages, but very few females. My guess is that army recruitment and participation in military construction may be responsible. They may be urban bound after they have accumulated some savings.

Most fellahin come into the city by train or bus with $30 to $150 in savings. It costs more than 75 cents a day for a single man to survive in Cairo. They have contacts through the coffee house to people from their district in Egypt, often also through middlemen or workers in one of the produce markets, and very likely have one or more relatives already living in the city. A buddy from military days is much more common now than ever before. A job is what is wanted, but none of their agricultural skills is relevant, because even if useful they will be in oversupply, so the military experience may make the greatest difference. Engine repair, for example, has a rising demand around the peripheral industrial districts and in the short rues (shari) of the French-designed city, drawing upon streets and ground floors of the six-story apartment buildings for work space. If there happens to be a demand for extra casual labor, word trickles back to villages very quickly, so that within a month the supply is again in surplus.

Recent migrants and traditionalists among urban residents wear a jalabiyeh revealing the district of their origin by their color and design, but the bulk of the male population now wear dark trousers and a colored or printed, but otherwise unadorned, shirt. Shoes are a better indicator of the degree of modernization, particularly among the crowds on the street after dark. On Kasr el Nil, Cairo's Fifth Avenue, shoe stores occupy the highest rent corner shops after the banks, and stop the largest crowds of gawkers.

In the room the migrants call home, a chair, table, and wardrobe are acquired relatively soon after entry into the city. In the native villages, houses are typically one-room mud-brick constructions often shared with the animals, which are expected to keep to their side. So not much is expected. Of course there must be a jar for water, a few water glasses or metal cups, dishes, and spoons. Light blankets are needed because Cairo can get cold in winter. The floor is the bed until a rug is obtained. Dirt and debris are pushed around, ending in piles, but only occasionally removed.

For people who find a niche before their money runs out, life does improve. City schools have better teachers, and their diplomas offer greater freedom to pursue personal interests. Small-scale opportunities resulting in windfall income are much more common. Somewhat better housing may then be found. Cairo today appears to have more small winners than losers, and that is enough to allow the local fellahin to accept their lot in life.

Egyptian urban migrants differ from other Mediterranean countries in the way they relate to the village. The Delta people in particular maintain a quite strict quid pro quo relationship with the family remaining in the village: "You get me some meat, because it is becoming very scarce in Cairo, and I will bring you some city-made shoes." The idea of working in the city to obtain a rural stake, is extremely uncommon. A man or woman who has found a niche in the city will not convert it into the status of a resident landowning peasant, but prefers to become an absentee landlord when investing in land. Family contacts become relatively superficial within a few years; there are very few known examples parallel to Greece and South Asia where marginal villages are supported by remittances from urban migrants. The exceptions are found among the migrants from the most depressed parts of upper Egypt who find their opportunities as servants and deliverers of produce. ("Though less educated," their employers say, "they are more dependable when they say they will do something.") The social distinctions provide the basis for a different kind of settlement.

The alternative — setting up a squatter's reed-topped hut in the rubble on the edge of the city or on a roof-top — initiates a slower process of change. Life in one of these marginal communities is more like it would be in a strange village because peasant societies also maintain quite high levels of rural-rural migration, often exceeding rural-urban, so that cultural adjustments have been made to outsiders who have come in to handle specialized crops, or are refugees from some "scourge of God" in their homeland. In Cairo the work of these semirural squatters is likely to be little different from village activities, since it revolves around the transport and processing of rural produce arriving in the city.

Middle-class migration is rapidly becoming the more significant form of immigration. Epitomized by the accelerating growth of the universities (the most prestigious of them now has 80,000 enrollment), and any other institution offering credentials, this flow is much more a trickling in of individuals supported by an extended family network. In this university-trained group one does find a few instances of exhibitionist modernism — striped trousers, often bellbottom, fancier shirts, the latest in shoes, longer hair, but definitely not blue jeans or sporty prints in fabrics, since such affectations could only be accepted by members of the most established families in Cairo, and even then displayed mainly within the confines of the exclusive Gezirah Club. At the moment every university graduate is guaranteed at least a clerical job upon completion at about $45 per month. Most of the jobs are in Cairo, but the promise is likely to be broken at the time of the next national emergency. Given the extreme reliance upon credentials in all Arab societies, instead of performance, personal achievement, competitive success, or lottery, the next crisis will be felt most strongly among middle class immigrants struggling to maintain a status their earnings do not allow.

Transactive Flows

The built environment of a metropolis in a contemporary society is designed to expedite public transactions of all kinds within rules laid down by the cultures of its peoples and the dominant political system. In the Third World, much more than in the socialist or the Western, diversity in transactions is achieved by specialization of the ethnic communities. The Egyptian identifies diversity among peoples in the form of dialectical shifts in demotic Arabic language and by the wearing of signs. The outsider can rarely distinguish even the Coptic remainder of pre-Arab settlers, the Maronite-rite Christian Arabs, or the Orthodox Greeks, unless he sees the appropriate gold cross or marked hand. A number of Jews remain in Cairo advertising their businesses and professions. Traditional goods and services are likely to be obtained through transfers between members of such communities, as well as those from the villages of upper Egypt. The lower Egyptians from the Delta are more involved in dealing with modern products and are becoming the middle class offering services.   The competitive position of future Cairo in this part of the world will depend much more upon their initiative in the future.

The middle class is adopting the automobile. As the number of posts in the ministries and the state-managed firms for which the chauffeur-driven car is a standard perquisite continues to increase, the streets in the post-Napoleonic city become increasingly congested. Egypt-made Fiat minitaxis are used heavily by the remainder of the middle class because the rates are less than 15 cents a mile with 12 cents for starters. The face-to-face transactions required to promote a project or start an enterprise require this kind of transport. As a result the road along the Cornish, paralleling the Nile on the east side, has become as noisy and hectic as any highway found among the Mediterranean settlements, but here gentlemanliness has disappeared; drivers take delight in tormenting pedestrians, missing them by a whisker or stopping dead within a few centimeters of their targets.

The twentieth-century portions of the city were built up around a streetcar network to which two mass transit lines were added. A few of those tram lines have been retired, and some have been replaced by buses and trolley buses, but the remainder keep going with miscellaneous equipment scavenged from dying tram lines all over Europe and America. We rode some streetcars that could well have been San

Francisco's Green Hornets of the 1940s, now enjoying a second or third life serving Cairene suburbanites. The French have been given the assignment of designing a subway connecting the two high-volume suburban lines and superimposing an elevated railway; although they claim they are ready to start construction any month later in the year, none of the other transport engineers advising the government has been apprised of the route and the size of the project. (My guess is that secrecy is used to hold back speculation in property.) Thus Cairo should have an adequate transit system some time in the 1980s if the encroachment of the auto can be contained and equipment can be replaced.

The Nile itself remains an unused transport resource of major dimensions. A few ferries operate where there is no bridge crossing, but exceedingly few watercraft ply the river in public service. Houseboat hotels for river cruises are moored next to the luxury hotels but there is nothing like the water-bus service of Bangkok, nor even its dashing water taxis. The ocean engineers of the University of Hawaii have the appropriate technology ready and waiting. This is a cheap mode of passenger movement eminently suited to the transition to megalopolis when Cairo's population is in the 10 to 20-million range.

A large share of the red public buses serve neighborhoods beyond the tram network. They are loaded to the limit and beyond because they feed the parts of the city most rapidly growing. Often agile young men await the bus three to five blocks before it arrives at the downtown station, catch it on the run, mount the side, and dive head first into the windows, so all the seats on the outward run are already claimed before it has drawn up to the station. Only in Karachi and Jakarta have we seen crowding of this intensity. About 10 percent of the equipment blows black smoke into the eyes of pedestrians and labors up the overpasses, so the engine maintenance is about as high as will be found in other developing countries. One difficulty with quick shifts in political winds is that they exacerbate the spare parts and preventive maintenance problems. An interesting outcome is an increasing dependence upon Tata of India for rolling stock, but the city is left strewn with the dusty carcasses of defunct vehicles as a result.

Goods movement is still mostly done in Skoda equipment, but Fiat is advancing; apparently a local plant produces the lorries appearing now on the roads. A miscellany of Nile barges carries the depleted supply of bricks (the silt from which the bricks are made was cut off from Cairo by the new Aswan Dam), stone, cement, and fertilizer. Agricultural produce moves by rubber-tired horse-drawn cart, but is distributed by donkey cart, particularly in the walled city. Camels with twin packs are seen quite often on the periphery of the metropolis and many I saw were carrying carefully husbanded manure.

Intermediate technology in transport is poorly represented in Cairo and what there is of it seems to be declining. Bicycles are moderately common on the periphery, particularly for journey to work and delivery of milk and bakery goods, but are more often playthings for juveniles in the interior of the city. Only one rather crude innovation can be seen –

a three-wheel cart engaged in miscellaneous delivery, pedal-powered from the back or front with reinforced wheels, often handed down from a light motorcycle. Mopeds, scooters, motorcycles, and motorcycles with sidecars are all present in the city but remain very rare.

Telecommunications are in a sorry state in Egypt. The telephone system is French, and even more overloaded than in Casablanca or Paris. Calling outside the city is more nearly impossible than inside, so Cairo is virtually isolated from 9:00 a.m. to 2:00 p.m. and again from 5:30 to 8:00 p.m., except on Fridays and Sundays. The telex is noise ridden, so the cables are garbled. The internal postal system has broken down, often requiring two weeks to catch up, so most ministries and firms are forced to hire courier services. Cairo seems to need four- to fivefold more communications capacity and people would be willing to pay for it, but because it is not in the five-year plan the stress on the systems will continue much as at present, unless they break down altogether.

One wonders if it is not possible to superimpose a totally new telecommunications system that serves all the high-volume users and also connects with other major cities. Then residential areas would have to set up their own antenna receivers that would connect either to an overhead satellite or to a tower on the ridge behind the citadel not unlike the one on Mt. Sutro in San Francisco. The capital cost per unit would be one-fourth that of an automobile, the energy required perhaps one-twentieth, and it would allow new standards for organizational performance to be set.

Behind the Built Environment

Highlights of the anticipated growth of Cairo have been stated in terms of population and social change, but the implications for land and the processes by which shelter is created have yet to be unraveled. Each metropolis evolves a unique combination of building methods, differentiated by history, culture, wealth, and natural environment; that of Cairo is no less distinctive.

Cairo's walled city tradition, followed by streetcar urbanization, has caused it to remain quite dense. The present settlement averages close to 300 persons per hectare (75,000 persons per square mile) on a gross basis. The typical building height is four to five floors, with the maximum around 30 floors. Almost everyone in Cairo explains this high density by asserting a truism — the soil of this overcrowded country is precious because it provides the food, or the foreign exchange for purchasing the food, that enters the mouths of the people of Egypt. The planners cite a figure that Egypt has lost 10 percent of its prime land since World War II for purposes of urbanization, including roads, reservoirs, and similar infrastructure, but mostly for industry and the military. At the same time, very little is lost to suburban sprawl. The primacy of the fertile soil for human survival in Egypt, however, is no longer valid in the technical sense, since it is the use of water that is now limiting agricultural production. Nevertheless people truly believe that the land is the mother of them all, so as long as the illusion remains, the country's decision makers are forced to bow to the demands for keeping the maximum amount of land in agriculture.

Actually the decision makers feel helpless in the face of the normal processes of speculation, combined with the lack of capital for transport, water, and electric power distribution, which together have greater leverage in the enforcement of high density. Buildable land with claims of relatively decent urban services, for instance, in Nileside, Heliopolis, and the western fringe, has reached the dizzying price of $150 per square foot, and occasionally quite a bit more for special sites. For luxury construction, where 50 percent ground coverage is allowed, costs run around 20 to 25 percent of the final price, which means that land rents have not yet caught up with conditions in East Asia or Tehran, but they are getting close. A lease on a livable apartment now costs more than the whole salary of top civil servants such as professors.

Monotonous tiny flats for blue-collar workers, built as sparsely as possible, with total costs running perhaps $3,500 for an apartment that houses on the average four to six persons, must be subsidized. It is a melancholy fact of life in Egypt that full-time workers in state-run factories cannot live on their wages and need to be helped by the remainder of the population in order to keep the factories running.

The formal sector accounts for only a quarter of the new housing produced, while the legitimate informal sector is estimated to account for at least half. To observe what happens there, walk along with me while we take a route to the edge of the city where the informal sector dominates the scene.

First let us amble along the 26 of July Boulevarde that takes traffic off the new, partially completed, high bridge across the Nile from the island called Zamalik for several kilometers. The boulevarde has a 50-meter median strip between two and three lanes of asphalt road, imperfect sidewalks, if any, starting at the Cinema Sphinx, where luxury apartments, new or still under constructions, rise 6 to 12 stories above the street scene. They give way to four-story tenements only a few years old but teeming with children and already showing considerable wear. Then we come upon several blocks of villa-type apartments, designed to announce that this is an appropriate residence for a foreign-trained medical specialist and his peers in this society, then more luxury apartments, whereupon the boulevarde stops dead at a railroad bund leading to the south of Egypt. So much for the formal sector.

On the wrong side of the tracks are the green plots of maize in graduated stages of maturation, cultivated so as to produce roasting ears over a long season, against a ragged skyline of raw red brick thrusting out of the plain. In the foreground is a blackened mud hut with small square portholes for windows, behind a pile of dusty debris. Careful inspection reveals that this is a charcoal business establishment, since there are stumps and loads of waste wood, and bits of smoke are coming through the rubble, which acts as insulating overburden. There are a half dozen similar establishments in the distance. The charcoal is, of course, used to roast the ears of corn to a luscious brown color on street corners throughout the city.

The one-and-a-half-lane road terminates at another like it paralleling a sluggish canal. At the corner is a traditional iron-working shop that bends rod and shapes sheet metal into such implements as an Archimedes screw. Nearby animals are at work providing the motive power for water wheels lifting water from dug wells and ditches. Yet around these vestiges of the past, houses go up step by step as the capital required becomes available for the brick, for the columns and slabs of reinforced cement, and the stucco which is sometimes added.

The informal building sector competes with the formal sector for materials of construction. Cement is very scarce, due to the export market in the OPEC world, but large new plants will be completed soon. Bricks are scarce because the Nile mud is settling behind the big dam upstream and is unavailable. Some of the formal sector is substituting a lighter "sand brick" that may be used for infill walls. For luxury apartments it is interesting to note that a wall begins with a course or two of brick, then most of the wall is done with large white, precisely formed, sand blocks, topped by another course of brick. There are no such innovations in the informal sector. The every-scarcer crude red brick was piled on floors awaiting the attention of the masons. Reinforcing rods seemed to be the scarcest of all. Sometimes a floor is used for living when the wall was half completed. (It does not really rain for years in this part of Egypt, but it does get very chilly during light showers in January and February, with temperatures down to 45° F at night.) It was these partly finished walls and piles of stacked bricks that created the ragged, as differentiated from stepped, skyline. Rooms are small, mostly four by six meters and they are occupied by a nuclear family or part of a complex extended family.

Work is proceeding in perhaps 10 percent of the structures, only a handful of which have been raised as yet to the temporary maximum of four floors. Half the workers, generally older men or boys, wear the traditional jalabeyas, indicating rural origins, and the other half wear dark trousers with homemade shirts, suggesting they are journeymen of a modern urban craft, very possibly employed by small contractors. Houses grow right out of the fields, and small channels for irrigation have been prepared within a half meter of the foundations. While three years ago this was a village of several hundred families and only the forge and a few shops had been built in pukka construction, there will soon be 20 times as many dwellings. The landlords of the peasants, often absentee, sell off part of the land to others to gain capital and invest it in housing, enabling them to become urban landlords, allowing the collection of five to ten times the rents. The ordinary settler from the villages at least knows how to relate to such landlords, whereas if a state corporation should be a landlord, he is at a loss when making fair demands.

On this growing edge daily village activities still dominate. The camels haul green fodder for the cows. Most of the traffic is by donkey cart and flat-bottom horse-drawn wagon. Occasionally a taxi will honk its way through the pedestrian flow. Regular bus service is not provided, but during opening and closing hours, factories may be served by dusty, ancient private buses. Women stoop at the canal side to wash clothes and clean pots in the scummy gray water while naked little boys splash around nearby and severely dressed little girls carry pottery jars of water or infants on a round of chores.

Following the road between the canal and the railroad tracks one can see what kinds of settlement this kind of building leads to five, ten, and fifteen years later. The five-meter streets begin to fill with debris, higher against the walls than in the dusty, trash-filled center. The canal is filled with rubble and litter, leaving only occasional pools of polluted green water. Elsewhere the canal space becomes a specialized market: one is a live fowl market, so the litter there contained many light-colored feathers. These accumulations occur because informal settlement has no claim upon urban services. For lack of standpipes, they must depend upon water carriers and no garbage or trash removal is provided. Our visit was too late in the day to see the "sewage treatment" process in operation; I assume it contributes to the growth of the maize nearby.

In this earlier constructed settlement we encounter a fascinating phenomenon – the second or third floor of a building is built to overhang the narrow street. In the original Cairo these overhangs were most often made of wood, sometimes exquisitely carved, but the availability of reinforcing rods with cement construction allows a continuation of standard building methods. The cantilevering is not done at the corners, but only in the center of the block, never consistently but at the whim of an owner with four- to five-meter frontage. Narrow dark alleys lead to the interior of a block. In old Cairo these overhangs had been abolished almost a century ago with the intent of modernizing the city by letting the air and sunlight in, but here we see the city-building propensities of the Egyptians in their purest form, with all stages of growth visible in a ten-minute stroll. The skyline that is fully built up remains ragged, with three to five floors completed to different levels and a solitary building in the block, usually with frontage on a midan or a corner, reaching six floors. In Cairo there was no brush on the roof to insulate it from the hot sun, as in Delta towns and villages, nor were there any of the belljar-shaped containers of mud reinforced with straw – presumably for storing food, such as grain and pickles – placed on the roofs of village dwellings. What we are seeing as we walk is village evolving into town and then into city.

In the fully urban stage we observe roads and other public facilities blasted out of the informal settlement, leaving signs of painted walls and floor on the street exposure, while in other cases landlords have reaggregated plots and put up proper buildings for which they are able to claim rents more appropriate to the rise in land value. In other instances the state claims the land and puts up regimented workers' housing. Some of this transformation of the original settlement begins after 15 years, but usually it takes much longer to impose major change.

Once one sees paraded before him this sequence in the evolution the present appearance of the older parts of the city becomes more understandable. The holes filled with rubble are due to the breakdown of the wood beams used for fires or the breakup of overburdened brick foundation, leaving some corners still standing up to five meters in height to reveal the type of construction originally occupting the site. Very likely some of the reinforced concrete and brick infill buildings will also collapse in 50 years, due to bad cement or rusted reinforcements, leaving similar disfigurements in the cityscape.

Distinctiveness in the informal sector is achieved through superimposition of a stucco plaster front followed by a coat of paint; adding tile to the front at ground level reinforces the distinction. The improvement of fronts, still quite rare, makes a statement to the neighborhood, drawing those neighbors who need some form of assistance.

Finally there exists in Cairo the true squatter, living on invaded land. Examples can be found in every district of the city. In a precinct containing luxury apartment houses (where this is being written) one need only go to the empty lot next door. There he sees small huts made out of found materials such as cardboard, crating, corrugated iron, dry palm fronds, broken brick, straw mats, but surprisingly little of the flattened tin cans that one sees in bidonvilles. The squatters are often construction workers or purveyors of fruits and vegetables on handcarts and they seem to take their eventual displacement for granted.

Architects and planners in Cairo assert categorically that there are no wooden houses in Egypt, except where wood may be a found material for squatter housing. One Harvard-trained architect admitted that it took him a whole year of living beyond his means in Cambridge before he could accept the idea that a wooden structure could be a house. All the wood for construction is imported from Canada and Scandinavia, they say, but I saw truckloads of four-by-four-centimeter poles suited for light framing which appeared to be Yugoslav.

Notwithstanding such assertions, we did see a tract of wood-frame houses in Alexandria not far from the waterfront. Of very simple design, perhaps 50 years old, and brightly painted in ochre, maroon, and deep blue, one and two stories high, these homes were well maintained. What could have been the reason for this anomaly? Perhaps they are a consequence of foreign aid. The age and the paint suggest that the tract might well be for Armenians, as their village people have worked with wood in the mountains. There are several Armenian Catholic churches in Alexandria.

If wood, or synthetic wood such as polyurethane foam, ever comes to Egypt, it must find an altogether new niche in the society. One use might be as a material for penthouses on buildings upon which the building of additional masonry walls is not possible. In the future the water pressure should reach to the top because the water supply program is now given high priority in Egyptian cities. This possibility tends to displace occasional squatters, who are willing to carry their water to the roof.

Organizing for the Future

I have argued elsewhere that the path away from a Malthusian crisis is paved with new organization. Expediting self-organization should be the intention of all state policy; the program must become particularly sophisticated in cities, where individuals should be expected to participate in many kinds of organizations.

How can the people of Cairo create the many needed new organizations? What kinds of new propositions can be launched in the present social, economic, and political climate, and what deficiencies remain? The answers to such questions are not easy to establish with solid information because the telephone system, a sine qua non of modern organization, is so badly serviced. There has been no telephone book since 1972 and it is only in Arabic. However, the Ministry of Social Affairs requires the registration of all voluntary organizations, presumably as a means of preventing subversion of the state; members of a nonregistered organization are subject to penalties. In 1972 it reported only 1,297 such organizations in Cairo. According to category these included:

Maternity and child care	31
Family care	17
Social aids	871
Care of the aged	2
Care of special categories (blind, etc.)	18
Education and religious services	237
Organization and administration	2
Care of prisoners	1
Family planning	2
International friendship	19

The category of "cultural" had no entries, perhaps because at that time culture and politics were too closely entwined. Day-care houses for children were included under "social aids," it is believed by local social researchers, and a capacity of 11,000 was reported serving 9,700 children.

The English-language newspapers are heavily censored (two are translated into English, one into French, and another German), although the society is open enough to allow free introduction of foreign newspapers, magazines, and books from both sides of the Iron Curtain, so that one can, with a lag, approximate the truth even about many internal issues not reported here. Western European periodicals, together with Time, Newsweek, and Business Week, predominate, the selection available determined largely by touristic demand (now about 900,000 visitors per year), which has been increased by Lebanese business-oriented refugees. The most informative monthly is an imitator of the Economist, called the Middle East which is printed in London by an Egyptian entrepreneur with the aid of a staff scattered from Iran to Morocco, Athens to Djibouti. It claims that most information is still obtained through the business intelligence systems of London, Paris, and Frankfurt. The Middle East is attempting to establish a standard for Arab objectivity — something that has never existed before in print. The journal publishes its total sources of income and capital in order to allay suspicions that it has been bought by some clever company or political entente and to demonstrate it has not become the voice of the CIA. The conclusions it reaches about the trend of events are sometimes different from those expressed in the Herald-Tribune or the Economist, but then the presumably objective Arab viewpoint is all the more important. This digression on sources of information is important because Cairo opinion about opportunities to organize is formed by rumors, which may or may not have substance, as influenced by such sources.

Egyptian national politics offers a good beginning for understanding the interplay of politics in Cairo. Since the break with Russia in March 1975 opportunity was provided for political forums (minbar). Forty were proposed, but only three were accepted, and they were allowed to be called tanzimat (group, organization). Theoretically the Arab Socialist Union possesses a political monopoly, a condition assured since the revolution of 1952, but now it is creating competition within itself between a moderate Right, Center, and moderate Left. The Right is best organized but is backed by only 30 percent of the members of the People's Assembly. Representing businessmen, craftsmen, and the rapidly expanding bourgeois, it believes that government should get out of the businesses it nationalized a half-dozen years back and stick to basic infrastructure. (The businesses were allowed to continue without so much as a change of name, so that even Weinstein's dry goods on the main stem, Rue Kasr el Nil, continues more or less as before.) To Egyptians, this means that ministers should be politicians rather than technocrats. The Center represents farmers, workers, and civil servants, and has attracted about half of the numbers of the People's Assembly, primarily because President Sadat's brother-in-law committed himself to it. Its program appears to be that of a balanced, mixed economy. The Left of center has only a fraction of the remainder of People's Assembly members — the three communist members have not joined — and appears to be badly split by the history of Marxist ideological divisions during this century.

The Sadat government moved quickly to expedite joint organizations with international firms. They claim to have the best law on the books anywhere in the world for the operation of foreign companies in Egypt, and in some ways they may be right, however the intent of the law has been undone by the precariousness of the Egyptian pound. Companies are caught in a set of exchange rates which run from 0.38 to 0.62 pounds per dollar. Representatives of interested firms calculate they would lose 40 percent of their capital upon repatriation. However, a program to float the Egyptian pound has been initiated; it is only deterred by the huge deficits faced by the government in years to come. The gap is even larger than the full cost of the military — a chit that might be picked up by the Saudi and Emirate governments. (The military bill runs $40 to $70 per capita, depending upon exchange rate.)

An indication of Sadat's eagerness to open up the society is the move to set up free trade zones which allow free movement of goods in and out, utilizing local labor in processing and fabrication. These free zones have been important to Taiwan and Korea, allowing them to compete with free ports such as Hong Kong and Singapore. They have been heavily used by the electronics, pharmaceutical, and garment industries. Egyptian labor is now available at bargain rates. The starting wage for clean work for literate women is approximately $40 per month, while experienced workers bilingual in English will gladly accept $100 per month. These rates may go up 10 to 20 percent after subsidies on nonessentials are removed later this year, but they remain in the same class with India, Pakistan, and Indonesia. Nevertheless there are no officially announced offers on the part of firms, even though the free zone program is six months old. If the moves are made, they will be very fast. The firms will try to be in production in six months. This outlook suggests prefabricated factory buildings — although any existing work space may be speedily declared a free trade zone — and perhaps also some prefabricated housing for key personnel. The government's preferred location for industry is in the Canal Zone, but Cairo's labor force is more varied.

Egypt is currently handicapped in an effort to expedite a "natural" winner among business opportunities. A sharpster from Brooklyn would note that the best long staple cotton is grown in the Delta and the government enterprises run four major cloth mills, with the great bulk of the cotton and cloth sent to the Soviet Union. However, the marketing is closely linked to that customer, and debts to the Soviets are huge. The Soviet Union is playing the role of tough lender; it has in effect a mortgage on the next 20 or so crops. Thus Egypt continues to pay for Nasser's adventures, since reneging on debts is no way to start floating a currency. It will take some truly creative effort to promote joint enterprises in the garments trade based upon Egyptian cotton.

Electronics is a better possibility. The intellectuals of Arab states are enthralled by the possibilities, but only Egypt has the homegrown talent that would allow it to move in concert with the firms. The big new boost to machinery given by microprocessors ("smart machines") was reviewed by Business Week in the last issue to arrive here. The projection to 1980 suggests that at least 100,000 jobs for women overseas could be created if the automatic manufacturing techniques do not beat them in the race to get on the market. At that time the demands from the automotive and electrical motor markets are also due to become very large.

The women in Cairo are liberated. They show this in their dress and their behavior. Soon they could even become a political force in the society. Thus far they have participated in bureaucracies and private enterprises but rarely have they been organizers, except when the Cairo Women's Club promoted family planning. The exclusiveness of the coffeehouses and similar places for negotiation means that this condition of passive participation is likely to continue for decades. Egypt has no institution equivalent to the Greek zacharoplasteion for women to get together. However, the abortion rate is said to have risen to half the level of births in Cairo. A two- to threefold further increase should open up options for women equivalent to those enjoyed in Latin countries. An electronics industry starting up in the next few years would accelerate the liberation process.

Some organizations are already effective, although apparently hopeless only a few years earlier. The military is one of these; it has become a meritocratic institution for expanding the modern sector. Water supply is another, and the Suez Canal organization is engaged in a huge expansion that is backed up by its unexpectedly high-level performance. The technocrats are intent upon adding to the list, which includes only those organizations I have personally encountered, either in Cairo or elsewhere, so there will be a diversity of government-sponsored organizations which will approach international standards of performance.

The reopening of Cairo to the Western world has loosened the fabric of its society. Tourism is awakening a number of the handicraft industries. Contractors are very busy overcoming the problems of shortages of materials. The hotels are pressed to the point that they must turn away business and be a little less than polite to the overflow. Airlines too are overbooked. Schools are open to more students, yet class sizes remain roughly constant, though still very large. Universities are exploding with students, including those who can pass stiff entrance exams. Through family connections, or coffeehouse contacts, a man has a chance to speak up about an injustice done to him, and there are instances where justice seems to have been achieved.

This note of extremely guarded optimism may be influenced by one unusual experience. Several times daily, while we walked through various back streets and artisan precincts, men looked up from their work benches, their pushcarts, or their games in the coffee shops, recognized us as Americans, and shouted "Welcome!" — one of the few English all-purpose words in the bazaar. Three times it was expanded to "Welcome Yanks!" The chief military enemy here is fully supported by the United States, and yet the common Egyptian has such a tolerant outlook.

10 Futures for Dubai*

It is difficult to think of Dubai, an oil-rich city-state on the Arabian Gulf, as part of the Asian Third World. For some reason we consider those who have hit the jackpot in a totally different category. Their potential wealth has removed the demographic stresses, the resource constraints, and the limits on rates of cultural improvement. But now they are fair game for exploitation by quick-witted outsiders.

Allah determined that Dubai should become rich, and attract five times as many guest-workers from South Asia and Egypt as were to be obtained from its own labor force so as to produce the wealth. Therefore, as visiting professionals, we see a small contingent of the Third World desperately seeking to be themselves again. The strongest motivation is to be a proper family man.

In Dubai the task was to find viable futures that could thereafter be elaborated by groups of public servants. The relevant information had been accumulated, sifted, and integrated by Paul Gabriel, an Arabic-speaking doctoral candidate, who used the material for his dissertation. He and Wendy showed off "their" city, enabling us to make visual assessments. An informal public address was scheduled. This was one of the few opportunities to demonstrate what the study of urban futures meant in terms of new policies. The present urban structure is not described because the audience was already familiar with it, and Paul Gabriel's forthcoming book would accomplish those ends so much better.

Therefore the reader must imagine being whisked from a luxury hotel serving food imported by air. The city is

*Estimated 1985 population — 250,000.

very much under construction, but the modern, prefabricated forms are readily separated from those of the old
city, created for pearling, coastal trading, and smuggling
only a few decades ago. Vestiges of squatter-type settlements, interim living quarters for the South Asian workers
who have now moved to apartments and residential hotels,
can still be seen. Heavy, serviceable cars, capable of
operating the largest air conditioners, are moving on
newly paved roads wherever they lead. Behind it all one
senses the taste and proprieties of a very small group of
British advisors to the sheikh. In the small, fully equipped
civic hall the white flowing robes of the Arabian members
of the audience stand out against the severe Western garb
of the merchants, administrators, corporation lawyers,
and consular corps who greatly outnumber them. All of
them are deeply engaged in contemporary Dubai.

AN "INSTANT CITY"

September 1978

A pulsing, young boom city has numerous futures open to it. Many
voices can be developed, and a variety of roles played — some
simultaneously and others sequentially in a normal cycle of maturation.
So much depends on the opportunities presented by conditions in the
region and the inherent constraints imposed by location, environment,
and precedent. Therefore, the most appropriate planning is not long
range or visionary, but opportunistic. A city that is alert to new
potentials and has conserved its resources can choose from among many
possible paths of evolution, even though it produces only one chronology
of events.

Dubai is one of the most interesting of the "instant cities" of the
twentieth century. Its future place in the constellation of world cities is
suggested by a brief retrospective. There were several instant cities in
the past century.(41) What are they today? What transformations did
they undergo?

In America, San Francisco was the entrepot for the California gold
rush. Within a decade raw pasture land was converted into real city,
recognized as such by established cities throughout the western and
eastern hemispheres. Its opera house attracted the leading entertainment talent in the world, and its tycoons generated respect in the
ranking salons of globe-girdling empires. The newly created wealth
went on to develop more durable resources in California and beyond, so
that it generated a century later the world's largest bank, the fourth
largest among the "seven sisters" petroleum giants, the largest technical construction firm, and "Silicon Valley," the fertile source of the
microcircuitry revolutionizing technology today. The fine arts and
popular creations flourish today in a golden age that promises to be
accepted as classic in generations to come.

Denver was the railroad terminus connecting gold, and later silver, strikes, with the industrial regions of America. It became a regional metropolis, surpassing all competitors through enterprise in smelting, banking, and merchandising. A century later it remains the hub of an area most attractive for educated, independent-minded young people. Therefore, it grows much more rapidly than its residents would like.

Virginia City was built on top of the fabulous Comstock Lode. Its elite failed to replace the surrounding forests or obtain the water necessary for follow-up industry, so they moved into the cultivated metropolises. Now it is a ghost town, restored to attract the tourist who has read Mark Twain and Bret Harte. It had surveyors and land developers, the physical planners of that era, equal to any of its competitors, but it failed to produce the entrepreneurs with vision who operated as the "real" planners, so its future was preempted by Las Vegas.

Cognizant of these phenomena, an experienced planner in America came to the University of California around 1970. He had been hired by the most affluent county of the most affluent state of the most affluent nation in the world. Always before his planning strategy had been based on an analysis of what was being done by the pace makers. He now felt insecure because he was out in front – there was no one to imitate. Dubai's affluence has not yet pushed it out in front, but it could, within its league of competitors, reach that stage within the lifetimes of buildings and facilities now being designed. This standard strategy of the top professional can be fitted to Dubai's prospects, and later other possibilities, based on current research on urban ecology, can be introduced.

Identifying Strategies

It is possible to decompose this planner's approach into a series of discrete steps. Each is easily fitted to the present circumstances in Dubai. The method involves:

1. Looking around at the competition for the city under consideration;
2. Identifying pace makers with endurance;
3. Searching for precedents and parallels in major arenas;
4. Discovering strategies employed by successful cities;
5. Formulating a mixed strategy based on imitation; and
6. Modifying it, employing comparative advantage in future competition.

The city-states within the United Arab Emirates comprise the immediate competition. Each has an urge to develop, but the disparity in resources is extreme. Petroleum production is the principal source of influence in the councils of the confederacy. Cash in hand is the source of power. Therefore, each state must either find oil or discover a substitute source of income. Those who have moderate quantities of oil, with unpromising prospects for the future, must look for ways of converting oil money into other kinds of income generators. Dubai belongs to this subclass within the United Arab Emirates. Its influence will decline if it does not discover the transition from the single original source of affluence to diverse, and therefore relatively stable, sources of livelihood. Dubai managed to gain the trust of British mentors in the 1960s sufficient to obtain a loan for dredging the creek, and adding to its port capacity, thus making itself the trading center in this part of the Arabian Gulf Coast. Finding oil in 1968 pushed it much closer to becoming a pacemaker itself among the states in the Emirates. It is complementary in most respects to larger, more prosperous Abu Dhabi.

The true pace maker in the Arabian Gulf region is Kuwait, a city-state whose name and whose policies come up daily in Dubai when discussing future projects. According to the calendar it is 20 years in the lead, although the head start was largely initiated by the sheikh's family members and their advisors, while the society as a whole needed to be virtually dragged into the modern era. Construction and modernization can now be compressed into a shorter span of time, so the lead of two decades has shrunk to perhaps half. Nevertheless, Kuwait has already carved out for itself the role of an international banking community. Within three years it has expanded from a circle of friends into a principal position in Asia – an eastern successor to war-torn Beirut and an outpost of the city of London. Its foundation has set a high standard in responsible giving, parallel in many ways to the Rockefeller dynasty that was founded upon the earliest development of petroleum. It is demonstrating that there is a future in making capital work for others, by collecting commissions and favors.

Outside of the immediate region the most relevant parallels are found in Southeast Asia. The bonanza that established Hong Kong was opium, but its distribution led into trading and banking. Modern Hong Kong was created from a huge refugee influx. The Shanghai contingent brought manufacturing skills and some equipment with them. Within a very short period Hong Kong learned how to manufacture textiles, fabricate plastics, build machines, and produce electronic equipment. Then it consciously expanded its airport, improved its tourist image, and set out to become the shopping center with the best prices and the most incredible variety. There were periods when Hong Kong overbuilt apartments and shops, but the activities introduced by new waves of refugees, many of whom brought their capital with them, pushed the city to ever higher levels of production and of income, so it was only a few years before the surplus space evaporated and a much greater boom in real estate was initiated.

Singapore has half the population of Hong Kong, but it competes in the same league. The discovery of tin deposits was the first boost it received, followed later by the servicing of rubber production and petroleum exploration. The promotion of tourism and free port shopping, followed by banking and management services, along with the industry collected on the famous Jurong industrial estate allowed it to complete a spectacular clean green city, made up predominantly of high-rise apartments, and an exemplar of entrepreneurial "rugged socialism." Singapore began its postcolonial existence as a city-state within the Malay confederation, and quickly recovered from the dissolution of those ties. Its labor force was imported from the Malay states and from South India. Though overbuilt several times over the past generation, it is again pushing against its capacity to serve visitors.

Although the "Asian dollar" was a financial device invented in Singapore, it now appears to be challenged by creative law formulated in Manila, where the Asian Development Bank is also located. With its current surplus of hotel space, Manila may now become a direct competitor of Kuwait for offshore banking. Its highly modern office and commercial center in Makati, providing headqua.ters for national enterprises, is being transformed into a base for multinational operations. Hong Kong has decided to tax offshore banking, thereby leaving the growth in this activity to other cities.

What this brief review of recent developments suggests is there appears to be room for a few more cities that are capable of converting the capital created by petrodollars into productive projects elsewhere in the world. If it is to compete effectively, the city must possess excellent telecommunication services, a free port, a liberal set of laws, a low level of crime and violence, and a minimum of political disturbance. It must accept immigrant labor, and encourage refugees to find a home which allows them to contribute their specialties to the local economy, their cuisine to the choices in dining, and their arts to add to the diversity supported in the city. It appears that the city-states of the United Arab Emirates could use the competitive advantage provided by their Arabic culture and their overbuilt services to find several mutually supporting roles as middlemen, and Dubai could very well be the local pace maker.

Elaborations on This Theme

Tourism mixes well with free port shopping and the management of capital, as both Hong Kong and Singapore have proven. The oppressive humidity of Dubai would force tourism into a limited season. The principal attraction seems to be sailing, since the beaches of other city-states are recognized to be superior.

The distance from Europe is not too great. After a tourist has "done" Tunis and Egypt, the next winter holiday could well be spent in the Emirates. However, a shakeout in room rents and labor-intensive services would be necessary. Otherwise, the clientele would fly on to Colombo, where the rates are half or less. A collapse in property values could very well occur before the end of 1979. Long-range planning must assume that it will occur, even though property owners will not accept the revaluation until long after it has happened.

An astute promoter of tourism would probably develop multiple attractions in the environment, some based on sailing, yacht racing, fishing, and "historic" tours retracing the routes of the gold smugglers of yesteryear. A little extra might be added by exploiting the attractions of nearby desert cases. However, an emphasis on tennis, squash, and court sports might well become more important.

The business clientele of the International Trade Center would depend on these services outside business hours. One imagines such facilities providing a partial substitute for the golf courses available in Europe and Japan where the principals in an enterprise use the sport as a means of gauging personalities of collaborators and competitors. The International Trade Center itself serves as a barometer of newly opening opportunities, and a place where new consortiums are negotiated or promoted, some of which may take root in the United Arab Emirates.

The planning and the promotion of the Trade Center, and the maintenance of its viability, is far more important to the future than any amount of physical planning. Its vision needs to be international, its sources of information global, while its spin-offs will occasionally settle down in the vicinity. It is the temple of business to which a special community — including the local offices of a hundred or so engineering firms, an equal number of financial interests, and several hundred consultants and free professionals — would repair. As compared to its principal competitors (expected to be the financial centers of Basel, Dresden, Brussels, Milan, Athens, Bombay, Seoul, and Honolulu) it appears too small to be viable, but the comfortable size of the entrepreneurial community and its petrodollar environment makes possible a very quick reaction time that should make it possible to survive major perturbations in the world economy.

Urban Ecological Strategies

We think of a community in an ecosystem as comprising a number of different populations interacting with each other and their physical environment. In an urban ecosystem man is dominant; diverse populations of men must interact continuously in many different ways. If they can manage it, humans aim for a stable state over the long run, because downswings from spurts of growth call for painful readjustments. Growth is intoxicating when first experienced, but the subsequent setbacks raise serious questions. Wise men are those who have experienced several cycles of expansion and setback and have survived so their counsel is sought. The advice is almost universally that of cooperation, so as to remove stressful peaks and valleys in welfare. Mutual effort is coordinated through organizations. Thus, a good measure of community potential for stabilization is a count of human organizations. An environment designed to enhance the formation and survival of organizations enabling specialized cooperation is ecologically sound.

Therefore, the answer for the aforementioned planner of a leading affluent community, whose prior strategies no longer were suitable, was given the following advice: 1) Identify all the voluntary organizations in the community that are viable. (These will have an address, at least one officer who deals with the public outside, a charter specifying his replacement, a membership, and a clientele for potential recruitment.) 2) Identify their principal common interests, remembering that some of these may not be respectable, and therefore remain hidden. 3) Discover the spaces and times they claim as necessary to the continued cooperative activity in which each of them specializes. 4) Mark out the overlaps and potential conflicts. 5) Then lay out a program for allocation of land, built environment, times of occupation, and community services that minimize the cost of conflict. 6) The result would be a community producing the highest level of human satisfaction for which the members themselves were willing to expend effort.

In his survey this planner found that an affluent community valued avocation even more than location as a basis for organized cooperation. For example, four different kinds of groups were formed to allow people to live with their horses, and each equestrian group demanded a different kind of turf. Similarly, more than 25 groups demanded a piece of shoreline which would allow them to live with their boat in an approved style. The possibilities for physical planning according to ecological principles are immediately evident. Because they are general principals they should apply equally well to Dubai.

In making proposals for change, however, one needs to be concerned with political processes. Changes must suit the dominant interests. In Dubai this means that planners must be conscious of the Makhtoum family, which will produce the shiekhs of the future, and most of the ministers as well. Fortunately, Dubai has wise leadership, as compared to other states in the region, and it has managed to stabilize the intrafamily contests for power so prevalent in the history of Arab states. Nevertheless, as elsewhere in the world, a shift of personnel in top posts will have predictable effects on the priorities assigned to interests sponsored by organizations. Ecological planning must take dominance into account to the same extent as cooperation or integration. If the elephant or the camel should displace the lion as king of the beasts, the relationships between all the rest of the species would noticeably shift.

When the Oil and Gas are Exhausted

Sometime, perhaps 40 years hence, the oil and gas of Arabia will have been reduced to a battery of marginal stripping wells. Will cities based on cheap energy have to die? The air-conditioned city of Dubai would operate at a tremendous competitive disadvantage. The thermal stress imposed by the environment might cause its affluent population to seek more pleasant locales, leaving behind another ghost city.

Recently a way has been discovered for overcoming thermal stress — it involves going underground at least three meters, and avoiding the high humidity adjacent to the creek. Israelis have demonstrated that comfort is readily achieved in the sizzling Sinai Desert without powered systems, merely through careful design.

If this technique for living in a desert environment is to be developed further, it would probably entail the establishment of a comfortable, energy-conserving Dubai with suq, offices, and dwellings located one, two and even three stories beneath the surface about where the bedrock rises above sea level. The surface above the city would be green, because its waste waters would be used for vegetation, mostly orchards and shade.

By that time the economical approaches to hydroponics will have been perfected. The highest quality water from wells would be used to produce the vegetables that add vitamins and variety to the diet of the future. Familiar foods will still be served for holy days and other formal occasions, but the cosmopolitan sources of the population of Dubai assure that many different cuisines – and newly created successors to the American fast foods, which seem to be popular with all ethnic groups already – will be made available. These adjustments to self-sufficiency and a steady state for the long run would require less than 10 percent of the present levels of commerce for feeding and clothing the population of Dubai.

The airport is likely to remain the principal gateway to the city, despite heavy requirements for liquid fuel. It is extremely probable that liquid hydrocarbon fuels will be the most highly valued sources of energy in the future. Extreme dependence upon aviation is due to the thinness of settlement in the Arabian peninsula. Dubai needs to remain intimately connected with many other cities if it is to develop and maintain new activities in business, trade, and tourism. Virtually all organizing tasks will require air transport.

The creek would no doubt fill up with sailing vessels and pleasure craft, displacing the working boats of the present, and silt would be allowed to collect again in most of the channel. Much of the mooring might be managed under the once luxurious towers of the city which would be closed off due to the inordinate air-conditioning requirements. Perhaps the bottom floor and the basements would find some continuing use, because for them the cost of comfort would be relatively cheap, and accessibility would remain high.

The ports and gateways that sustain the city more than those so far described will be largely invisible. The petroleum industry itself has been responsible for the introduction of sophisticated telecommunications. The global networks will continue to be contacted through communications satellites in the sky. Their existence will cause most of the office work of the future to be conducted through interaction with fluorescent screens. The overall energy cost to maintain this gateway is trivial.

Switzerland's Basel and Berne, which possess functions now most nearly equivalent to those expected in the future for Dubai while operating within a confederation similar to the United Arab Emirates, will have much greater difficulties adjusting their physical form to the scarcities and opportunities of the twenty-first century. Yet Swiss citizens and guest-workers are confident that the cities will reconstruct themselves appropriately.

With planning that is possible today, the future of Dubai may be assured to at least an equal degree.

11 A Postscript on Method

Much of what has been recommended here to the futures-oriented tourist and untourist turns contemporary social science on its head; yet for the Third World it is good science. As emphasized everywhere, but particularly in the reports on Korea, and Dubai, Third World urban societies are undergoing growth and change unprecedented in their history. The standard procedures for problem formulation, study design, funding, research team mobilization, instrument development, sampling, data collection, coding, data processing, analysis, report writing, and the recommendation of policy or behavioral change to interested parties, tend to take two to five years in Western societies when everything goes smoothly. In the more chaotic and error-prone environments of developing metropolises a respectable study will take even longer. Given these conditions the study can only reveal a past that has been left far behind; the policy and behavioral change proposals that depend upon the study will look backward rather than forward, unless the decision makers add an unusually large component of personal experience and immediate observation at the time they implement the final report.

Consider the aspect of growth alone. Urban population grows by four to ten percent per year – even more if there is stress of some kind in the countryside. Moreover, most of the growth is not in the form of infants yet to be acculturated but is made up of active young adults bringing disparate traits and externally acquired experience to the arena of action. The rate of economic growth is usually substantially greater than that of population growth, so formally organized urban activity growth is expanding at a net rate of 5 to 20 percent per year, sometimes even more. Some of this growth will accelerate physical and organizational obsolescence in vital sectors; thus the foundations for old life-styles will erode away.

People on the scene will often single out the extraordinary rises in the price of land as an underlying reason for the disappearance of traditional organizations and for shifts in social function noted in specific precincts. In two to four years land prices may be expected to rise an average of 50-100 percent in real terms, but much of this is quite naturally concentrated in areas of economic prosperity or improved accessibility. Land price is a proxy representing many forces operating from a distance; it is an excellent indicator of shifting expectations. Since the abrupt rise in the price of petroleum, land prices in these cities have leveled, and often dropped. The meaning of this reverse shift is not at all clear, but it is suggestive.

All the indirect evidence taken as a whole suggests that a third to a half of the identifiable social relationships connecting individuals and households to sites and institutions will have been changed between the time a study is designed and the time a report can be digested. Indeed, it is quite remarkable that cities retain a recognizably unique lifeway when experiencing the kind of change under way in much of the Third World. This impression of characteristic order can only be explained by the fact that a roughly equal proportion of "invariant" relationships have been preserved so they can be used for orientation and reference by residents.

Given this fluidity, and the unavailability of many familiar kinds of current data, how does one organize the collection of new information so as to achieve a stable set of expectations? Obviously he needs to build a theory about Singapore, Calcutta, Katmandu, or whatever places he visits, that might also affect his thinking about other Chinese, Muslim, and Indian-influenced cities. The theory may not be comprehensive or subtle, but should serve to condense a huge amount of information. At the same time, when serving as a theme for intellectual conversations, such a theory should elicit the recent contradictory instances which challenge it. There is also a bonus: other people's generalizations can be incorporated into one's own framework.

Sociologists have recently suggested methods for building theory without engaging in extensive sample surveys or processing bundles of statistics. Arthur Stinchcombe's Constructing Social Theories(42) illustrates such a method; it has been followed up in an article by Nicholas C. Mullins.(43) The theories most suited to middle-range forecasting are continuously compared and reviewed in Futures, a serious international periodical published in London.

Reliable methods for observing behavior in public have been worked out by psychologists, although most of the examples they report focus upon short sequences of behavior in similar settings and do not come close to the demands of observing a metropolis. They may, however, be used persuasively for spot checks designed to test an interesting hypothesis. In such work it is important that the stranger does not change the behavior by his presence on the scene. With this problem in mind Webb, Campbell, Schwarts and Sechrest compiled Unobtrusive Measures,(44) which demonstrates methods that are particularly useful for plotting the influx and diffusion of imported styles and forms.

A method of investigating urban ecology that comes closest to yielding the quick appraisal desired is that of Grady Clay.(45) He searches for the "undisclosed evidence, the patterns and clues waiting to be organized." With maps, camera, and a sketch pad as instruments, and depending upon a wary reporter's ear as a filter, he aims to penetrate whole industries of propaganda, seeking out the public's consensus. The intent is to work out a better fit between language and urban environment, always testing to discover the amount of communication actually achieved.

Grady Clay's procedure also starts with an introduction to a new locale and orientation within it ("getting a fix"); it leads on from there to the special places, or epitome districts, that draw the crowds. Fronts − in all the meanings of the term and in all scales of presentation − are identified; they lead the explorer to representative "strips" and "beats," two kinds of association based upon human mobility. Inventory buildups ("stacks") play a prominent role in city routines, while the refuse and discards collect in out-of-the-way "sinks." Finally the tourist-investigator enters the territories claimed by the differentiated ethnic and life-style communities ("turf") for an understanding of the diversity provided.

Techniques of ethnomethodology were specifically applied to the exploration of foreign places by Dean McCannel.(46) Tourism, he argues, is the antithesis of revolution, since traditional orders are respected, sometimes restored, rather than overturned or transformed. The standard contemporary tourist is recognized to be a representative of the postindustrial era in search of destroyed cultures and dead epochs, or strange remnants of the past. An ambitious tourist hopes to obtain a holistic insight into human concerns, seek out his own roots, and discover alternative relationships to a constructed environment; a tourist expresses shame when he is not tourist enough.

Sightseeing implies a "system of attractions," or cultural productions, for which there is staged authentication. The Baedeker and Guide Bleu are manuals prepared for "sight sacralization" − "Yes, I saw the Mona Lisa." McCannel developed a semiotic formulation for an environmental transaction:

(tourist / sight / marker)
                                        attraction

(role / object / sign)
                                        phenomenon

which can be extended to cover the approach of a futurist as follows:

(futurist / datum / indicator)
                                        expectation

The futurist must see through the cultural productions prepared for both the tourist and the resident; his shame is expressed when confronted with subsequent events he should have foreseen, but did not.

Somewhere in between the sociologists and the psychologists stands the observer who notes the establishment of social boundaries or frames of behavior. These mark out the lines of defense in the battle to preserve what is held to be proper and also the frontiers that must be crossed to become notably deviant. Erving Goffman describes these phenomena for us in Frame Analysis, an invaluable work for planners and designers who are conscious of the ways in which settings for public behavior are constructed.(47) They know that recognizable cues must be installed on the scene in order to elicit playfulness in one locale, for example, and business negotiations in another, extending to those calling forth such extremes as respectable gambling, diplomatic formality, theatrical posturing, religious solemnity, etc. Such signals, when frozen into the physical environment, are easily recognizable across language barriers; the kind of behavior contained within the setting is almost always interpretable from clues provided by the action. The two forms of evidence corroborate each other. The original frame may be askew, whereupon covert cues, usually behavioral, dominate the situation, revealing a new frame behind the facade. The rent in the curtain could be caused by a car crash and the attendant commotion, or it might be the arrival of the underworld boss with his bodyguards who "hold court" in some defensible position. The problem is to take these overlaying versions of "what is really going on" and what is "out there" for a modestly involved participant and convert them into a set of expectations about nontrivial happenings and relationships for specific periods in the future. Frame analysis deals with episodes, often multilayered in meaning; futures study seeks to discover which of these episodes seem likely to be relevant for anticipated objective conditions, in what proportions, with which modifications, and with room for what kinds of innovations.

Forecasting from Modernization Trends

Standard methods for viewing modernization processes employed to test a handful of hypotheses are almost always too crude and oversimplified a means for understanding a city. They are not worth reassessing here. Hypotheses are numerous and cheap for the exploratory investigator, but time is short, so the limited observations and sources at hand must be matched against the population of hypotheses to see which are strengthened or weakened by the evidence. Most will not be affected at all.

Modernization is almost always viewed as a process of "catching up" with the contemporary norms; we most often assess it in terms of the degree to which the gap between "them" and "us" is being closed. Not only is such an attitude patronizing, it is inefficient to employ in the field. Every tourist and untourist should be warned, however, that the cultural and economic gap is felt very strongly by the bilingual layer of the society with which an outsider is thrown into contact; the subject crops up in conversation so often it appears to be a cultural obsession.

The bias can be avoided by regarding the phenomena of modernization as a diffusion of artifacts, images and traits to be estimated in much the same way that one traces the Japanization of the West through style in cameras, color television, autos, architecture and landscaping or notes the Indianization of fabric prints and philosophical groups.

Until recently the prime objection to this equivalence of approach was the political and economic forcefulness by which Western images were being transmitted; however, the disappearance of the British Empire, the fall of the dollar as the basi medium of exchange, and the failure of the American military in Viet Nam and Cambodia suggest that the aura of power inherent in the Western image has dissolved. Power remains exceedingly important in guiding the direction of influence – particularly for external appearances and public rituals – but there are multiple sources of power today in the Third World. Yet power by itself is not enough; for example, Saudi images have penetrated very few countries, despite the expenditure of billions of dollars in subsidies, mainly because they had a very limited cultural base at the time of emergence into world politics.

Everywhere in the Third World it is possible to see conditions so contrasting and disparate that it is claimed that a "dual society" exists – modern overlaying the traditional. One apparently simple method of understanding development – remembering that only very simple methods are useful to a short-term tourist – is to trace the transitions of people and specialized activities, such as education and sanitation, from traditional conditions to a modern state. The individuals usually go through some kind of a conversion process which causes them to reject a large part of the tradition that has been shown ineffective and to adopt an alternative with an excellent external reputation. The pathways are trod many times after they have been pioneered, so the tabbing of the recently opened pathways should give a futurist some leverage for forecasting the direction and rate of change. The newly modern people collaborate to create the new schools, new institutes, and modern organizations for supplying services.

It will be noted that this simple, two-sector model was introduced above with a caution. It has several limitations. The first is that the concept of modern itself has multiple levels. One of these might be called colonial; it would be epitomized in the relatively unchanged hill station retreats of the Western elite of an already historic era. These outposts of the metropolis are now used by the imitators of the old elite, and often even the followers of the imitators; they make up a backward-looking stratum of the society whose values and symbols are obsolescent, though far from dead.

A second level of modernity is postindependence – the consolidation and early realization of the ideals of the freedom fighters. What was borrowed as modern was an ideology, almost always that of socialism, which proceeded to transform traditional and colonial institutions. The traceable sources are limited to Laski's coterie in the London School of Economics, the Left Bank in Paris during the 1920s and 1930s, and Greenwich Village or Spanish Harlem in New York about the same time.

Almost always there were also a few odd, accidental influences that flavored the individual political puddings.

Still more recently – almost entirely in the jet age – a cosmopolitan impetus has been given to public services and popular culture. For the first time in history "modern" has a reproducible set of outcomes regardless of locale instead of pale approximations of the appropriate imperial hub – London, New York, Paris, Amsterdam, Brussels, Rome, Lisbon, Madrid, or Moscow. Cosmopolitan tends to mean Chinese or French cuisine with American snacks; the images that flow through the telecommunications nets and the mass media – Time magazine, the Beatles and their successors, and the singing commercial; footwear styles based upon Italian designs with the merchandizing pace set by Bata, a firm launched by Czechs; blue jeans, sport shirts and knit jerseys that have now become universal indicators of informality and unpretentiousness; know-how that is defined comprehensively by textbooks from New York or intellectually by elegant monographs from Oxbridge; or antibiotics with nonsense names coined in America by a computer. But all of this is unfixed, impermanent, short lived and speedily replaceable by something better or temporarily of greater interest. Cosmopolitanism is the antithesis of ideological commitment to any of the living religions or to nationalism and socialism, which it increasingly displaces. Therefore cosmopolitanism is fought by both the establishment and the opposition, not only in Havana, New Delhi, Nairobi, Phnom Penh, and Rangoon, but almost everywhere else.

These three strata of modern are readily distinguishable even in countries like Thailand or Ethiopia which though conquered in battle by imperialist powers were never reduced to colonial status. The levels are apparent mainly because the specific influences have a "period quality." Colonial features and forms are visibly decaying, so one expects revivalist movements among older people with money and influence. They create new institutions like museums and academies dedicated to the preservation of imperial artifacts, rituals, skills, and historic places. One can predict with a high level of confidence that these features will survive for a long time to come and that sociocultural changes will wash around the fringes of these bulwarks of the past. Soon the preserved items will stand out as quaint but revered landmarks.

Postindependence elements are peculiarly governmental. However, with a third generation coming onto the scene, few new opportunities to demonstrate this independence remain for the newly educated professionals. The newest classes of graduates are better critics than builders; therefore, their ideological goals, whether nationalistic or political, do not predict future states of being.

The new immigrants to the city, and those absorbing standard urban concepts from a distance in the rapidly expanding middle schools of towns and central villages, are acquiring nationalism and multiplying its service symbols, translated into regional idioms and languages. Labor union organizers and local politicians are acutely aware of the strength of ideals and principles made sacred by the blood of martyrs. So we can confidently forecast a continuous expansion of formal social services, such as schools, hospitals, and public transport, and the growth of their urban bureaucracies, even if it does not make economic sense. Much of the local news will be about the conflicts between these contending bureaucracies; from the translations available even a visitor can sense which institutions will continue to grow as the economy expands.

The latest phase of modernization – cosmopolitanism – may be regarded as a myriad of interconnected fads, many of which have shallow roots and effect little significant change; nevertheless a few fill previously unexpressed needs and evoke consequences that become visible. Many of these are associated with the increasing independence of women, the decline of the arranged marriage, new channels of courtship, postponement of the entry of youths into the labor market, and the search for controls over environmental exploitation.

Judging Cosmopolitan Influences

In the Third World private sector new capital is very scarce. (Prior to the global inflation short-term business loans were quoted on the street at 2.5 to 4 percent per month, while if one qualified for imported capital the rates were only 1/2 to 1 percent per month.) Therefore a potentially successful entrant into the business sector of the metropolis emerges into view first in the financial pages of the English-language periodicals. Recent installations and proposals – taking one category of industry at a time – that appear in the monthly business journals should be reviewed. The spot news on each project will be noted by the dailies and weeklies. Advertisements are also sometimes informative, particularly when a new product is being added to a line already marketed. An announcement of investment commitment in these media leads to actual production two or three years later (longer for steel mills, heavy machinery, and power generation) about 60 to 80 percent of the time, thus offering a good foundation for linking up the more indefinite forecasts of social change.

Corroborative information can be obtained from the English-language section of the telephone book. If one starts from Fortune's list of leading multinational firms, he can readily identify those that are represented in such a way that their reputations are at stake. (Use of locally dominated consortiums, joint enterprises with nonrevealing names, and licensing do not really amount to much more than a testing of the industrial climate.) A metropolis like Hong Kong will become a new home for hundreds of major multinational enterprises, and their names are excellent indicators of industrial competences, current and prospective, that can be tapped. However, most metropolises in the Third World will have branch offices and plants belonging to only a score or more corporations. Noting the locations on a map, and the number of telephone lines to various subdivisions enables a person with professional experience to arrive at quite a few inferences about the scale of operations for the respective firms. Other multinational organizations, some state-owned corporations, others nonprofit groups, with a few representing professional associations, are responsible for almost all of the other newly introduced expertise and technology.

The chamber of commerce or the local industrial development corporation may sponsor a commercial library or this service might be provided through the consulates of the technology-exporting countries. These libraries will probably prepare their indexes according to the name of firm, and a file of clippings will very likely have been assembled. For cities like Singapore, this approach would generate too much information to digest, but the library nevertheless remains a prime resource to explore after the building sites have been visited.

Perhaps the quickest means of getting a cross section of the fundamental differences between cosmopolitan versions of modern and the others is to arrive at the central market in the morning. There one will see peasants in their weekday village dress, porters (still coolies in many Asian cities) in the minimum clothing respectable for the poorest working class, shop attendants and small shopkeepers conforming to standards set by crafts and guilds, and an occasional policeman, public official, or professional, each of whom must distinguish himself from the crowd. The mass of purchasers is made up of trusted servants and householders who reveal the spectrum that lies between rural traditions and modern Western styles of dress. Note also the sex ratios, since markets in Bangladesh will be 100 percent male, but in a society just as predominantly Muslim, such as Java, they will be predominantly female. Where religious and ethnic groups are mixed, as in Penang or Jerusalem, the variety within a kilometer of the central market becomes kaleidoscopic, and could require days to sort out, even with the help of a sophisticated guide. The products that are displayed, ranging from the latest California potato to portable television sets, are indicative of what is accepted by the masses.

Everyone has learned a set of intuitive rules for assigning social status to people around him. He starts with the morphological clues which still work quite well with the westernized sector of the Third World, but encounters severe difficulties with the indigenous indicators. Considerable mystery will be generated by his preconceptions. Using all the means provided at the interface of this culture with the rest of the world, the new visitor should be able to discriminate several score different roles or types based purely upon the local rules for the presentation of identity by means of color, style, clothing, and action, even though most of the names, functions, and special contributions have yet to be sorted out. Through subsequent observation, reading, and conversations it will be possible to discover which of these are major contestants in the competitive games that play out the future in a given locale. South Asia is the richest region for displaying role types, while former American dependencies, such as the Philippines and South Viet Nam, have begun to use these stigmata much more to express personality.

Fortunately, helpful bilinguals are rarely reluctant to explain in their own terms the major cues exhibited in uniforms, apparel types, head gear, and portable implements of a trade. It is part of the public knowledge of their city; the patterns elucidated are more distinctive than the architecture of the city hall. The visitor should be warned, however, that these reporters tend to assign images and patterns according to an urban ordering that "should" exist and is therefore idealized to some degree. An empirical study, which would require many months, even years, to complete, would reveal a large number of exceptions, sometimes demonstrating that a generalization no longer holds in a practical sense — such as when women should be wearing black in Mediterranean countries.

Local observers are particularly untrustworthy when assessing rates of urban change. Most believe that fundamentally there has been little movement in their immediate environment and will so state even when it is undergoing unprecedented transformations, while the sectors of metropolitan society most distant for them are felt to be in the throes of abrupt change. These biases stem directly from active participation at a single focus; they do not match the biases of the future-oriented outside observer trying to gauge the changes likely to be observed later by journalists and other outsiders.

Making Contact

Actually venturing out into an utterly strange environment is quite different from theorizing about it. A very first step, particularly for the untourist, is to become acquainted with the network of streets and public services in the immediate environment. Upon leaving the portal of the initial refuge the strategy is to make close note of the openings to the left, right and center, exploring each a little way, perhaps a hundred meters. Then the most promising of these ways should be taken for a round-the-block excursion. (This sounds utterly safe, but in Dacca where the signs are 99 percent in Bengalese script, I never did get back to the starting position because high walls disguised the back of the hotel. I came out through a narrow opening onto a road already traversed but in a way that was not readily recognizable, eventually discovering that a loop had been made but not knowing where to turn to get back to the launch site.) The alleys should be explored because in many oriental cultures they contain much of the public life of the city. When the starting point is again in view, it is useful to offset and make a crude spiral away from the point of origin, or else follow an intriguing boulevarde or corridor, both of which allow one to employ a straight line return to the starting point.

The standard tourist's reaction to becoming lost is to hail a taxi. In the poorest cities of the world no functioning taxi system exists. The nearest equivalent may be a scooter which serves the local population as an alternative, or a pedicab, which goes by a different name in almost every society. These vehicular arrangements are organized to fit the needs of the middle classes, not those of the occasional tourist; the operators are rarely bilingual. Often they do not even know the city and depend upon the fare to guide them to the destination.   (This is particularly true after the crops are in and the labor market is flooded with peasants who pick up these low-paying jobs to fill in the off season.) Even if there are taxis, the fares are often determined by bargaining but the tourist does not know the rules of the game. Even if he is willing to pay triple the normal fare, he may unwittingly be taken for a ride into unknown parts of the city where a frequent destination exists that sounds the same in a local language. (For example, KAL resembles Tower in Seoul.) Eventually the personal transport specialists, by consulting each other, will deliver the tourist to his intended destination. Tourist hotels reduce this confusion by providing neighborhood maps on cards, although even then there can be ambiguity. The untourist living in informal or cheap accommodations has to be more careful; he must undertake much more extensive explorations on foot in less accommodating neighborhoods before starting to ask serious questions of the environment or of the community that are relevant to its future. Reassurance of the presence of public toilets, if any, will be helpful. He will want to be shown also how to use the bus or tram system as well as the personal transport vehicles.

Habits acquired in using Western telephone systems must also be curbed. It is almost always necessary that one be introduced to the instrument by a local user who has learned to discriminate the various "busy" and "disconnected" signals and similar challenges. Only the airlines and intercontinental hotels will respond in English when spoken to in that language; in most places even the bilinguals at the other end of the line will hang up for fear of becoming involved in a complicated situation. In metropolises with overloaded telephone systems (in the Third World this constitutes the predominant majority) a top administrator or professional will have a special telephone secretary whose principal duty is to outwit the system by using roundabout tactics or through dialing the same number interminably, such as twenty, or even a hundred, times. Once he is through to the desired number, a strangely accented caller has an exceedingly difficult time making his desire for information understood. Yet some visitors do very quickly acquire the knack and retain the patience necessary for telephone use, just as others learn to use the street networks without getting lost within two days of first contact.

All through this review of the central districts the designer-futurist will be on the lookout for good pictures. Most of his story cannot be told in words. During the first exploration a few shots may be taken, particularly of small-scale phenomena, but for most of the day there is too much interfering activity. Notes should be made where early morning, or late afternoon, shots can be taken advantageously. In the humid tropics early morning is almost always the best. After dark the local stock of postcards and commercially prepared slides can be sifted; a few of them tell much more than intended by the tourist promotion agency that sponsors their production. Near the end of the stay, a cab or cycle rickshaw can be commandeered at dawn and a roll or two of film can be profitably spent on the most revealing large architected forms in the metropolis, with the examples of landscaping reserved for midday.

Perhaps a better method of representing the novel twists to design in a city is suggested by the old-fashioned members of the profession less dependent upon the latest photographic technology. They have learned to sketch and are able to ignore crowds, traffic and inconvenient shadow in the course of reducing the image to a representation. Also the police and counterintelligence forces of the Third World are less concerned about an artist. In this respect the untourists have a special advantage – they look like artists according to the public image and are seldom disturbed while at work. The likelihood of becoming a victim of thefts is also very much reduced. An added feature is that neither the superstitions held by those who might be caught inadvertently in the picture nor the antics of the poseurs need be a concern. A series of sketches can be rendered comparable in weight at one's leisure, according to the requirements of a convenient technique for reproduction or display.

With the repertoire of images and elementary conjectures acquired in a week or so spent in this way it becomes possible to talk meaningfully about the various constraints laid upon the architect and the landscape architect. One learns about the best clients to be found in the public sector, and the special political difficulties faced by designers. Does corruption free the designer, as in the Americas, or limit him, as in most Muslim countries? The public building is almost always a monument to a person or to a concept, but according to what forms and precedents is the monumentalism defined? The academic faculties can refer the visitor to the interesting offices in the central city where the differences between a feasible design and one that is better, even outstanding, may be compared. Before the two weeks are over the visiting designer should be able to sketch out the kind of proposals that would surely be acceptable in the next round of projects in a metropolis and could suggest a few others that might attract the attention of an aggressive, innovating client.

The industrial designer and the advertising copy specialist are not likely to find the task so straightforward. They are much more likely to be tied to catalogs and the slick magazines – both of which are hard to find as indigenous publications. Too often they are direct translations from imported English, French or Japanese versions with very minor adjustments for local taste. Advertising graphics in the vernacular sometimes do produce blurbs for styles in clothing and fronts for establishments in astonishing color combinations, but these presentations are intended for the cabaret and massage parlor strata of society. They make interesting souvenirs but portend little for the future.

Designers of artifacts and graphics will be especially sensitive observers of local attire. They appreciate somewhat better the techniques of fabrication based upon looms, knitting machines, needlework, dye vats, buttons and zippers. In the less educated parts of the Third World clothing is used to establish membership in a community – rarely the full dress, but a fez, turban, or skullcap for the head, or a color combination in a sari, or sometimes only a hairstyle or caste markings. In a complex city sheltering many communities, the communities are encouraged to fill a restricted set of roles which are understood by everyone else, so these communal markings also serve to differentiate urban service roles. (In Calcutta, it was noted, traditional Hindus will keep cows in the city, but Muslims can slaughter them, tan the hides, and work the leather, while Chinese control the styling and marketing of shoes, and cosmopolitan Marwari export house agents and madrassi bureaucrats are expected to manage the export to Russia and Poland.) Well-established roles may well draw people from many origins, but the role players affect a homogeneous appearance in public, sometimes to the extent of adopting an unofficial uniform, especially in the lower ranks of the civil service. More revealing and predictive than their dress or their behavior in public are the artifacts such people work with – the typewriter, hand-held calculator, printed forms, etc.

New terms appearing in the official language and changes in the slang signal the acceptance of new styles. In a place as organized as a metropolis the communicators are alert to the appearance of new objects and actions and will attempt to standardize reference to them, so as to minimize ambiguity, by preparing a list. In Japan, where the publication and communication industries are highly centralized, complete dictionaries are put out annually; in other countries such lists of neologisms are the exclusive property of editorial offices and circulated in university departments. They reveal most succinctly the many dimensions of cultural growth and the particular pathways for borrowing and invention involved in current organizational growth; the organizations need these additions to the language to teach improved procedures to their members, to prevent errors, and to sell novel services to their clients. Since completion of the borrowing process rarely takes less than a year after a term has been added to the speech of a city and often takes a decade or two, the technique has fair potential for middle-range forecasting. It requires local informants who are multilingual and sensitive to the undercurrents of talk in the city. Fortunately such people are also most interested in meeting strangers and are almost certain to be found among the persons recommended for contact to the visiting specialist in the public sector.

For the public sector the new projects appear in the five-year plan documents, which are most often initially drafted in English, but the delays are very great and the likelihood of cancellation is naturally increased. Quite a few five-year plans still do not have a regional breakdown so the prospective location of the production facilities is not published. However, because public corporations are more sensitive to public opinion, they are more careful to describe their projects on billboards at the construction sites. In most countries a futuristic image is sketched in color on the hoarding; in quite a few the size of the prime contract accompanies the name of the contracting firm. In a democracy this is done to diminish the likelihood of citizen disapproval; in the gradations leading toward an authoritarian regime one notes an increasing necessity to applaud the wisdom of the chief figure in the political limelight and to emphasize the glory he is bringing to his people. An abbreviated reminder of the first official announcement of the project is quite often proudly displayed at the site by the contractor.

Whether socialist in viewpoint or intent upon maintaining a mixed economy, the Third World countries encounter their most obstinate problems in the service sector that produces either free goods, such as education, water supply, or family planning, or those that are distributed for fixed fees. Recognition of faults in the administrative process by ministers and top officials leads to many invitations to outside experts and managers in the hope that improvements drawn from their experience will take root, grow and multiply. The continuous flow of foreign specialists attracts others, most commonly medical personnel, who are footloose and still idealistic.

The simplest method for appraising future public-sector projects with long-term consequences is to discover a friendship circle or professional network that includes such professionals as engineers, doctors, economists, architects or bankers. Most often it is necessary to invent some kind of plausible deal involving one's own professional connections in order to make contact; for ethical reasons, it must be a project that is worth full commitment should the conditions be ripe for implementation. Placing oneself in the role of a social entrepreneur of some kind is likely to reveal the style of the behind-the-scenes competition that these projects must survive, and the extraordinary risks that may be encountered. (The untourist is at a considerable disadvantage in this kind of evaluation. Because of his desire to move about either informally or as an "outsider," the networks he is likely to contact are smaller in size and narrower in function.) These contacts usually require a great deal of time when spare hours are precious, so they should not be used exhaustively.

Working in this way one should understand the nature of an obligation in the culture of the city being studied. Koreans have vastly different expectations from, say, the professor-student relationship, as compared to the Indians, the Latins, or even the overseas Chinese. These are matters that the attaches in the diplomatic service will understand and be able to convey, if they are available for consultation. Otherwise one should consult the old-timers — expatriates who are fully conversant in the language and have been residing in the metropolis for years.

It is particularly useful to discover whether the new projects, programs, or reforms appear to have a broad spectrum of political support. If that is the case, there is a good chance that they will survive some fairly drastic political shifts during the course of implementation. In most societies political scientists and journalists are two kinds of professionals accessible to the tourists; they can provide critical insight regarding political risks. Ultimately, of course, the visiting futurist must be his own odds maker.

The writing, as suggested earlier, must proceed in fits and starts as the interesting information accumulates. Therefore, one departs with a file full of fragments. The preparation of a first draft with conclusions supported by data and observations requires disciplined pruning which will leave a number of smaller-scale insights unreported. These items should be preserved as part of one's personal repertoire. Whenever events occur that were presaged by such notes the prescient paragraphs can be dredged up and the connection between the anticipatory phenomena and the new event can be incorporated in any subsequent comments. It constitutes a confirmatory test of the forecasting model or logical scheme employed and of the method. Significant events that were not forecast or foreseen are much more important, however, because they will reveal new options and suggest how the forecasting model for that metropolis can be improved.

Notes

(1) A systematic approach to assessing Third World elite opinion was applied to young Thai. Surprisingly, it revealed a preoccupation with existing inequities and individual expectations of massive violence. Robert B. Textor, "Cultural Futures for Thailand," Futures 10 (October 1978): 347-360.

(2) The international airport has become the principal gateway to the world. Although originally much attention was paid to the appearance of the "VIP road" that connected the terminal with embassy row and the luxury hotels, the present effort is devoted to extracting the maximum economic benefit from its unique access through changes in law, customs regulations, and land use. By 1978 the most advanced planning was being installed to expedite the Industrial Promotion Zone and tourism for Colombo in Sri Lanka. The Ceylonese reported that most of the technical assistance was provided by Singapore.

(3) John McHale presents a wide-ranging review of current forces for cultural change and growth, drawing from his experiences as artist, architect, and futurist in "The Future of Art and Mass Culture," Futures 10 (June 1978): 178-190.

(4) Richard L. Meier, "Exploring Development in Great Asian Cities: Seoul," Journal of the American Institute of Planners 36 (November 1970): 378-92.

(5) Korea Journal, 1969.

(6) R.L. Meier and Ikumi Hoshino, "Adjustments to Metropolitan Growth in an Inner Tokyo Ward," Journal of the American Institute of Planners 34 (July 1968): 210-222; and R.L. Meier and Ikumi Hoshino, "Cultural Growth and Urban Development in Inner Tokyo," Journal of the American Institute of Planners 35 (January, 1969): 2-9.

(7) Under Mayor Yang in the period of 1970-72 an extraordinary new program for low-income housing was evolved. It emphasized family self-help, neighborhood cooperation, artisan contractors, and metropolitan planning of essential services for both squatter area upgrading and creating communities for industrial workers.

(8) Ronald Dore, City Life in Japan, (Berkeley: University of California Press, 1958).

(9) These plans were largely fulfilled or exceeded for Tokyo as a whole, although the "automobile substitute" has been restricted to the "executive minibus," which has a very limited role. Changes in currency relationships have brought income levels closer to the United States targets than could be imagined at that time. Growth in electric power use virtually stopped at the end of 1973, however, so that "climate control" is less widespread than anticipated.

(10) Japan Times, September 26, 1969.

(11) Arthur L. Robinson, "Semiconductor Competition: Airing the U.S.-Japan Issues," Science 202 (1978): 405-408.

(12) The Japanese points of view are analyzed by Gene Gregory, "Computing the World Industry in Japan's Favor," Far East Economic Review 102 (December 15, 1978): 75-79.

(13) Richard L. Meier, "Analysis of the Contemporary Urban Ecosystem: An Appraisal of Hong Kong's Future," in Issues in the Management of Urban System, H. Swain and R.O. McKinnon, eds., International Institute of Applied Systems Analysis, (Vienna: 1975).

(14) Richard L. Meier, Planning for an Urban World (Cambridge, Mass.: MIT Press, 1974).

(15) Vehicular population growth in Hong Kong already seems to be slackening, a trend that is attributed more to administrative measures than to increases in the cost of fuel. The cost of the operating license was doubled, and the queue for obtaining a driver's license was allowed to lengthen to six months. Parking charges are brought up to a level that is felt by the operator, even though they are still less than the charge that would meet the current land rents. Traffic law enforcement has been noticeably tightened. An excise tax on passenger cars exists, but until now has not been high enough to act as a serious deterrent.

(16) Robert Edward Mitchell, Levels of Emotional Strain in Southeast Asian Cities, 2 vols. (Taipai: Orient Cultural Service, 1972).

(17) The best current indicators are obtained from the annual reports on fisheries in which estimates of those actively engaged in fishing occur

periodically. The total has dropped from 70,000 in 1965 to 46,000 in 1973. Moreover, many of the water people who still fish have moved into flats in harbor towns, some of them involuntarily, in the course of the cleanup programs. The number of vessels has been reduced to 5,600, not all of which are used as residences. This represents a huge reduction from the 150,000 to 200,000 estimated to be living in that manner after World War II. The hurdles that they needed to overcome are described by E.N. Anderson in his monograph, <u>The Floating World of Castle Peak Bay</u>, (Washington: American Anthropological Association, 1970). Crowding was the least of their worries.

(18) An admirable paper analyzing the possible political futures for Hong Kong was published by Professor P.B. Harris, "The International Future of Hong Kong," <u>International Affairs</u> 48 (January 1972): 60-71. It is unusual that the conclusions should remain valid after the cessation of the American participation in the Viet Nam War, the Nixon shock, and the Kissinger miracles. The passage of time has allowed only a slight sharpening of the alternatives which he was able to perceive.

(19) An exercise in aggregating expert opinion was conducted with "China watchers" in an attempt to assess a "population-food balance" failure as compared to other outcomes that are imaginable. Its likelihood is rated quite high by these experts over the middle run. Cf. Vaclav Smil, "China's Future: A Delphi Forecast," <u>Futures</u> 9 (December 1977): 424-489. A response to this risk by Hong Kong businessmen and professionals is to keep half of the family capital in gold or deposited outside the colony, and make sure they have a way to the outer world, either legitimately by means of up-to-date visas or by underworld routes.

(20) The resolution of the political issue of Taiwan through American recognition of China had immediate repercussions for Hong Kong. Its role in Chinese development was enlarged. Cf. <u>Far Eastern Economic Review</u> 102 (December 15-29, 1978).

(21) The Australian human ecologists also focused their attention upon Hong Kong, and a fascinating series of studies has appeared:

A.R. Aston, "Water Resources and Consumption in Hong Kong," <u>Urban Ecology</u> 2 (1977): 327-353.
S.V. Boyden, "Integrated Ecological Studies of Human Settlements," <u>Impact of Science on Society</u> 27 (1977): 159-169.
J. Kalma, M. Johnston, and K. Newcombe, "Energy Use and the Atmospheric Environment in Hong Kong," <u>Urban Ecology</u> 2 (1977).
K. Newcombe, "Energy Use in Hong Kong," <u>Urban Ecology</u> 1 (1975): 87-113, 285-309.
_____. "Energy Use in the Hong Kong Food System," <u>Agroecosystems</u> 2 (1975): 253-276
_____. "From Hawkers to Supermarkets," <u>Ekistics</u> 43 (June 1977): 336-341.

_____. "Energetics of Vegetable Production in Asia, Old and New," Ecology of Food and Nutrition 6 (1977): 9-22.

(22) Richard L. Meier, "The Measure of Metropolitan Performance: Singapore and Bangkok," in Metropolitan Growth: Public Policy for Southeast Asia, Leo Jakobson and Ved Prakash, eds., (New York: Halstead-Wiley, 1974).

(23) Estimates of mid-1977 suggest that the national population growth had been reduced to 2.5 percent per annum due to the administrative innovations diffusing out from Bangkok, although the technical innovations, such as the new injectable contraceptives, are tested first in regions served by special hospitals before being introduced into Bangkok. The growth in acceptors in the 1975-77 period is estimated at 20 to 25 percent per year for the country as a whole, where the acceptors of contraception have reached 40 percent of the households (1978). Compare this with Taiwan, a leader, at 65 percent. W. Kolasartsenee and T. Narkavannakit, "Thailand," in Studies in Family Planning 9 (September 1978): 251-252.

(24) Allan G. Rosenfield, "Thailand: Family Planning Activities, 1968-1970," Studies in Family Planning 2 (September 1971): 181-191.

(25) Interestingly, the Malaysian economy experienced all these stresses and emerged four years later stronger than ever. A safer automobile tire moved in from Europe to sweep the American market; it required a significant amount of natural rubber for its compounding. Therefore natural rubber has excellent prospects for another five years. Palm oil prices did not become quite as depressed as expected, so the expansion in plantations continues. Moreover, UMNO came out of the election with strong new leadership, and its opposition tainted by scandal. In addition, a remarkable new institution, the Tabung Haji, mobilized savings of the bumiputra by expediting the pilgrimage to Mecca from the Penang airport in an ultramodern fashion. Far East Economic Review 102 (November 17, 1978): 32-36. Meanwhile, a sophisticated industrial promotion program is sponsoring low-wage industries linked to the world market for the smaller cities in Malaysia, leaving the higher, more skilled wage group for Penang and Kuala Lumpur.

(26) V.K.R.V. Rao and P.B. Desai, Greater Delhi: A Study in Urbanization (Bombay: Asia, 1965).

(27) Some of this appears in W.F. Ilchman and Trilod N. Dhar, "Student Discontent and Educated Unemployment," Economic and Political Weekly 5 (July 1970): 1-8.

(28) The Basic Development Plan for the Calcutta Metropolitan District (published in 1966 and again in 1967 by the Calcutta Metropolitan Planning Organization) remains a remarkable document. Ford Founda-

tion funds, along with an unusual body of consultants, expedited a much clearer conception of what was feasible for a very poor metropolis than had existed ever before. Unfortunately, the almost total cessation of industrial investment in 1966-68 brought about by the hundred-year drought and consequent food shortage, followed by a period of political extremism, delayed implementation for five to ten years.

(29) City and Industrial Development Corporation of Maharashtra, New Bombay – The Twin City, Bombay, 1970.

(30) Meier, Planning for an Urban World.

(31) The nuclear-powered agro-industrial complex (NUPLEX) involves the use of a nuclear reactor to expedite simultaneously the production of water, fertilizer, chemicals, electrometallurgicals, and power, which are combined to develop previously unused soil resources. Its significance for the feeding of an expanded Bombay is demonstrated in my Planning for an Urban World. The Indian counterproposal involved the use of nuclear reactors for multiple-cropping in the Indo-Gangetic plain. India's unwillingness to sign agreements that prevent it from making nuclear weapons has led to uncertainty that even the existing contracts for nuclear fuel for its power plants would be fulfilled, therefore the Atomic Energy Commission has postponed the food processing efforts. At the beginning of 1979 India's problem was one of finding sufficient storage capacity for surplus grain and sugar, so there was no pressure from consumers.

(32) Ibid.

(33) E.P. Eckholm, "The Deterioration of Mountain Environments," Science 189 (1975): 764-770.

(34) Jiro Kawakita, "Technical Assistance in the Himalayas – Native Participation and Volunteer Efforts," The Wheel Extended (Toyota Quarterly Review) (Summer 1975): 26-36.

(35) Terry G. McGee and Y.M. Yeung, Hawkers in Southeast Asian Cities: Planning for the Bazaar Economy (Ottawa: International Development Research Center, 1977).

(36) R.L. Meier, "Multinationals as Agents of Social Development," Bulletin of the Atomic Scientists 30 (October 1977): 30-35.

(37) Edward Hoagland, "Cairo Observed," Harper's 252 (June 1976): 65-78.

(38) Generalizations about fertility controls which apply to Egypt are portrayed by W.P. Mauldin and Bernard Berelson, "Conditions of Fertility Decline in Developing Countries 1965-75," Studies in Family Planning 9 (May 1978): 90-147.

(39) R.L. Meier, "A Stable Urban Ecosystem," Science 192 (June 4, 1976): 962-968.

(40) Janet Abu-Lughod, Cairo - A Thousand and One Years of the City Victorious (Princeton, N.J.: Princeton University Press, 1971).

(41) Gunther P. Barth, Instant Cities: Urbanization and the Rise of San Francisco and Denver (New York: Oxford University Press, 1975).

(42) Arthur Stinchcombe, Constructing Social Theories (New York: Harcourt, Brace, and World, 1968).

(43) Nicholas C. Mullins, "Theory Construction from Available Materials," American Journal of Sociology 80 (July 1974): 1-15.

(44) Webb, Campbell, Schwarts, and Sechrest, Unobtrusive Measures (New York: Rand McNally, 1966).

(45) Grady Clay, Close-up - How to Read the American City (New York: Praeger, 1973).

(46) Dean McCannell, The Tourist: A New Theory of the Leisure Class (New York: Schocken, 1976).

(47) Erving Goffman, Frame Analysis (New York: Harper Colophon, 1974).

Index

About the Author

RICHARD L. MEIER (Ph.D., Organic Chemistry, UCLA) is Professor of Environmental Design at the University of California, Berkeley. He is a planner, geographer, systems theorist and sociologist, and has been interested for a long time in the way cities can become "engines for development," pulling whole territories into a modern world. Professor Meier is the author of Planning for an Urban World - Design of Resource-Conserving Cities, published in 1974 by MIT Press.